Thinking Volleyball

Mike Hebert

Human Kinetics

Library of Congress Cataloging-in-Publication Data

Hebert, Mike, 1944-
  Thinking volleyball / Mike Hebert.
    pages cm
  Includes index.
1. Volleyball. I. Title.
  GV1015.3H43 2013
  796.325--dc23

                              2013023996

  ISBN-10: 1-4504-4262-5 (print)
  ISBN-13: 978-1-4504-4262-6 (print)

Acquisitions Editor: Justin Klug; **Developmental Editor:** Cynthia McEntire; **Assistant Editor:** Elizabeth Evans; **Copyeditor:** Mary Rivers; **Indexer:** Katy Balcer; **Permissions Manager:** Martha Gullo; **Graphic Designer:** Nancy Rasmus; **Graphic Artist:** Julie L. Denzer; **Cover Designer:** Keith Blomberg; **Photograph (cover):** AP Photo/Jeff Roberson; **Photographs (interior):** © Human Kinetics, unless otherwise noted; **Photo Asset Manager:** Laura Fitch; **Photo Production Manager:** Jason Allen; **Art Manager:** Kelly Hendren; **Associate Art Manager:** Alan L. Wilborn; **Illustrations:** © Human Kinetics; **Printer:** Versa Press

Human Kinetics books are available at special discounts for bulk purchase. Special editions or book excerpts can also be created to specification. For details, contact the Special Sales Manager at Human Kinetics.

Printed in the United States of America   10 9 8 7 6 5 4 3 2 1

The paper in this book is certified under a sustainable forestry program.

Human Kinetics
Website: www.HumanKinetics.com

United States: Human Kinetics
P.O. Box 5076
Champaign, IL 61825-5076
800-747-4457
e-mail: humank@hkusa.com

Canada: Human Kinetics
475 Devonshire Road Unit 100
Windsor, ON N8Y 2L5
800-465-7301 (in Canada only)
e-mail: info@hkcanada.com

Europe: Human Kinetics
107 Bradford Road
Stanningley
Leeds LS28 6AT, United Kingdom
+44 (0) 113 255 5665
e-mail: hk@hkeurope.com

Australia: Human Kinetics
57A Price Avenue
Lower Mitcham, South Australia 5062
08 8372 0999
e-mail: info@hkaustralia.com

New Zealand: Human Kinetics
P.O. Box 80
Torrens Park, South Australia 5062
0800 222 062
e-mail: info@hknewzealand.com

E5861

I dedicate this book to all of the athletes who played for me. This includes club, college, and U.S. teams. You are the young people who motivated me to stay with it. I extend my thanks to every one of you. It was a great run!

CONTENTS

ACKNOWLEDGMENTS

Aside from the editing staff at Human Kinetics, only a few people read passages from this book before publication. I asked former U.S. national team coach and current University of Minnesota head coach Hugh McCutcheon and current U.S. women's head coach Karch Kiraly to give it a test run. I also asked my good friend Jay Van Vark and my longtime mentor Dennis (Aame) Amundson to do the same. And finally, I leaned heavily on my wife, Sherry. Many, many times I would hand her a stack of manuscript pages and beg her to tell me if any of it made any sense. She always presented a meaningful response, delivered while cooking dinner, feeding the cats, tending to her gardens, or perhaps while lost in a book of her own. Thank you, Sherry, for your love and patience.

I'd like to add a shout-out to all the guys on the first tee at San Diego's Coronado Golf Course for tolerating my lack of game and making me feel like San Diego is now my home. And let me hear an amen for my beautiful daughters, Becky and Hillary, and my grandsons, Mateo (who at age three could identify almost any airplane that ever flew and is planning to be an astronaut by the time he starts kindergarten), Farris (who has appeared as Jimi Hendrix for the past two Halloweens and badly wants to be a motorcycle daredevil), and Aliya (who arrived already poised to create her own future).

INTRODUCTION

I think I first questioned the status quo in the early 1950s when I was in third grade at St. Bernardine's School in San Bernardino, California. My hands were in ready position, and I was about to take a swing at Panfilo Rubio, the younger brother of one of my best friends, Jose Rubio. We were arguing about something and decided to square off against each other outside on the school handball court. All the action fights took place on the handball court, usually in front of big crowds. The "sissy" fights were in the cafeteria courtyard.

I was a certified nerd. I had glasses, braces, and a lunchbox (with thermos). In my front shirt pocket, I carried a book of bus tickets to get to and from school. I also went to clarinet lessons on Saturday mornings. What was I doing at the handball court gearing up for a schoolyard fight?

Out of the corner of my eye I was watching for one of the sisters (as in Sister Marie; we didn't call them nuns at St. Bernardine's) to swoop in and break up the fight before it even started. This was exactly how she had saved my life a few weeks earlier when I somehow got in Danny Winker's way while he was running the bases during a kickball game at recess. He was the toughest guy in school, and I knew it was only a matter of a few seconds before I was going to get my lights punched out. I had raised my hands to guard my face as Danny ran at me. But just as he was about to unload his notorious straight right hand upon my nose, Sister Marie grabbed him by his hair and pulled him into her classroom. He spent the rest of the day sitting in the principal's office, growling at everyone who walked by with his standard greeting, "Who are *you* lookin' at?"

This earlier episode was justice in its purist form, I thought. I hadn't done anything wrong. Sister Marie showed up just in time to prevent Winker from rearranging my face. And on top of all that, he got suspended for three days. I was beginning to believe that when things threatened to go against me, all I had to do was wait for Sister Marie to appear and put things in order. This is what I had taught myself to expect. She was the personification of justice at St. Bernardine's. There was no reason for me to doubt that anything was about to change. I trusted the status quo.

Fast-forward to the scene at the handball court. At the very moment I drew my fist back to smack Rubio, I fully expected Sister Marie to appear and stop the fight. But she was a no-show; I was on my own. Rubio blasted me with a left hook that came out of nowhere, and I was down. From then on it was a flurry of fists from Rubio and a weak attempt by me to mount a defensive strategy. The crowd started booing and, one by one, began drifting away.

It was a crushing defeat for little Michael Hebert. My glasses were broken. My shirt was torn. Never mind that the street-savvy Latino kids had added one more notch to their total while the hopelessly nerd-ridden white kids had to suffer another humiliating loss. I could handle all of that. But what really ate at me was that I had allowed myself to trust the system. I really believed that Sister Marie would always be there to fix things.

My naiveté was exceeded only by my anger. I could not believe that I had never questioned the legitimacy of my contrived status quo. It was then and there that I promised that I would never let that happen to me again. I would ask questions. I would carry with me a healthy skepticism wherever I went. I would rely on Sister Marie (and all of the future Sister Maries that would make an appearance in my life) only if I had researched and evaluated the situation with a careful eye.

I stuck to that promise. I made a series of decisions that surely left friends trying to figure out where I was going in life and why. I turned down a college basketball scholarship to an eastern school and instead I enrolled at BYU for a year even though I wasn't a Mormon. Next, I transferred to UCSB, joined a fraternity and, in the same year, was both a varsity athlete (volleyball) and a cheerleader (don't ask). After college I chose the Peace Corps over the military. While in the Peace Corps in Nigeria, I taught my cook–steward how to veer from the local culinary orthodoxy by showing him how make tacos and burritos. Upon my return to the states, I married an African-American woman and earned a PhD in philosophy of education from Indiana University where I participated in an assortment of leftist causes. After a few frustrating years, I left teaching to pursue a career as a volleyball coach. At every stage of this journey, I asked the same questions. Is this the right thing to do? Have I looked at the issue from all sides?

By the time I launched my coaching career at the University of Pittsburgh, I was profoundly accustomed to questioning the status quo. It had grown into a full-fledged instinct. It seemed that I always had to know what I was getting into. It had become a way of life, for better or worse.

This book picks up my story in 1976, describing how I learned to apply the principles of critical thinking to each of the decisions that my new job was going to hurl at me. It is not a book that attempts to teach you how to pass, set, and hit. There are several books on the market that do this very well. Instead, this book will discuss ways to *think* about how to teach people to pass, set, and hit. There is a difference, as you will see.

Chapter 1 asks the often-overlooked question "How does one find out what to coach and how to coach it?" Chapter 2 suggests ways in which a program can be erected and maintained on that foundation. These two phases of development remind me of the sign I looked at every day in high school as I entered the building: "As the twig is bent, so the tree is inclined." As a high school student, I never knew what that meant, but now, as a coach, it seems to express the very core of what I was then after.

Chapter 3 develops one of my firm beliefs but one that is rarely discussed in volleyball literature. It recommends that all coaches teach their teams to embrace a signature style of play that is unique to their team. There is no such thing as a universally accepted way to teach volleyball skills, nor is there only one way to design systems of play. Coaches must make decisions about how to accomplish both.

My unorthodox approach to discussing defense and offense continues in chapters 5 and 6, preceded by a reasonably academic discussion of the proper use of motor-learning theory in chapter 4. Chapter 7 walks you through difficult questions regarding the establishment of a positive gym culture. Then chapter 8 catapults you into the book's most controversial chapter where I claim that teaching the chemistry-related skills is more important than coaching the technical skills. And before you even ask, my answer is "Yes, I really believe this." Chapters 9 and 10 invite you behind the curtain where I share many of the issues and solutions I thought to be valuable during my career as a volleyball coach.

As my career evolved, I was careful to take advantage of every conversation I ever had with the giants of the game. Doug Beal gave me a solid theoretical start. His eye for the game is unsurpassed. The late Jim Coleman, one of the brightest volleyball minds I have ever known, was a national treasure. Mary Jo Peppler, Chuck Erbe, Dave Shoji, John Dunning, Bill Neville, Marv Dunphy, Terry Pettit, Don Hardin, and Russ Rose were voices that I paid close attention to. Another coach who has made a significant impact on how I see the game is Shelton Collier. Later I learned to appreciate Brian Heffernan, John Cook, Hugh McCutcheon, Kevin Hambly, Christy Johnson-Lynch, and Karch Kiraly.

This list is woefully incomplete. Some of my greatest insights have come from late night conversations among coaching friends when we were all on the road recruiting. I also connected some important dots as I listened to players on long bus rides.

Yet now, as I scan the volleyball literature available throughout the world, I still see a large hole. There are hundreds of books, articles, and videos that break down the technical and tactical features of the game and how to teach them. But none, or at best only a few, are devoted to a discussion of how to *think* about asking the right questions and how to *search* for possible answers. Coaches must be critical thinkers, not protectors of the status quo. This is one of the only books that can come close to being able to fill that void. It doesn't provide everything you need to know about the game. But at least it's a start.

KEY TO DIAGRAMS

O	Player	——————▶	Player movement
OPP	Opposite	- - - - - ▶	Ball movement
MH	Middle hitter		
OH	Outside hitter		
S	Setter		
P	Passer		
L	Left blocker		
M	Middle blocker		
R	Right blocker		
LB	Left back		
MB	Middle back		
RB	Right back		
⊗	Blocker		
●	Opponent attacker		
🏐	Volleyball		
⊗	Back row defender		
<u>MH</u>	Front row players are underlined		

CHAPTER 1

Learning and Decision Making

Throughout my career I received hundreds of unsolicited requests from volleyball coaches asking for my advice on just about every topic imaginable. Some coaches wanted me to send them my entire philosophy of coaching, complete with handouts. Others asked for my offensive and defensive system diagrams so they could be copied and handed out to their teams. On one occasion, I received an e-mail asking for the details on a game-plan sheet that I was using during a television match that the coach happened to be watching. I always felt ambivalent when reacting to these requests. Part of me wanted to say, "Do your own homework." But I also felt a twinge of sympathy each time I read one. These were coaches who simply wanted to get a foothold in the profession and didn't understand the magnitude of their request in relation to my availability.

Still, I rarely complied. There was not enough time to respond to each case. One particular question, however, kept getting through to me. "I want to learn how to coach" was the refrain. "Can you tell me where I should start?" That was the toughest question of them all. How do you begin the process? Where do you start? What do you do?

Well, I was in that place in 1976. I had played the game at a reasonably high level on the beaches and in the gyms of Southern California, primarily in Santa Barbara where I went to school. But when I accepted the job to coach the women's volleyball team at the University of Pittsburgh in 1976, I was unprepared for what was ahead. I had never coached, never taken a coaching class, never attended a coaching clinic, and never planned a team practice. And for good measure, I had never even seen a women's volleyball match. I had to come up with something, and I had to do it quickly. The start of practice was only a few weeks away.

It didn't take long for me to wish that I had not taken the job. I knew how to play the game, but I didn't know how to teach it. The only source of volleyball knowledge available to me was my experience as a player. I knew how to perform the skills and could demonstrate each of them. I had learned to emulate the better players in the Santa Barbara volleyball community. The give and take among these players, the modeling of each of the skills, the sharing of ideas about how to play the game—all of this gradually became crystallized in my mind as a reasonably structured body of knowledge that could be packaged and passed along to my players. I just had to figure out how to coach them. So I decided to accept the $2,500 salary (yep, that's right) to lead the University of Pittsburgh Pantherettes into battle.

What follows is a firsthand account of how I learned to coach. It is *not* a book that will tell you, for example, how to pass, set, or hit. There are plenty of good books and videos that can do this better than I can. Instead, this book will encourage you to think for yourself as you confront the multitude of questions and decisions that will line up at your desk on a daily basis. I am more interested in helping you think creatively about solutions than helping you with your memorization skills.

Nor do I wish to enlighten you about worn-out volleyball concepts that others may try to pass along as cutting-edge knowledge. The best way to lose a reader would be for me to explain, once again, how to play a perimeter defense. Instead, I encourage you to create your own justifications for buying into a specific volleyball concept. But more important, I want to *add* to the current dialogue surrounding these concepts. I don't want to simply repeat what others have already said.

My first practice session was memorable. I must have violated every possible motor learning principle that ever existed. I provided no demonstrations. Instead, I told the players to just try harder. Try *what* harder? they must have been thinking. I set up drills that involved only one ball and 12 players, good for no more than one contact per player every 30 seconds or so. On occasion I found myself tutoring one athlete while the rest of the team stood by waiting for instructions regarding what to do next. I neglected to equip my assistant with a plan for what to do should I peel off to work with an individual or small group. But mostly, I found myself stopping a drill and talking for long segments of time. I must have thought that my long-winded explanations would enable my players to be able to walk onto the court and execute the skills. In essence, my practice was a complete mess.

To put it succinctly, I was in over my head. I must have been quite a sight, with my football-style coaching shorts, my whistle, and my clipboard. After all, my only role models had been my own coaches in football and basketball. I tried to talk with a gruff voice. I even threw in a few swear words to make the environment more "athletic."

To this day I carry a lot of sympathy and respect for those brave pioneers who were marooned with me in those early practice sessions at Pitt. Hopefully, I've gained some knowledge since then. You can make that determination in the pages that follow. But of one thing I am certain: As coaches, whether rookie or veteran, if we ever believe we know it all and cease our pursuit for good information, we are abandoning a key requirement of our role.

Learning to Coach

I knew that I had to get better. I had to actually learn how to coach. One of my first decisions was to attend a coaching clinic, and I chose a good one. The instructor was Doug Beal, who was to become the head coach of the U.S. men's gold-medal-winning volleyball team at the 1984 Olympic Games. That clinic was exactly what I needed. I never knew that volleyball could be broken down in so many ways and from so many perspectives.

I learned the difference between cognitive and motor learning and the importance of knowing how to apply this difference in my coaching. I learned to create drills and to structure and plan a practice. Buoyed by this experience, I attended more coaching clinics and became exposed to a variety of ways to think about teaching the game. My mind began to explode with questions. What is the best technique for playing defense? What serving tactics should I employ? What should be the role of punishment in practices? How should a setter be trained? Should I pass with 5, 4, 3, or 2 players? Is the 5-1 a better offensive alignment than a 6-2? Should I design a system to fit my athletes' abilities, or should I choose a system first and force athletes into that system? The questions kept coming.

I next figured out that I could learn a lot about volleyball by becoming a clinic presenter myself. I knew that I was no Doug Beal, but I knew that the topic preparation would help me begin to feel comfortable thinking my way through volleyball-related issues. So I sent out a flyer to members of the local Pittsburgh-area volleyball coaching community. I was stunned to find that nine registrations had arrived by the deadline date, each accompanied by a $15 check to cover the participation fee.

Are you kidding me? I suddenly had $135 in my newly created Pitt volleyball promotions budget, and I had a captive audience of nine who were showing up to listen to me talk about volleyball. Life could not get any better than this.

I also began to cultivate a teaching style that would serve me well throughout my career. Instead of always telling a player what to do, I frequently formulated a series of questions that would lead the player to a level of self-discovery that would empower her to arrive at the desired solution by herself. This was no accident. At the same time I was launching my coaching career, I had just completed my PhD in philosophy of education at Indiana University. This version of the Socratic teaching method (leading the learner to a desired conclusion through the skillful asking of questions) was a natural spin-off from my academic studies.

"Why do you line up with five receivers exposed in your serve-receive pattern?" I would ask participating coaches at my clinics. "Does this mean that all five of your passers possess an equal skill level?" If they said yes, I would challenge them to demonstrate this to be the case through the use of passing drills and statistical results. Of course, no volleyball team can claim to have five equally skilled passers, and their statistical evaluations inevitably proved this to be true. "So if some of your passers are not as good as the others, why do you expose them equally in your serve-receive pattern?" I would ask. "Have you considered reducing the number of passers in your formation, thereby freeing your better passers to receive more balls?"

And so it would go. Not everyone appreciated this method of learning. Many coaches would rather be told exactly what to do. They would have been fine with something like this: "Coaches, here is a three-receiver system, and this is what it looks like in each rotation. Write this down and go use it with your team." But I was never happy with this approach. There was no dialogue. I wanted to produce critical thinkers as much as I wanted to help coaches win matches.

My frustration with this mode of inquiry was captured, somewhat tongue in cheek, in a blog entry I wrote for the American Volleyball Coaches Association (AVCA) in 2012.

Avoiding the Herd Mentality

I am a huge Monty Python fan. My next pet peeve is illustrated in a scene from one of their movies, *Life of Brian.* I realize how dated and obscure this reference will be for most of you, but stay with me.

The movie is a spoof on the Christian belief that three wise men visited the baby Jesus and his parents, Mary and Joseph, in their home in Bethlehem. The wise men delivered gifts to the family in honor of the newborn infant. But in the movie the wise men got it wrong and walked in on a different family whose mother was single and whose infant child happened to be named Brian. The wise men soon realized their mistake, snatched the gifts back from Brian, and delivered them to the rightful address where Jesus, Mary, and Joseph were living.

But somehow the word got out that Brian, as a result of the earlier visit by the wise men, was in fact the Messiah. The movie is a chronology of events that Brian, reluctantly, is forced to confront as the local population continues to pursue him as their sacred leader.

In one of the scenes, Brian, now in his 20s, is running from his spiritual flock as they chase him through town in an attempt to worship their master. As the chase ensues, one of his sandals accidently slips off. But Brian keeps running. The throng of disciples stops momentarily as one of their leaders declares, "Look! It's a sign. He has given us the shoe. Follow the shoe!" And, with the shoe in hand, the multitude resumes its pursuit, presumably to enshrine the shoe and learn its secrets from the Messiah himself.

So here is my pet peeve. As presenter or participant, I have participated in hundreds of volleyball coaching clinics throughout my 35-year career. And in each case I can guarantee that most of the attendees were taking notes or participating in topical discussions related to volleyball. However, my distinct impression has been that many of these coaches talked about volleyball concepts with the same misguided passion that Brian's followers had attributed to the shoe. They assumed the presenter's legitimacy, captured the clinic material with the efficiency of a Rhodes Scholar, and praised clinic concepts as if they were self-evident truths.

During one such clinic in Chicago many years ago, a presenter stood before a large audience to declare that he had just returned from an international coach's clinic and was prepared to reveal some of the "secrets" he had picked up from the world's best coaches. The first of these secrets was what he called the Pakistani chop serve. This new technique, he said with a touch of drama, would revolutionize the game. Pencils were poised and brains were locked in the "on" position as he began his demo. He described in great detail the toss, then moving to the high overhead position of both hands, palms facing and touching each other, cocked backward at

> continued

5

> continued

the wrist hinge with fingers pointing skyward. Then came the actual chopping motion as he swung both hands straight forward, contacting the ball with the narrow edge of the palms-together grip, creating a topspin effect.

Predictably, the Pakistani chop serve produced no insightful result. It looked the same as a pepper partner spiking the ball into the floor to her partner, only done with two arms instead of one. But to my surprise as I scanned the audience of at least 250 people, most were furiously drawing diagrams and taking notes. They wanted to go home from the clinic with the secret, and the Pakistani chop serve was right there for the taking.

The presenter—I wish I could remember his name—quickly changed gears. "What are you doing?" he asked. He admonished everyone for embracing what he called a ridiculous concept (the chop serve) without critical examination. He then went on to conduct a very interesting discussion of serving technique that did indeed include the level of critical thinking that he was after.

Through the years I have witnessed this phenomenon in action. In the 1970s we were led to believe that we must spend hours and hours of training time learning how to dive and roll. This was because the gold-medal-winning Japanese teams of the '60s and '70s were doing it. Forget that they did it because their lack of height required that they emphasize defensive technique. And forget that these techniques were deployed to receive only 5 percent of all the balls sent into the defensive court. We did it because it looked really cool, and it gave us something new to do in the gym that was different from any other sport. Volleyball could now claim a set of skills and drills that brought attention to our sport. We were tough, and we were athletic. We had a new shoe to follow.

Years later the "tanden" fascination captured the American coaching community, along with related terms such as "down-up" and "up-down." These concepts came from our then-U.S. Olympic coach Toshi Yoshida. Toshi is a good friend of mine, and I can tell you that he was baffled by the way these concepts swept the nation. Tanden was just a sophisticated term for center-line passing. The other two terms were concepts he created for one or two specific players on the national team who needed isolated training; these concepts were never intended to become national catchphrases. But to this day there are coaches who believe that Toshi intentionally created a brand new set of universal techniques for teaching the game. They had found their own shoe to follow.

More recently we have seen the growing popularity of the gold medal squared (GM²) menu of coaching concepts. Some coaches are buying into these concepts as though they hold a superior position in the universe of coaching philosophies. The cauldron, the white board, swing blocking, and pancake digging, among others, are concepts upon which the GM² methodology rests. These concepts have been packaged in a way that reminds me of the TV pitchmen who sell the Shamwow, the Veg-O-Matic, and the Popeil Pocket Fisherman.

There are many great concepts embedded in the GM^2 approach, but they deserve to be scrutinized. For example, I spoke with Anson Dorrance, the originator of the cauldron concept with his North Carolina NCAA champion women's soccer teams (with props to Dean Smith who was the *original* originator). I asked him if he actually used daily cauldron results to determine his starting line-up (this is a popular practice among GM^2 advocates). "No," he answered. "The cauldron is for a few players who find it motivational, but mostly it's for the parents."

I have spoken to three of his ex-players who confirmed what he told me. This doesn't pull the rug completely out from under the cauldron concept, but it does suggest that further investigation of its usefulness should be undertaken. I would argue that the same interrogation process be applied to all of the GM^2 concepts before they are accepted as the truth.

We are a profession of coaches who are chasing the shoe or, more accurately, chasing the person who is thought to have direct knowledge of the shoe and its powers. I welcome the day when we morph into a community of critical thinkers, devoting our time and effort to the search for coaching concepts that make sense to us. I will rejoice when I see people lay down their pencils as soon as the speaker starts talking about the Pakistani chop serve. I will go all Zorba the Greek when I see coaches ask *why* the principles of GM^2, or any other collection of concepts, should be implemented in their gyms. I want coaches to pull themselves out of the pack as they chase after the shoe and ask themselves why? What does this particular shoe have to offer?

Adapted from M. Hebert, 2012, Getting it right! Part III. [Online]. Available: http://avcavolleyball.blogspot. com/2012/02/getting-it-right-part-iii.html [June 25, 2013]. Used with permission from American Volleyball Coaches Association.

Continuing to Learn

I never stopped seeking new avenues for learning. I even became certified as a high-school and USVBA referee and officiated hundreds of matches, including the Pennsylvania State Championship finals in 1977 and 1978. I wanted to understand the game from the point of view of an official. What better way to accomplish this than by working as one? I developed an excellent knowledge of the rules and how to apply them. I learned how to calm emotional players before their emotions escalated to a point of no return. I learned to listen to coaches to determine whether their confrontation warranted compassion or sternness. I began to recognize the common ingredients of winning teams and how they behaved during competition. I learned a lot about coaching while managing the match as an official, and I applied this knowledge in developing my coaching philosophy.

As my career unfolded I was able to identify additional sources of volleyball information. I discovered technical journals, both domestic and international. There I found sophisticated discussions of every volleyball-related topic you could imagine. I worked my way into the U.S. National Team Program in 1981 as an assistant coach for the World University Games in Romania.

This was the first of many U.S. assignments that took me around the globe and into fascinating discussions with coaches from Cuba, China, Russia, Japan, Brazil, Korea, Holland, Germany, Turkey, and just about every country that fielded a women's national team. I built my own library of volleyball videos and eventually produced several of my own. I read every coaching book I could get my hands on. I never stopped presenting at clinics and camps. I became one of the most widely published authors in our sport. I was obsessed with chasing down every morsel of volleyball insight available to me.

But I am getting way ahead of myself. Let's return to the original question. How does one prepare to become a volleyball coach? Where do you start?

Conventional Wisdom

My first suggestion is that you scroll through your personal memory bank and delete every lingering image of volleyball as you have seen it played in your Tuesday night recreational league. The "bump and a beer" approach to learning the game of volleyball can be a lot of fun, but it is unlikely that it will serve as a reliable source of technical and tactical information sufficient to launch your career as a volleyball coach.

Most recreational sports—flag football, pickup basketball, softball, baseball, soccer—seem to be played at a higher technical level than one would find in a recreational volleyball match. I believe there are two reasons for this. First, the skill base for these more mainstream sports includes at least one of the big three skills common to American recreational team sports: kicking, catching, and throwing. Being able to do any one or combination of these three skills qualifies the average American recreational athlete to participate in virtually any team sport except volleyball. None of the big three are necessary when playing volleyball. Learning to play the game, and how to coach it, will therefore require a journey marked by very few familiar road signs.

Second, volleyball's four main skills—forearm ball control, overhand setting, blocking, and spiking—are completely unique to the sport. They are not important in the playing of any other recreational sport that I can identify. This fact disables any crossover benefit that might result from playing another sport. Volleyball players and coaches are, for the most part, left to their own devices. As a result, technical progress is slow, especially at the beginner levels. This, in turn, leads to the perception among many that volleyball is being played at a lower level than other sports. Many also believe that volleyball's perceived slow rate of skill development prevents the sport from providing adequate role modeling for aspiring players to copy. "Volleyball," a Division I basketball player recently said within earshot of where I was standing, "is the sport you play if you're not good enough to play any other sport."

Most of us first come to know the game by copying the playing styles exhibited in the environment where we first learned to play. In my case I enrolled at the University of California at Santa Barbara and joined a fraternity. The fraternity house featured a sand volleyball court. The routine for learning the game went something like this. New Guy wants to play. He writes his name on the sign-up sheet to get in line for the next available opening in the queue of players waiting to get on the court. He and his partner (usually a veteran player who has been assigned to check out the New Guy's skill level) take the court against the winners from the previous match. New Guy is immediately exposed as a rookie without skills. Veteran partner calls time out and takes New Guy under his wing. Here is how you pass. Here is how you set. Here is how you dig. This preliminary lesson often lasted less than the length of the time out.

Conventional Wisdom at Work

This was my introduction to the game. There was no coach, no recognized interpreter of volleyball knowledge available to tell us whether or not we were doing it the "right" way. We learned the game from the local players who had it passed along to them by the previous generation of players. This transfer of skill and tactical knowledge from one generation to the next is similar to the role of oral history in many Native American cultures. But instead of calling it oral history, I'll call it the conventional wisdom. It is the residual product of all the contributions from all the players who ever participated in shaping the game as it came to be known on the UCSB campus.

Tracking down the conventional volleyball wisdom in your community is a good place to start your search. It provides an excellent source of volleyball-specific information for those wishing to learn how to play or coach the game. Every volleyball community has a cadre of local gurus who seem to be the keepers of all local volleyball knowledge. You need to find these people and start asking questions. Are there any camps or clinics that I can attend? Are there any club or high school programs that would allow me to observe a practice session? Search the Internet for every volleyball reference. Do your best to file away each scrap of relevant information. Build an informed knowledge base from which you can craft your own approach to coaching the game of volleyball.

I believe every volleyball community possesses its own conventional wisdom. I reached this conclusion as I witnessed the steady parade of visiting players who would stroll down to the campus beach at UCSB looking for a game. I can remember vividly that, when these visitors from another volleyball community would step into our world to challenge for court time, they were treated as if they were lepers. They were ignored, or worse, banished to the bottom court to be stuck with low-level players all day. This was especially true of visitors from the Midwest who showed up at our sand courts wearing the wrong shorts, the wrong sunglasses, the wrong tee shirts, and no flip flops. But occasionally the informal power structure that governed each court would relent and allow the visitor to play. This concession was executed with a nod of the head that resembled the nod given to the keeper of the lion cage in the Roman Colosseum when it was time to release the lions to feed on the Christians.

Although there was never anything formally established, it was clear that the visitor would be performing under intense pressure. All the regulars would gather around the visitor's court to critique his game. If he would put up a set with spin and wouldn't call a violation on himself, there would be eye rolling and muffled exasperation from the gallery. And if he were to tip a ball over the net with an open hand? More eye rolling. More exasperation. These techniques weren't allowed by the rules governing our courts. But apparently they were allowed in the gyms back home where he played. Each visitor came equipped with his own version of legal versus illegal. Every time this happened, I was reminded that every player, no matter where he is from, comes stamped with the brand of his own conventional wisdom.

In my case the campus-based volleyball community had decided how the game was to be played, and we were not bashful about letting outsiders know it. Volleyball techniques are subject to more idiosyncratic interpretation than any sport I know. For example, there is a ball-handling rule that prohibits the ball from coming to rest anywhere on the player's body (such as hands or forearms). The ball must rebound off the player's body within a certain time frame. If the ball stays in contact with the player too long, then a violation occurs, the referee blows the whistle, and the offending team loses a point.

The problem is that each referee and each player interprets this time frame differently depending on the conventional wisdom that shaped his game. Still, for the brand new volleyball coach, the conventional wisdom is the place to start. This is where you begin to understand the broad strokes of the game. But be mindful of the differences that might surface. There are often local, regional, and national styles that lie in wait as you build your understanding of volleyball.

Nontraditional Approaches

The earlier reference to the Midwesterner who brought his own ball-handling interpretations to the courts at UCSB provides a typical example. On the beaches of Southern California, it is considered illegal to set the ball with your hands unless it comes out with no spin. This technique is often called the "deep dish" and is considered legal even though the ball clearly comes to rest when compared to the quicker release style used in the indoor game. But in the indoor game, the ball is allowed to spin as it exits the setter's hands. The outdoor release would be a violation indoors, and the indoor release would be a violation outdoors, but both releases are linked to the same rule. The ball must not come to rest. The differing interpretations of the rule result from the evolution of differing ways of executing ball-handling skills from region to region.

These sorts of conflicts in rule interpretations often victimize volleyball. The double contact rule is another example. According to the rulebook, the ball must be played with a simultaneous contact of the ball by both hands. Any successive contact, first one hand and then the other, would be ruled a fault, and the offending team would lose a point. But even this rule can have different interpretations, depending upon how egregiously the double contact is executed. What might be allowable in one region of the country might not be in another. I would recommend that you familiarize yourself with the standard ball-control expectations embedded in your community's conventional wisdom.

This was never so clearly revealed to me than in the 1964 Olympic Games in Tokyo. In September, right after the conclusion of the Tokyo Games, the men's collegiate team from UCLA visited UCSB for a dual match. After the match both teams gathered at Jensen's, a traditional postmatch watering hole for volleyball players near the UCSB campus. Sitting next to me was UCLA star Ernie Suwara, a highly regarded U.S. starter who had just returned from Tokyo. We saw this as a rare opportunity to hear about the Olympic experience firsthand. I can still recall the hazy portrait of the scene. Our tiny bar table had managed to balance an evening's supply of beer and peanuts on its precariously wobbly foundation. Everything was perfect. We were definitely floating in our little corner of volleyball heaven.

The Nightmare in Tokyo

The 1964 U.S. men's team was loaded with elite players. We were all anticipating the possibility of the U.S. team winning the first-ever Olympic medal in the sport of volleyball. Instead, things went terribly wrong. The Americans unexpectedly ran into what many of us came to describe as the nightmare in Tokyo. Here is what happened.

Prior to the Games, the American players had worked hard to develop an effective overhand serve-receive style. This had been the conventional reception technique used in both the indoor and outdoor game in Southern California at the time. Naturally, our team arrived in Tokyo expecting to pass every serve with their hands. But within the first few minutes of the match, according to Ernie, the Americans were whistled for three or four ball-handling violations. It turns out that the International Volleyball Federation had decided prior to the Olympics that the overhand reception of serve would be illegal, but no one had informed the U.S. delegation.

Harry Wilson, the U.S. coach, was furious. He had selected his team based, at least in part, on the ability of his players to receive serve using their hands. He left most of the good forearm passers at home, thinking that their skills would not be needed. This miscommunication put the American team in a deep hole. The shock of having to retool their serve-receive game on the fly—being forced to switch immediately from overhand passing to forearm passing—coupled with the fact that the U.S. team had been together for a total of only three weeks prior to arriving in Tokyo, left the Americans in a difficult situation. Not only were they going up against seasoned national teams who had been training together, in some cases, for years, they were also asked to adapt to a ball-handling style for which they were unprepared.

Not surprisingly, the U.S. team finished ninth out of ten teams at the Tokyo Olympics. Ernie's detailed and vivid account of his experience left a lasting memory in my volleyball consciousness. The U.S. lost because they failed to keep up with evolving volleyball techniques. They had remained isolated and stuck in the past as the game progressed to newer and higher levels of play. Ernie wrapped up the evening by issuing a heartfelt promise. He and his teammates returned home with a resolute intention to modernize the American style of play. They would immediately begin training forearm-reception techniques. They would be ready for the next time.

The 1965 U.S. Open in Omaha

But a year later, at the USVBA National Open Championships in 1965, a similar event occurred. This time, however, the Americans were the benefactors, not the victims. A college team from Mexico had entered the collegiate division. They were very talented. But despite the fresh memories of the disaster in Tokyo involving the clash of ball-handling styles between the U.S. and the rest of the world, a new and equally devastating controversy had been building behind the scenes. The team from Mexico was about to find itself in the center of the storm.

The restrictive ball-handling rules regarding what the setter could or could not do while playing outdoors on the beach had begun to drift into the gyms where the indoor game was taking place. These rules stipulated that a hand set, forward or backward, must be sent directly within the body line established by the setter's stance as the ball was contacted. Any set that strayed from this directional requirement would be called a fault. The result was an excess of whistled violations by overly zealous referees who were already poised to penalize players who created even the slightest amount of spin on the ball.

It was a frustrating game to watch. The tight rule structure encouraged a simple style of offense that discouraged any sort of deception. Setters were handcuffed. They were under great pressure to avoid committing errors, especially since the second referee in those days, positioned on the floor opposite the first referee, was also empowered to whistle a ball-handling violation whenever the urge prompted him to do so.

The USVBA Open in Omaha was to become a flashpoint. On the one hand, an army of officials was hellbent on protecting the conservative American Puritanism applied to ball-handling rules. On the other hand, the team from Mexico had ball-control skills that represented the creative, more dynamic future of the game. This was the backdrop for the Mexican team when they took the floor in Omaha.

It would be an understatement to say that they were unaware of what was about to occur. The rest of the world in the early 1960s had been developing a very different style of play that featured deceptive side-setting, diagonal jump-setting, acrobatic back sets while sliding on the knees to save a bad pass, and so on. It was a dynamic, risk-taking style that was the polar opposite from the U.S. style. The problem for the Mexican team was going to be that, even though most of the volleyball-playing countries in the world had adopted these newer ball-handling techniques as the new conventional wisdom, the U.S. was not among them.

The Mexicans were caught by surprise, just as the Americans had been in 1964. They were setting the ball acrobatically and executing a fast-paced offensive system. But as a result of the restrictive officiating culture of American volleyball at the time, the officials were blowing a whistle almost every time the Mexican setter touched the ball. The officials were calling the matches according to the American rule structure, and the Mexicans were being whistled out of the gym.

They finished last in their pool and headed home early. I can still visualize the Mexican players leaving the arena to board their bus. Some were in tears. Some were angry. Some were still too confused to understand what had just happened. They, like the U.S. team in 1964, had been ambushed by an unanticipated difference in the ball-handling rules governing the tournament, only this time in reverse.

By the way, Rudy Suwara (Ernie's brother who also had competed in the 1965 USVBA Open) told me that one of the members of the Mexican team was Ruben Acosta. Acosta was later to become the president of the International Volleyball Federation (IVBF) and would be considered by many to be one of the most influential leaders ever in the sport of volleyball. I wondered, as the years flew by, how many bad breaks in

Lang Ping used the experiences and technical knowledge she gained as a player in China to fuel her passion as coach of the U.S. Women's National Team. Coaches must use every opportunity and resource available to better their skills and improve their players.

Associated Press

the seeding of U.S. teams in international competition might not have occurred had Acosta and his teammates been afforded a more positive experience in Omaha.

In any case, to a volleyball coach hoping to put those first few building blocks in place, the conventional wisdom is the place to start. Despite the occasional detour, the conventional wisdom will equip you with many of the answers needed to teach the basics of the game. For most of you, this will be sufficient, but at some point many of you are going to want more. When that time comes I recommend that you consider looking into additional sources of volleyball-related knowledge.

Framing Issues and Making Decisions

When we step outside the box to weigh the merits of the accepted conventional wisdom versus less traditional ways to teach the game, we immediately face the challenge of clarifying how the new way is different from the old. Only when this level of clarity is achieved will a coach be able to frame the issue properly and make informed decisions. Let me illustrate what I mean.

As a coach addresses the many questions, challenges, and uncertainties that emerge on a regular basis throughout a career, it will be important to cull out and investigate these issues one by one. Once an issue is identified, the coach should identify the various alternative solutions for resolving it. These alternatives can come from anywhere. The methodical review of volleyball-related science, instructional videos, defining moments that leave an indelible memory, one's own trial-and-error experience from a coaching past—these are among the idea-laden destinations that should be regular stops on your coaching journey.

Finally, after evaluating each option, the coach selects one and moves forward. The ultimate goal of the process is to accumulate a comprehensive collection of decisions that can be sorted into topics that cover the waterfront of coaching volleyball. The process requires three stages:

1. Articulate an issue.
2. Identify and evaluate alternative solutions.
3. Select an option and justify it.

Let's give it a try. Several years ago, while watching a volleyball match on television, I noticed that one team was committing twice as many service errors as the other, yet was still in control of the match. In other words, the team making the most errors was winning. I wondered about the dynamics of a match that would allow this to occur.

The TV color analyst explained that the team making more errors had decided to use an aggressive high-risk/high-reward serving philosophy for the match. They didn't believe they could win unless they served tough. But, I thought to myself, at what point does this strategy bring diminishing returns? In other words, serving tough often results in an increase in serving errors, and an increase in serving errors leads to an increase in free points for the opponent. This match and the unusual number of serving errors committed by the winning team may have been, statistically speaking, an outlier, but I was intrigued by the question and decided to pursue it further.

Articulate the Issue

The issue is the level of risk I am willing to live with as I develop a serving philosophy for my team.

Identify and Evaluate Alternative Solutions

Option 1: Serve tough and don't worry about service errors. This option comes from those coaches who believe that there is a strong correlation between serving tough and winning the match. It is a popular strategy among men's teams. Serving conservatively in the men's game will enable your opponent to pass more accurately and lead more often to a successful attack. Most feel that anything less than an aggressive serving philosophy will reduce a men's team's chances of winning. But this is not true for the women's game. Even conservative serving, such as serving at a weak receiver, serving to a specific location to force a predictable offensive pattern, and serving into a seam between two receivers can still result in scoring points. Nevertheless, those who claim that the tough, aggressive serving style leads more often to victory even in the women's game say they have statistical evidence to prove it. So far, I have not seen it.

Option 2: Serve conservatively to reduce errors. Another subgroup within the coaching population is the conservatives. They like to coach a low-error game, giving up as few points through their own mistakes as possible. They want to *earn* their victories and not rely so heavily on opponent errors. They believe that blocking and hitting points, plus the free points given to them via opponent errors, will be enough to get them the necessary 25 points to win the set.

Creating a serving system that helps your team score points seems to be a fundamentally sound principle. I kept statistics that told me who my top scoring servers were. By "scoring" I mean points scored by our team in each server's rotation. Those statistics, taken through the years with my women's college teams, reveal that in a typical 25-point set, the winning team's point scoring distribution would look something like that shown in table 1.1.

TABLE 1.1   Typical Point Distribution for a Winning Team in a 25-Point Set

Scoring method	Points
Kills	12
Opponent errors	8
Terminal blocks	2.5
Service aces	2.5
Total points	25

Here is my take on this data. If we were able to earn 17 points per set by hitting, blocking, and serving (12 kills + 2.5 blocks + 2.5 aces = 17), all we had to do was sit back and collect the free 8 points from the opponent. But conservative serving usually results in the opponent committing *fewer* mistakes. Eight errors might be too much to expect given how much easier it would be for our opponent to play a cleaner, more error-free game. Consider also that a conservative serving philosophy would lead to probable increases in the number of kills against us, along with a decrease in our blocking numbers. Given all these probabilities, I would have a difficult time using this option. Conservative serving would likely decrease our number of point-scoring opportunities and increase the number of opportunities for our opponent. In addition, I would expect a decrease in the number of errors we should expect from our opponent. Frankly, none of this sounds appealing. Serving conservatively seems to have fewer advantages than serving aggressively.

Option 3: Combine both styles into a hybrid serving philosophy. This would mean that your team would serve tough when your best servers are at the line but serve more conservatively when your weaker servers are up. This strategy seems to be a popular choice among coaches whose philosophy is to maximize strengths and minimize weaknesses.

Select an Option and Justify It

My next task would be to analyze each option by reviewing the information I had gathered on the topic. This would include my recollection of past experience with each of the proposed solutions, consultations with other coaches, the talent level of each of my servers, the efficiency of my team's blocking in each rotation, and the passing strengths of our opponent. Throughout this analysis I would reach back to my experience when coaching in Cuba with the U.S. national team. I was on staff as a consultant in charge of evaluating serving strategies. It was then that I began to understand the value of serving tough and risking an error. I was able to see firsthand how serving easy led to Cuba's scoring easy reception points.

Not surprisingly, there was a psychological component embedded in the clash of serving styles employed by each team. While the Cubans were serving rockets from 50 feet behind the end line, the United States was engaged in the conservative "don't miss" strategy. Predictably, our conservative serving philosophy gave the Cubans a reason to increase their confidence level when they realized we were not going to challenge them from the service line.

This was a defining moment for me, and it impacted my decisions about serving strategies for the rest of my career. I learned that by serving tough throughout a match, no matter how many serving errors might result, an opposing team could eventually be worn down mentally in the face of the constant and heavy bombardment thrown at them by the serving-tough team. However, a team can serve its way out of a match if every server is allowed to pound away with his most risky serve. If the high-risk philosophy begins to result in such a high number of errors that your team becomes mired in a demoralizing psychological slump, it may be time to reign in your service game until the team's confidence returns.

My choice of strategy would be option 3, the hybrid system, for these reasons:

- My personal preference as a coach is to play aggressively and avoid conservative solutions when possible.
- I learned my lesson about the psychology of serving from my defining moment while facing the Cubans.
- I believe that many of my servers preferred and were competent using an aggressive style of serve.
- The conservative-only option creates an atmosphere of vulnerability among my players.
- The aggressive-only option can result in too many service errors and lead to demoralization.
- The hybrid style fits my coaching personality of maximizing strengths and minimizing weaknesses.

Sport-Specific Training

Let's take a look at another issue. Somewhere along the line every volleyball coach wants to teach players to increase their vertical jump. This usually occurs early in the coach's career, and I was no exception. I began by developing simple jumping exercises that I would lead in practice. After a while, I added weight room resistance and plyometrics. I did my best to keep up with the latest in training methods.

But over time I began to notice a problem. Most of the jump-training regimens were aimed at increasing a player's vertical jump as measured by how far off the floor an athlete could move her center of gravity, but there were no restrictions on the footwork that should be used when executing the training jump. For example, players were allowed to point their toes straight ahead when planting for the jump. This made me uncomfortable. I knew that if a spiker were to accelerate into a plant with her toes straight ahead, she would fly forward into the net. In order to jump straight up using maximum speed into the plant, the player would have to turn the trailing foot to a position roughly perpendicular to the line of approach. This would allow for the maximum conversion of lateral speed to upward explosiveness.

This is what distinguishes volleyball jumping technique from other forms of jumping. Although it can be argued that many different types of jumping can contribute to some degree, only the jump training that emphasizes the correct foot position to convert lateral speed to vertical lift will provide volleyball players with the sport-specific style they need.

Additionally, when testing how high a player could jump, there was little or no emphasis placed on what the player needed to do while in the air. Hitting, blocking, and jump serving come to mind. But we were getting results only on how high the player could touch, not how successfully she could control her body while in the air. It became apparent to me that the hand and arm movements coming out of the plant were critical to the player's ability to be in maximum position to execute a block, spike, or a jump serve. So whenever we jump trained or jump tested, we did so with the proper foot and arm mechanics coming into and exiting from the plant.

Quick hitters, for example, need to get up quickly using a bent elbow (abbreviated) arm lift. They must have excellent trail-foot mechanics since they attack in such proximity to the net. Jump servers and back-row attackers must learn to broad jump into the plant while using a long-lever pull-through as they execute the arm lift. There is no need for them to be as concerned about avoiding contact with the net; therefore they can position their feet to maximize the distance covered as they broad jump toward the net. Pin hitters' mechanics lie somewhere in between. In any case, these additional movement patterns must become part of your jump-training regimen.

It is important to remember that you are training volleyball players. Their sport-specific jumping mechanics may differ substantially from basketball's rebounders and shot-blockers, football's defensive backs, track's high jumpers and pole vaulters, and soccer's goalies. And while it is acceptable to use generic gravity-jump training, such exercises should not dominate your workout routine. Choose your training methods wisely by including sport-specific jump training. This recommendation is underscored by Carl McGown in a 2012 e-mail discussion with John Kessel highlighting the important principle of specificity in motor learning:

> Training is specific. The maximum benefits of a training stimulus can only be obtained when it replicates the movements and energy systems involved in the activities of a sport. *This principle may suggest that there is no better training than actually performing in the sport.* [my emphasis] This text maintains that the principle of specificity is the single most pervading factor that influences the improvement of performance from a physiological perspective. Training effects are, in the main, so specific that even minor departures from movement forms, velocities, and intensities result in undesirable training effects. This means that incorrectly designed training activities will have no carry-over value for a particular movement form, and may even have the potential to negatively influence activities.*

Later in my career I conducted a Level 5 USA CAP coaching seminar with my instructor from the early days, Doug Beal. A biomechanics expert had been asked to conduct a session on improving vertical jumping for volleyball players. It became clear that he was presenting a program of exercise for athletes not encumbered by the proximity of a net nor the need to spike or block while suspended above the floor. We concluded that it wasn't clear that trying to execute a max jump in all situations was even desirable. Sometimes a lower-than-max block jump would be preferable to a max jump if the blocker needed to get down quickly and move outside for an additional block attempt. Jumping too high would prevent the player from even having a chance to recover and block in the secondary zone. The same is true for spikers. There is

---

*Source: John Kessel, October 8, 2012, "Stop Teaching Running," USA Volleyball blog, www.teamusa.org/USA-Volleyball/Features/2012/October/08/STOP-Teaching-Running.aspx?p=1.

a difference in the way one would approach to hit a quick set and the way one would approach to attack a high set to the pin. In other words, there is a tactical element to jump training in volleyball. It is not simply an exercise in maximum lift.

Articulate the Issue

The issue is how I should design a jump-training program for my players.

Identify and Evaluate Alternative Solutions

Option 1: Turn the matter over to the strength coach and trust that he will do the right thing. This has become a popular option for today's coaches who actually have access to a strength coach but who find themselves wrapped up in an ever-growing pile of paperwork, an exponential increase in the number of daily phone calls (recruiting, scheduling, and so on), and all the other mounting responsibilities that encroach on a coach's time and availability. There comes a time when coaches decide to buy back some time by trimming items from the daily checklist. For some, designing their own jump-training program is one those items. So they turn it over to the strength coach. This is understandable, but it is not a legitimate option for coaches who want to remain intimately connected with all aspects of their program.

Option 2: Design a jump-training program combining traditional Olympic lifts with plyometric training. This is the traditional approach used to improve an athlete's vertical jump. It involves a series of Olympic lifts such as the clean, clean and jerk, snatch, deadlift, full squat, and front squat. This type of resistance training is usually done in a weight room. The purpose is to build strength in an athlete's core. Core strength enables an athlete to increase the speed and explosiveness of attempts to propel the body weight vertically from the floor.

Plyometric training aims to overload the eccentric contraction of the muscles used in jumping so that the muscles generate as strong a contraction as possible in the shortest time. The Russians and their Eastern Bloc allies introduced this style of jump training in the early 1960s. Since then it has been accepted in the biomechanics world as an important piece of any jump-training program. In fact, the sport science community argues that the combining of both resistance training and plyometric training will have a better effect on jump training than if an athlete chose one or the other exclusively.

Option 3: Use resistance training and plyometric training *plus* sport-specific movements. This is an option that I developed with the help of some forward-thinking strength and conditioning coaches. Most notable among them was Sarah Wiley, the 2007-2008 National Strength

Coach of the Year at the University of Minnesota. We spent hours talking about how our jump-training program could be more sport specific. We eventually concluded that while not every exercise could be modified to fit sport-specific movement patterns, there were enough that could. For example, a plyometric repetition using a straight-up jump could finish with the upward thrust of the athlete's arms held in spike preparation position, instead of being allowed to let the upper body strain to reach as high as possible at the top of the jump. We would sometimes finish reps by executing a line swing or a crosscourt swing.

We would also take this same exercise to the baseline where jump servers could train their specialty, complete with the modified foot position, toes pointed forward at plant. Jumping into a blocking position that emphasized penetration at the top of the reach would be another example of sport-specific jump training. Plus, I felt that measuring a player's skill height—how high over the net a player could hit and block—was usually more important than her straight-up vertical jump height. I tended to discourage jump-training programs that failed to include volleyball-specific movements.

Finally, we developed a series of jumps that replicated some of the off-balance positions in which volleyball players find themselves, such as jumping backward, jumping from side to side, and going to the floor to defend a tip and recover to approach for a spike with a maximum jump. We found that adding the sport-specific movements to our jump-training program equipped our players with the versatility needed to play the game at a higher level.

Select an Option and Justify It

I would choose option 3, to add volleyball-specific movements to the traditional resistance and plyometric program, for these two reasons:

- Handing the jump-training program over to a strength coach without my review seems to be irresponsible. The head coach must have intimate knowledge of every aspect of the program.
- I approve of the traditional approach to jump training as outlined in option 2, but it is incomplete without the addition of sport-specific movement patterns.

This is exactly how I learned to clarify each issue that made its way, in rapid-fire fashion, to the pages of the volleyball coaching journal that I kept during those early years. Some issues were easier to resolve than others, but I became extremely disciplined in the use of this methodology as I constructed my philosophy of coaching.

Through the years I insisted that it wasn't just about discovering one way of doing things. I was always keenly aware of the fact that by choosing one direction, I was choosing to reject the other options. It is important that a coach understand the reasons not only for *selecting* a particular option, but also for *rejecting* the others.

Conclusion

To become a grounded, confident professional, a coach needs to experience the entire decision-making journey. A coach can't read just one book, go to one clinic, talk to one coaching mentor, or read one biomechanics study. A coach needs to identify and evaluate the issues that regularly bubble to the surface. The coach then accumulates the sum total of these decisions to create a checklist that will guide her career. The remaining chapters of this book will illustrate how this approach can be applied to virtually any topic facing any coach at any level.

CHAPTER 2

Structuring and Running the Program

One of the skills that I developed unintentionally through the years is the ability to walk into a practice gym or a competition arena anywhere in the world and determine which of two paths a coach has chosen to follow. I know this because I have visited—as a recruiter, a speaker, a spectator, a scout, or a visiting coach—hundreds of gyms and arenas around the United States and around the world.

On the one hand there are some who have decided to channel most of their efforts into being a practice and game coach. I call them clipboard coaches (CC). Coaches in this category focus almost exclusively on those things that will affect their team's performance. Their daily schedule includes very little else.

On the other hand, there are coaches who choose to be program developers (PDs). They, too, target the team as a primary focus, but they also take on diverse projects that will enhance the scope of the volleyball experience they have committed to provide. They want to successfully market their team and draw large crowds. They engage in aggressive fund-raising efforts. They take part in community-service activities. They go out of their way to meet and engage potential program boosters. For the PD the overriding question is this: "Can I do both? Or will the quality of the team's performance suffer if too much time and energy are spent on all of these program-building activities?" This is one of the first decisions to be made by the coach.

Clipboard Coach Versus Program Developer

In any case, before your first match, actually before your first practice, you should declare your intentions. Either you are going to be primarily a CC or you are going to be a PD. Both styles are capable of winning, but there is a big difference between a collection of coaches and players who are sequestered in a practice gym all week and a comprehensive program that seeks to capitalize on every opportunity available in the quest for support and reputation.

I often would find myself, along with at least a few other college coaches, watching a high school or club practice to evaluate potential recruits. Players would sometimes walk across the floor, stand in front of us, thank us for coming, and introduce themselves to us. These were the PD programs. When watching the CC's practices, the opportunity to interact with a club representative was rarely provided.

I knew that I was in the midst of PDs when the number of spectators at a home event was greater than the sum of the players' family members, when the arena projected the administration's decision to compete in a volleyball-specific environment and not in a place where volleyball is only allowed to set up shop temporarily until the impatiently waiting basketball hoops are returned to their rightful place on the floor, when the players demonstrated a commitment to keeping their shared spaces (such as a locker room or meeting room) organized and free of debris, and when members of the booster club would approach to talk about their love of the game and the program.

Though these kinds of items are often absent from the landscape in the CC environment that emphasizes coaching the team, I reiterate that there is nothing wrong with this approach to coaching. My point here is that I would encourage every coach to declare which of these two paths she intends to take. The clarity achieved for all concerned is worth the effort. But the decision to build a comprehensive program requires much more than a command of skills and tactics. It requires a major investment of time and resources on the part of the head coach.

Table 2.1 suggests a few sample areas that might help to illuminate the different approaches to the same issue taken by the CC and by the PD.

TABLE 2.1 Comparison Between Clipboard Coach (CC) and Program Developer (PD)

Clipboard coach (CC)	Program developer (PD)
Plans and runs practice	Invites local club and high school teams to watch practice and build strong relations
Is indifferent to crowd size	Actively works with administration and community to promote attendance
Has no interest in marketing	Contributes time and energy to working with marketing staff
Has no booster organization	Helps to build a booster club and attends meetings to show support
Has limited social networking	Is involved in active updating on Internet and regular speaking engagements in community
Has little interest in press relations	Cultivates positive relations with members of local and regional press (print and electronic)

Division of Labor

To the PD, I suggest the formulation of a division of labor among your staff. This will provide further clarification as you seek to piece together the foundation of your program. Here is a sample breakdown of responsibilities that could apply at any level. Notice the specificity supplied by the following assignments.

Head Coach

1. Develop and manage program.
    a. Create organizational plan.
    b. Establish staff division of labor.
    c. Perform staff training and evaluation.
    d. Establish staff protocol and ground rules.
2. Develop and manage budget.
    a. Develop annual program budget.
    b. Monitor budget expenditures to ensure fiscal responsibility.
3. Plan and conduct regular staff meetings.
4. Coordinate team and player development.
    a. Schedule and conduct regular player meetings.
    b. Develop annual goals and goal-pursuing strategies for the team.
    c. Supervise the technical and tactical development of players.
    d. Develop and implement a system of play.

5. Develop and supervise a plan for scouting opponents and preparing game plans.

6. Develop and supervise a plan for managing matches (prematch, during, postmatch).

Assistant Coach

1. Assist in developing a plan for training the team in coordination with head coach.
   a. Create year-round training schedule.
   b. Draw up daily practice plans.
   c. Assemble and supervise scrimmage team.

2. Develop a strength and conditioning program for the team.
   a. Create year-round plan.
   b. Conduct the physical-training segments of practice.

3. Assist in coordination of team and player development in coordination with head coach.
   a. Schedule and conduct regular player meetings.
   b. Develop annual goals and goal-pursuing strategies for the team.
   c. Supervise the technical and tactical development of players.
   d. Develop and implement a system of play.
   e. Develop a year-round player education program for players.

4. Develop a system for scouting and game planning in coordination with head coach.
   a. Create opponent scouting files.
   b. Prepare game plans.

5. Supervise team managers.

6. Coordinate facility reservations and equipment transfer.

Director of Operations (Manager)

1. Coordinate statistical evaluation program.
2. Create and distribute postmatch reports to staff and players.
3. Coordinate all team travel.
4. Administer camps.
5. Coordinate hiring of camp staff.

Program Infrastructure

PDs, having clarified the responsibilities and roles for each staff member, now turn their attention to creating a normative structure within which the program will operate. I'm not sure that there is a widely accepted term that describes this constellation of policies, philosophies, expectations, rules, personal beliefs, goals, and accommodations, but I like the term *infrastructure*. All teams function, whether they are conscious of it or not, within a network of directives and resources that make up the program's infrastructure.

One element of this infrastructure is the formation of a team culture that reflects the coach's philosophy of team building. At times, philosophies seem to come from everywhere. Players are bombarded with different ideas about how they must reshape their behavior to fit into the team's evolving culture. This enculturation process will occur with or without input from the coach. I always felt that it would be in my best interest to direct this process rather than allow it to occur in a random fashion. There is no telling what you might end up with if you turn your attention, even momentarily, away from the process.

It is always important to imprint among your players some of the most basic beliefs you possess as a coach. I read the letter (see the sidebar Dear Team) aloud to my team every year at our initial team meeting. Even though this was written for a college-level team, I believe it can be translated to address the realities facing any team at any level.

Dear Team,

Most of you will find that achieving our program goals will be difficult. You will be expected to manage a wide range of demands on your time and energy. While juggling all of these demands, you will be expected to keep everything in perspective. You will be asked to develop the skills of self-discipline in a way you have never experienced up to this point in your life.

- I want you to respect and appreciate your family, but I also want you to grow independently and become your own person.
- I want you to succeed academically, but your time will be limited, and the distractions will be many.
- I want you to push yourself to excel, but you must remain optimistic in the face of frustration.

> continued

> continued

- I want you to take great care in keeping your body and mind poised to perform at peak levels while avoiding injury, but I also want you to enjoy the full range of college experiences.
- I want you to be available to help in off-court team activities, but I want you to have time away from volleyball-related responsibilities.
- I want you to behave aggressively as a competitor, but I want you to show compassion toward your teammates.
- I want you to develop an unshakable confidence in yourself, but I don't want you to become arrogant.
- I want you to learn to resolve issues with diplomacy and skill, but I don't want you to cave in to others who are being insensitive to you.

Underneath all of this lies the nucleus for success—the development of personal discipline. In my mind, the disciplined person is the one who does the right thing even when no one is watching. Discipline means doing what you are supposed to do even when you don't want to do it.

The pursuit of discipline—this will be a common theme throughout our interactions. The coaches want you to know that we understand how very demanding this experience can be. There will be ups and downs for each of us. But in spite of how difficult the challenge, we want you to work very hard to fashion your own sense of discipline on a daily basis.

Each time you act in a disciplined way, two good things happen. First, as you exercise the discipline muscle, it gradually becomes stronger. Second, you invest in the same things your teammates are investing in. When you invest in a group, you achieve ownership. When you achieve ownership, you develop a passion for the group and its goals.

Despite the heavy volume of information contained here, the reality remains that individual and team discipline ultimately comes down to practicing a small set of principles over a long period of time. Success is not a matter of mastering subtle, sophisticated theory but rather of embracing common sense with uncommon levels of discipline and persistence.

Said in yet another way, discipline is to an athlete what scales are to a musician. Mastering the scales is what allows the musician to perform music. Mastering the skills of self-discipline is what enables a person to become an accomplished elite athlete.

My next message to you is an important one. It is always inconvenient to be on a team. In the challenging world of team sports, team goals must supersede individual agendas. Self-absorbed behavior must be replaced by selflessness. Individual agendas must be replaced by sacrifice. Taking the easy way out must be replaced by the acceptance of inconvenience.

Throughout the championship manual, you will read about things that, on the surface, do not seem to be related to learning how to play volleyball. In fact, you may find yourself becoming bored and frustrated during meetings. You will feel overwhelmed at times by all that I will ask you to do. There will be times when all you want to do is just play volleyball, have fun. You are asked to think all day in school; why should you have to come to practice and meetings to think some more? Sometimes you just don't want to think.

I want you to know that I understand your frustration during these moments. There is a fine line between pushing you to process tons of information and pushing you so hard that you become fatigued and unable to think any more. I will try to do my best to be aware of this line.

Meanwhile, I want you to leave your comfort zone behind and understand that the topics in this manual, if mastered, are absolutely the difference between winning and losing at an elite level. So while you are saying to yourself "I can't handle any more of these meetings," I am asking you to interrupt yourself at that point and say, "I know that I'm tired, but I'm going to power through and try to get the most out of all those occasions when Mike is going to ask us to think."

Finally I want to talk to you about keeping the arteries clear. Team chemistry is an elusive thing. There are likely to be as many definitions for it as there are coaches. "Let's all pull on the same end of the rope" and "Let's have some fun out there" are examples of appeals to team members to play with chemistry. But what do we mean when we say these things? What are we asking our players to do? Well, here is what I think: Team chemistry is the daily rehearsal of the championship behaviors that you have already outlined for yourselves.

These behaviors flow through the team's arteries to each player, coach, and staff member. They carry life to the team's mission. For a team to achieve its goals, the arteries must remain clear.

My way of making sure that we never lose sight of this process is to conduct regular artery check-ups. It might occur before or after practice, before or after competition, on a bus, in an airport lobby, or at a hotel meeting. I provide ample opportunities for players and staff to identify any blockages that might prevent those arteries from pumping valuable life to every corner of our team environment. If we find a blockage, we examine it, suggest a strategy for treating it, and work hard to make sure that the blockage is minimized. Keeping the arteries clear. This has become a staple in my list of coaching principles.

Self-discipline, the acceptance of inconvenience, and keeping arteries clear—these are the three pillars of personal success as an athlete. Keep them in mind as you undertake your journey through the topics that follow.

Sincerely,
   Mike Hebert

   The championship behaviors referenced in the letter were the product of a series of team meetings aimed at naming the specific behaviors that would enhance our chances of contending for a championship. At each successive meeting, the team would whittle the list of behaviors down until they were happy with the overall results. I also created a championship manual each year that contained all of the necessary schedules, meeting topics, selected writings, program information, team policies, and guidelines.

   The sidebars Championship Behaviors and Nonchampionship Behaviors are examples of the championship and nonchampionship behaviors that were created and adopted by one of my teams in the mid-2000s.

Championship Behaviors

Confidence

Use a lot of communication.

Use positive body language after a mistake; reassure teammates.

Be aggressive.

Take risks.

Use an acknowledging tone or nonverbal cue. (Avoid having the last word.)

Make eye contact.

Poise

Carry yourself positively.

Relax.

Accept challenges.

Presence

Communicate loudly.

Be competitive.

Maintain an open, upright posture (stand tall).

Practice good technique.

Be willing to face challenges (try new concepts).

Acknowledge tough drills (don't look defeated).

Respect for the Game

Do the little things—stay low, get homework done to have quality time to recruit.

Be more concerned with your team.

Listen to teammates and what they have to say.

Take criticism well; ignore the tone.

Hold yourself accountable (never cut corners).

Team

Be all about the group.

Know your role and accept it.

If someone struggles, others need to make a move.

Winning is more important than one's own accomplishments.

Always push teammates.

Keep players accountable.

Change yourself for the team if you need to.

Respect differences.

Consistency

Play every match like it's against the best team.

Bring same level of effort no matter what the drill.

Don't prejudge a team.

Practice good techniques and don't fall into bad habits.

Be aware of how your emotions affect the team.

Be ready to take on anything.

Competition

Swagger.

Understand common goals; acknowledge your role.

Push your teammates.

Be unafraid to call others out for lack of effort.

Compete to win, not to avoid punishment.

Embrace pressure rather than shying away.

Come back after a loss.

Acknowledgment

Nod your head.

Make eye contact.

Accept criticism.

Be willing to change techniques and attitude.

Understand nonverbal cues.

Belief

Maintain common goals through practice.

Show confidence and trust in the program and each other.

Harbor no doubts.

Don't be afraid to challenge teammates.

> continued

> continued

Sharing

Don't rely on the same players to cover every ball.

Distractions

Don't bring outside life on court.

Don't be a distraction (by looking at clock, making no effort).

Don't show frustrations.

Don't make stupid errors.

No complaining.

Sacrifice

Stick to a diet; take care of body.

Make sure to eat.

Drink alcohol in moderation.

On recruiting weekends, hang out with team.

Sacrifice body for play.

Keep grades up.

Maintain good sleeping habits.

Manage time well.

Roles

Coaches and teammates must be straightforward with roles.

Get your job done.

Honor your teammate's role (she earned it).

Don't be jealous of your teammates.

Technique

Always stay low.

Be conscious of what you're working on.

When peppering, use correct hitting form even when coaches are not watching.

Emotions

Don't get too amped.

No snapping, no complaining.

Keep emotions even.

Know how your emotions work and how to use them (if you play well while mad, be mad).

Don't get annoyed with a teammate and yell in anger.

Don't cry!

Nonchampionship Behaviors

Uncontrolled Emotions

    Crying

    Bringing outside drama onto court

    Letting emotions affect people around you in a negative way

    Showing frustration in self or others

Absence of Communication

    Being dishonest during confrontation

    Using poor body language

    Not acknowledging teammates or coaches

    Contradiction among coaches; lack of clarification to players

Taking Criticism Personally, Leading to Lack of Confidence

    If you give criticism, then not accepting it from others

    Being selfish: unable to accept that others are trying to make you better

    Dwelling on it: talking about the person after he has criticized you

    Counterattacking: finding fault with the person who has just corrected you

Lack of Confidence Making You Fearful

    Afraid to make mistakes

    Doubting/not trusting yourself or teammates

    Using bad body language: bad eye contact, slumped shoulders

    No communication

    Look of fear on face

Error Prone Because of Distractions

    Not respecting the game

    Unaware of when to take chances

    Not taking care of the ball in crucial situations

Complacency

    Living life just on the plateau; not wanting to move up

    Going through the motions

    Complaining

    Not giving 100 percent effort

Letting Distractions Affect Play

    Overemotional

    Bringing outside drama onto court

> continued

> continued

Complaining

Using white lies to get out of uncomfortable situations

No Leadership

Relying on only one person to always lead the team

Not fulfilling your role on the court

Nobody willing to step out of comfort zone and confront teammates

Not following the championship goals and not calling others out for their mistakes

Nobody stepping up when teammate is struggling

Policies and Guidelines

All teams have policies. Some call them guidelines. They are an important part of the team's infrastructure. Many of them are generated by the coaching staff's identification of issues within the program that are in need of a solution. They can arise from a simple, innocent observation such as "Let's make sure that the players bring their championship manuals to every team meeting." Or they can take shape over a longer period, eventually requiring a programmatic solution. Here is one such episode that provides a glimpse into this process.

Many years ago I received a phone call in my office from one of my starting players. She wanted to tell me something, and it was very important. "Of course," I said. "Come right over." This type of phone call rarely brought joy to my life. So I felt relieved when I saw her disarming smile appear in my doorway. This would be no catastrophic issue thrown on my desk. She was smiling. How bad could it be? My naïveté was on display.

She was almost in tears as she told me that her sister was getting married. And furthermore, she was going to be in the wedding! It was then that I realized that she had not come to *ask* me if she could miss any team responsibilities. She had come to *inform* me of her decision to miss our matches on the upcoming wedding weekend. In her mind this was a no-brainer. Her smile broadened as she started explaining the details of the wedding, the shower, the reception, and her dress, never realizing that she had placed me in a state of shock.

I started backpedaling immediately. It was inconceivable to me that a full-scholarship athlete would be allowed to miss practice and competition to attend a wedding. My answer was no. I told her that her sister would have to find someone else to be in the wedding so that this player would be available for our match. It was approximately at that moment that I learned about the sacred status of weddings among family members. For a moment, she simply stared at me. Her tears of joy gave way to tears of anger and disbelief. She was too distraught to discuss it any further. Her parents would be in touch with me, she said. And she got up and left.

A Guideline Is Born

I'm not sure who was more dumbfounded by the outcome of the conversation, the player or me. Neither of us could believe that the other was serious. But when I was called into the athletic director's office the next morning, I knew that something had gone wrong. Her parents had threatened to pull her from the team permanently if I refused to let her miss the match. I went to the team before practice that afternoon and conducted a straw vote. Should Jane (not her real name) be allowed to go to the wedding? *Yes*, they bellowed at me. And they looked at me as if I were a dictator without feelings for his players' emotional well-being. I looked back at them in silence. I realized that this was not a battle I was going to win. My speculation was confirmed when the AD called to inform me that Jane would miss our matches and attend the wedding.

This occurred many years ago, and I am certain that the issue might be handled differently in today's climate. I am also certain that this is an issue that is not confined to the college level. But the incident stands as an example of how normative guidelines can evolve to become a part of the program's infrastructure. Beginning with the following season, this policy was in place.

Wedding Policy

The staff understands that the wedding topic can be a sensitive one. Most players feel as though they have a right to attend weddings, especially the weddings of relatives or close friends. We agree with this, except when it conflicts with a volleyball activity such as practices, meetings, and matches. Players will be expected to be present at all team activities.

Your job is to anticipate that a wedding might be taking place and to tell the newlyweds-to-be that you will not be available during your season. If they want you to be a part of the wedding, ask them to schedule it for a time when you will be available.

Program Guidelines as Part
of the Infrastructure

Identifying issues in need of a solution was never a problem. Issues were readily available. Solutions, however, were often in short supply. I viewed each issue as an opportunity to invent a solution. The wedding policy is an example of this process. These solutions would morph into guidelines for managing the issue each time it would appear.

The use of cell phones is another issue that eventually led to the formation of a team policy. For the team, cell phones posed no problem. This was because all of the team members had been swept into the cell phone generation. (Go to the section titled Millennials in chapter 10 for further discussion of this issue.)

We should have been more prepared for what was to take place in American culture as a result of the proliferation of electronic communication technology over the past 50 years. One of the iconic voices during the 1960s period of student unrest in the United States was the Canadian social psychologist Marshall McLuhan. His signature contribution, explained in *Understanding Media* (McGraw-Hill 1964), was the quote "The medium is the message." His new-age thinking introduced my generation to the concept that the literal exchange of ideas that might occur in a face-to-face conversation was being replaced by the invention and widespread use of TVs, radios, land-line telephones (along with a hand unit called the telephone remote), and then later by the emergence of headphones, pagers, personal computers, e-mail, cellular phones, and texting.

The new devices allowed us to communicate more efficiently. But over time these new forms of sharing information established a new reality among each generation of tech-savvy Americans. It became clear to many observers that, as McLuhan put it, the medium indeed became the message. Face-to-face conversations have been replaced by electronic conduits that allow users to enjoy immediate access to each other. A new language (lol, u r next, bff, and btw are examples) has been steadily evolving, which is an additional expression of the impact of newly adopted forms of communicating.

In the athletic arena, this tension is felt whenever a coach old enough to have been enculturated in a previous era comes face to face with players molded by today's matrix of communication methods. The coach is considered old school when she attempts to slow down the pace of what appears to be a runaway train. New gadgets are being developed at a sizzling pace, and players routinely absorb each of them into their lifestyles.

When the coach wants to conduct a team meeting to teach players how to appreciate the use of critical thinking in making decisions on the court, she is confronted immediately by the expectation among players that for best results, the coach needs to speak in short, information-only segments. Any attempt to explore a topic beyond its bare bones content will be met with restlessness and impatience. If it can't fit on a texting screen, it is too cumbersome to be processed. Players are perfectly content with this version of the medium being the message. This is what they know, and they are comfortable with using it as their primary method of communication.

But coaches are rarely comfortable when attempting to communicate within these new parameters. Coaches would rather reach back into their own era for guidance when formulating a communication style that would be effective between and among their players. But therein lies the cultural collision that prevents the smooth sailing we all are seeking as we attempt to build our programs. This is an inevitable consequence of members of different communication generations joining hands and marching toward the finish line together. Unless someone decides to resolve the dilemma before it undermines the possibility of mutually pursuing team goals.

This is where cell phone policies take center stage. By regulating the use of cell phones, the coach can guarantee that there will be certain blocks of time free of the invasive presence of the cell phone. For example, the coach who is annoyed, rightfully so, when everyone reaches for her cell phone and lays it next to her plate at team meals can create a policy prohibiting cell phones to be used at team meals. Instead, the time can now be used to converse with one another in a relaxed, uninterrupted setting. And by providing specific times when the players are allowed to use their phones, the players know that the cell phone embargo will be only a temporary inconvenience.

The advent of the texting feature of the cell phone has complicated things. Before texting, it was easy to spot violators of the no-cell-phone policy. But now the new generation has honed their texting skills to a level where they can converse and text at the same time, *with two different people*, all the while concealing the phone's location. It is truly something to behold.

The battle rages as we speak. For every cell phone policy drafted by a coach, there are cadres of cell phone zealots dedicated to finding ways to circumvent that policy. The coach has to stay at least one generation ahead of the players. This is the only way to manage today's coach-player communication issues. By making the attempt to understand the communication patterns of your players, you should be able to secure their support in your effort to establish meaningful cell phone policies.

Just remember that you are powerless to stop the relentless drive to create new forms of communication. Right now we have Skype and other forms of face-to-face electronic communication filtered only by how clearly your computer or cell phone can present screen images. What about 10 years from now? What new devices will be available in the marketplace? If you wish to avoid the worn-out posture of the coach who constantly berates the newer generations of players for being selfish, lazy, and unappreciative, make sure that you do your homework. Pay attention to how players communicate and learn to understand the waves of cultural change that have shaped their being. You thought you were through taking foreign language classes, didn't you? Well, more lies ahead. Suck it up and learn the language of each generation. Yes, it's that important.

Here are some of the cell phone policies I used as a college coach.

No-Cell-Phone Zones

- All designated team-gathering places
- On the bus (on long bus rides, the coach may designate a block of time for phone use); texting OK
- Airport and hotel check-in and other transitions (the busy times between airport arrival, baggage claim, and ground transportation to and from hotel)
- Practice and competition arena
- Training and weight room
- All team meals

Times and Places for Cell Phone Activity

- Airport gate
- Your hotel room
- Outside the bus (after matches and before departure)
- Locker room
- Emergency or crisis situations

No-Texting Zones

- During *any* team meeting regardless of location
- During team meals

Times and Places for Texting

- On the bus
- In the locker room
- At the airport

Other guideline topics also made their way into the infrastructure. Here are a few examples:

Access to parents, family, and friends at competition site

Substance use and abuse

Team prayer

Academic standing

Community service

Equipment and apparel

Travel protocol

Setting Goals

Why have goals? There is no need if you do not believe that how a player thinks impacts his performance. For those who do believe this—that psychology plays a role in determining who wins and who loses—goals are an important part of the coaching process.

There are two kinds of goals: outcome goals and process goals. Outcome goals are clear, bold statements referring to intended team results. These results can be measured through wins and losses, conference finish, postseason tournament participation, and so on.

Outcome Goals

Outcome goals target what the team will achieve by the end of the season. They are important because they provide a destination that becomes imprinted in the minds of everyone in the program.

For example, these were our outcome goals at Minnesota for the 2009 season. Everyone was asked to buy into them. They served as a compass to guide us through the season. The buy-in had to be complete and without hesitation.

2009 Outcome Goals

- Finish the preconference segment with at least 9 wins (9-3).
- Finish at least second in the Big Ten.
- Win our first and second round NCAA matches.
- Qualify for the Final Four by winning our own NCAA Regional.

These goals must be imprinted in all of our minds, I explained. We will not talk about them very much. Instead, we will let them take root in our consciousness and grow throughout the season. They will eventually take over our every waking moment. This must be so. Otherwise, we will never reach our goals.

Process Goals

Outcome goals are accomplished through execution on the court. Process goals function in the realm of psychology. They are enabling goals. Process goals provide the psychological foundation for pursuing and achieving outcome goals. Here are some sample quotes taken from actual accounts of athletes as they explain how they achieved their outcome goals—the upset, the unexpected victory—through the use of psychological process goals.

> "We simply believed we could do it. We never stopped believing in ourselves."

> "From day one, we set our sights on beating them. Every day in practice we talked about how we couldn't wait to see the shock on their faces after we beat 'em."

> "It all boils down to pride. You have to have the feeling; without it you can't win."

> "We were able to stay connected on the court. We've had great chemistry all year."

> "It's about respect. After what they did to us last season, we felt they didn't respect us as a team."

Belief, visualization, pride, connectedness, chemistry, respect—this is the language of psychology, not technical execution. It is the language of process goal setting. But for now I want to stay with the topic of outcome goals. Process goals will be discussed in detail in chapter 8.

Performance Baseline

To build infrastructure, it is necessary to establish a program baseline. This baseline is an assessment of the current level of team performance. I conducted an annual statistical review to determine which areas of the game we would need to improve in order to compete for a conference championship and for postseason tournament play. I called this the championship template (table 2.2), and I used it as a compass to guide my planning of the upcoming training segments.

Since it was my intention to reach the Final Four in every year I coached, I decided to construct a template of Minnesota's performance in the area of attacking. I have always felt that a team's hitting stats, more than any other statistic, correlated with winning matches. So, using the Internet to collect the statistical information I needed, I compared Minnesota's hitting stats with the stats of each of the Final Four partici-

TABLE 2.2   Championship Template 2009

School	Kills (K)	Attack errors (E)	Total attack attempts (TA)	Kill efficiency (K − E/TA = KEff)	E% (E/TA)	K% (K/TA)	Kills per set (K/S)
PSU	1734	428	3352	.390	.128	.517	14.9
Stanford	1731	454	4069	.314	.112	.425	14.7
Nebraska	1714	590	4166	.270	.142	.411	14.5
Texas	1719	447	3795	.335	.118	.453	14.6
Average	1725	480	3846	.324	.125	.449	14.7
Minnesota	1680	626	4512	**.234**	**.139**	**.372**	**10.6**

pants from the previous season. This comparison, I believed, would tell me roughly where we needed to improve if we were to contend for a Final Four berth. So, for example, I used the statistical summary from the 2008 Final Four to provide data that could be used in planning for the 2009 season.

A look at the championship template from the 2008 Final Four teams revealed some useful information as I looked ahead to 2009:

- The numbers in bold in the Minnesota row stood out to me as problems.
- Our KEff was 90 percentage points below the Final Four average.
- Our E% of .139 was very good, but 6 points above the Final Four average.
- Our K% was 77 points below the average.
- We averaged only 10.6 kills per set, well below the Final Four average of 15.

It was clear to me that we had to improve our offensive efficiency. Our off-season emphasis would have to shift to the following:

- Increase our K% when we get an open swing.
- Hit away from body line; wipe off; high hands; and off speed.
- Our setter must improve her set location and set selection.
- Left-side hitters have to become better "erasers" when our ball handling breaks down. (Erasers are hitters who are talented enough to kill the ball even when the pass and set are poor. Thus they erase the poor ball control that preceded the swing.)

As a coach, I managed to qualify for five Final Fours. I believe that the conclusions reached after examining the championship template were among the most important tools I used to chart my planning strategy. They provided a baseline read on my team's ability level. I used that baseline as a starting point for almost every outcome goal we established for our off-season training. A team without goals is a ship without a rudder. Or, to use another analogy, you've got it floored, but you're in neutral.

Identifying Resources

Resources are another category of elements that reside in the infrastructure. It is important to identify the resources available to you at your school or club. This seems like an obvious task, not worthy of separate treatment in this chapter, but the number of coaches who have trouble negotiating these obvious steps would surprise you. These resources include volleyball equipment, clerical help, facilities, coaches, event management crews, operating budgets, medical personnel, and anything or anyone else that can be recruited to assist in your effort to build a volleyball program. All of these resources should be sorted onto a spreadsheet titled Inventory. Once completed, the coach should review the list to select items for action. Once selected, these items are assigned to one or more staff members, a completion date is fixed, and a three-year plan is constructed.

Players: The Most Important Resource

A program's most important resource, of course, is its players. This was apparent the moment I stepped into the gym at Pitt. I took a hard look at how my players compared to the region's best. It was clear to me that to make my players competitive, we needed improvement in four areas. First, I had to start recruiting prospects that possessed similar or better athletic ability than our opponents. Second, I had to assemble a staff that could teach the game well enough to defeat these opponents. Third, I had to create a player-centered culture that would motivate them to buy into my method of program building. And finally, we needed a practice and competition facility that would create a sense of pride throughout the program. Attention to these four items was imperative. They became my personal mantra.

Each of these issues is a no-brainer and exists at all levels of coaching. Many of the solutions can be identified and put into place by exercising sound planning skills. But sometimes the need for a resource can materialize in unexpected ways. The following example provides a brief history of how one such resource came to exist during my early days at Pitt.

Event Management: The Birth of a Resource

I kept a notebook. It included notes on just about everything volleyball related that I didn't know enough about or couldn't do. There were so many things that I had not thought about as I began the job. What equipment should I order? How do I scout an opponent and present a game plan? What about fund-raising?

By the way, our first fund-raiser called for our players to scour the faculty offices and hallways on Tuesdays to secure sandwich orders. The sandwiches would be delivered in cardboard boxes to my office on Wednesday morning. Our players would pick up their orders in time to make their deliveries by lunchtime. We made 50 cents per sandwich. One week we took in a whopping total of 58 dollars. I suspect that not many of today's active coaches can relate to the bottom-feeding fund-raising schemes hatched in the old days. Nor was there anything in the notebook that would guide our fund-raising efforts.

There wasn't anything in that notebook about event management either. This was no surprise. Was there any reason for me to be concerned about putting together an event management team? It was 1976, and there was no history of large crowds at a women's volleyball match. My focus was on training my team, and I had settled in as a CC. But I was soon to learn that event management would become an essential component in creating a successful competitive environment.

I offer the following account not only because it is an accurate sequence of events that preceded the implementation of a director of operations for volleyball, but also because I hope it opens the eyes of today's readers so they look to a time when volleyball struggled to gain a foothold in the athletic department's hierarchy.

Thirteen. This was the total number of spectators who fought their way into Trees Hall at the University of Pittsburgh the evening in 1976 when I made my home debut as a coach. At that time, we charged a dollar for adults. Students were free.

The gang of irate pickup basketball players, who were routinely booted from our competition arena just before the teams took the court for warm-ups, also would have been charged a dollar. But they never stayed for matches. They chose instead to hang around and harass our staff and players with glares and verbal insults as they stormed out of the gym. I don't think they appreciated my tone when, knowing they weren't students, I sarcastically asked them to show ID for proof of adult status.

Surely on this night, opening night, the basketball advocates would relent and allow us to conduct our volleyball match in an atmosphere of negotiated peace. But we were naïve. As the veteran, city-toughened street basketball players saw it, our women's volleyball match was an affront to their way of life, and they would do anything to protect their domain. This was the case prior to every home event. By match time, even though their scheduled time on the court had expired, their numbers swelled sufficiently to give the appearance that they had established late afternoon control over our competition court. And this fueled in them a sense of righteousness.

It was clear that our volleyball match mattered little to them. It all boiled down, in their minds, to the fact that we stood in the way of the natural order of the universe. They believed that gym space belonged, first and foremost, to the legions of pickup basketball players everywhere who possessed the right to walk at any time into any gym and claim it as their own. Add to all of this the fact that they had to give up the court to a bunch of girls playing a sissy sport like volleyball. We were in their way, and we had to be removed.

It is against this backdrop that I prepared to make the long stair-descending walk from our second floor arena to our basement locker room. I was intending to conduct a final prematch meeting with my team. But before I could even pass through the door, a representative from the basketball militia stopped me. He spoke with an air of uncommon passion on behalf of all victims everywhere who were forced to witness volleyball supplant basketball as an official court activity. With his posse standing behind him, he loudly accused me and my team of infringing on their constitutional right to play pickup basketball!

Constitutional right? Are you kidding me! "Defiant" comes to mind as the word to describe the level of disgust radiating from their leader. It was as if the group had recently discovered the term *constitutional right* and had convinced themselves that this newly hatched strategy would trump anything we could say or do. So you can imagine their frustration when the security guards appeared to chase them from the building.

As an aside, I should mention that every home competition this first year started with the same confrontation. Both sides would brandish their sabers and then retreat to their respective habitats. In the end we always got the gym, and they got the exit door. But the verbal abuse directed at me and my program, the embarrassment I felt for my team and fans, the giving and receiving of verbal threats that define the battle for court time in most urban facilities—all of this began to take a toll on me. Nevertheless, no matter how stressfully these prematch confrontations played out, I always invited the basketball terrorists to stay and watch the match. But, of course, they never did. They likely would have viewed this as an unacceptable concession to the enemy during the ongoing turf war in Trees Hall.

Back at our first match, our crowd had temporarily increased to 15. Two students had entered the arena. But instead of taking a seat in the bleachers, they walked across the warm-up court and stopped directly in front of me as I sat on the bench. I'm not sure what I was expecting. Maybe some lost basketball junkies looking for a game? So I was crossed up when one of the students asked me if I could direct her to the tai chi class in an adjoining gym.

I gave them directions and returned to my prematch preparation. But my focus was immediately interrupted by the sound of a sheet of lined paper being ripped out of a spiral notebook. The two students were still in front of me. They explained that they didn't want to be late for their class. I watched her scribble a note that said, "Tai chi—turn left and go straight to the far door." This was a path that would take the tai chi students right through our spectator seating area. But before I could protest, I was handed the note and asked to find some tape to attach it to our entrance so that other students would not be confused as she had been. And off they went. For the record, I did find a piece of athletic tape, and I did tape the sign to our entry door. And yes, some of the tai chi students walked right through our event as the match was being played.

It was as if we weren't even there. This match was one of those defining moments for me. I knew immediately that something had to change. If I were going to coach volleyball, I would have to create a culture that would not only discourage these kinds of disruptions but would also result in the presentation of volleyball as a sport to be respected. I knew that the quality of my program would be revealed with each and every decision I would make.

So I made up my mind. No more sweaty, arrogant basketball players trying to stay on the court past their assigned time. No more insults hurled in our direction. No more using our court as an exit ramp to tai chi. And no more crowds so small they could all fit into an elevator. It was time to step back, ask all the tough questions, and begin the long process of developing a comprehensive volleyball program that would provide solutions to these kinds of issues.

It was then, in the fall of 1976, that I committed myself to becoming a program developer and not a clipboard coach. I couldn't get that opening night scenario out of my mind. My first decision, therefore, was to meet with my administration to assemble an event management crew to prevent a repeat of our opening night misadventure. And we did. It was a skeleton crew in the beginning. But over time these folks took care of things such as game programs, court security, ticket taking, finding and paying officials, supervising pre- and postmatch court protocols, overseeing press room availability, assigning ushers, initiating a marketing and promotions plan for volleyball, and, I was happy to learn, clearing the arena of all the new friends I had made within the world of pickup basketball.

This was my first run at our administration to ask for something new, something in addition to what I was told I would have. I had identified a problem in need of a solution and, presto, the problem was solved. I liked the feeling. I had made a difference in how things were to be done around Pitt volleyball. A protocol had been born. My job was to identify the program's needs, and the administration would help me solve the problem. Little by little, I was building an inventory of resources that would carry the program to the top of the AIAW eastern region.

Later, during my tenures at New Mexico, Illinois, and Minnesota, I continued and refined this process, bringing even more specificity and detail to the search for resources. Failing to acknowledge this first step in program building could only lead to uncertainty and confusion. Resources determine what is possible. And if I wanted to be the best, I had to know that the necessary resources would be in place. I had settled the event management issue at Pitt. Now it was time to apply this same protocol to as many additional issues as possible.

I started to look more closely at potential resources as I walked across campus. For example, I noticed that Fitzgerald Fieldhouse, located across the street from the Trees Hall all-access recreation facility, would be a more desirable arena for showcasing my program. Spectator seating configurations were more desirable. On game day the place was buzzing with some genuine energy. The constant warfare being waged with the basketball warlords would be left behind in Trees Hall. Relocating to the Fieldhouse became an immediate priority. I also noticed that Pitt's lifting and conditioning facilities were open to football and basketball athletes, but not to volleyball. Title IX legislation, I hoped, would soon take care of both issues. And it did.

I then began to carefully assess what I could find out about the region's top teams to determine what made them successful in terms of program support. Where I detected a deficiency in our own program, I began to push for improvement. I needed to know if it would be possible to accumulate the resources, particularly in terms of budget and facilities that could support the ever-increasing demands of my vision of a program.

Recruiting Budget for College Coaches

I can't recall the exact figure, but I believe my annual recruiting budget hovered somewhere near the $1,000 mark. In other words, from a financial standpoint, this meant that we were limited to the recruitment of local in-state players. One or two recruiting trips to California or Chicago would easily have devoured the entire budget. Under AIAW rules, athletes were allowed to pay their own way to visit any campus they wished, thereby shifting the financial burden of the cost of the visit from the institution to the athlete.

While a handful of athletes took advantage of this opportunity, the rule did not yield substantially large numbers of recruits taking and paying for campus trips. Pitt continued to come up short in the recruiting wars. Imagine trying to showcase your school and your volleyball program to more than 50 prospects per year on $1,000 or less; in other words, you have about $20 available to spend on each recruit. The solution to this problem would require some administrative help, but there was no significant budget increase in sight.

Fortunately, I had started and coached a local junior volleyball club that kept supplying the Pitt collegiate team with solid, local talent. Schools without this advantage and without a national recruiting budget had to rely on the occasional superstar athlete who would show up every few years. We were fortunate to be able to field an extremely competitive team without the luxury of being able to recruit nationally.

Locker Room and Team Room Spaces

Remember, the year is 1976. Women's NCAA sports were in their infancy. Athletes who enjoy today's streamlined, well-equipped spaces would have a hard time believing the conditions within which their volleyball ancestors were forced to survive. Follow along as I describe the conditions we encountered during one of our early road trips. While this was not true of Pitt's facilities under our watch, it will open your eyes to what some believed to be an acceptable facility experience.

As we squeezed out of our van (traveling by van in those days, yikes, another story altogether!) to enter the small, unkempt arena where we would be competing that night, I commenced my search for the human being who might be in charge of unlocking the building. We were scheduled for a noon practice. It was 11:45, and there wasn't a sign of life anywhere. All the doors were locked. Wind had blown leaves and assorted trash items onto the building's front steps, preventing us from sitting down for what could be a long wait. Very clever gamesmanship, I thought to myself. Keep the visitors off balance.

I sent scouts in all directions to seek the keeper of the keys. No luck. The cell phone would not make its appearance for another 20 years. As we began to pile back into the van for the trip back to our off-campus motel, I heard the bang of a door being thrust open behind me. I turned around to see the home coach as she kicked leaves from our entrance path. She was sorry for her late arrival, she explained, but she was look-ing for some athletic tape and a Sharpie pen. Hmm, this was proving to be great entertainment.

We followed the coach into a dimly lit gym where one of her players was sweeping leaves off the court. I really thought the lights would grad-ually brighten, but they didn't. Down the hallway and down the stairs we trudged. "In here," directed the coach. "This is your locker room." To us it looked like a maintenance closet. If you looked carefully, you could see that a 2 x 4 had been attached to one wall about 5 feet from the floor. Starting at one end of the 2 x 4, nails had been driven diago-nally so that there was a nail protruding from the 2 x 4 about every 12 inches or so, about 10 nails altogether (we had traveled with 14 players). I also noted that there were 3 metal folding chairs in the vicinity. They would come in handy, the coach explained, when it came time for the team to have a meeting.

The coach then asked the players to line up behind her. One by one, she wanted each player to spell her last name so that she could print it with her Sharpie on a torn-off length of athletic tape. The plan was to place one name above each nail. "Just make sure you hang your stuff on your own nail," she implored. "This way, you will know where to find your belongings after the match." She was priceless. Fortunately, my sense of diplomacy summoned me to my senses and I held back from asking her how I should approach the dilemma created by too few nails and only three folding chairs.

To be fair, this was not the norm, but it did provide one end of the spectrum for rating locker room and team room facilities in 1976. Most schools had what Pitt had. Our athletes dressed and showered in the public women's locker room shared by every female on campus. We had no meeting room, except for the often-used classroom next to the handball courts, but we didn't meet there often. The sound of the handball banging like a metronome against the room's back wall was too distracting. The era of volleyball-exclusive locker rooms and elaborate video and meeting spaces was still years away.

The arms race had not yet begun, and the facilities at Pitt would do for now. I don't know exactly how our team felt about their accommo-dations in Trees Hall, but there is one thing I do remember. Our players were noticeably happier following their visit to the "Dungeon of Death," which was how they referred to the closet with the 2 x 4 on the wall.

Travel Budget

In the early days it was common to travel by van. Volleyball players were expected to pile into 12- or 15-passenger vans and drive for as many as 12 hours to and from a competition. The drivers? None other than the coaches who were understandably tired from coaching a team throughout a weekend tournament. It is one of the most dangerous things in my life that I can recall doing. I still carry vivid memories of long van trips that found everyone asleep at 2:00 am with an exhausted coach at the wheel.

It was also common for athletes to share a bed with a teammate. That's right. Four players per room. This practice lasted into the early 1980s when, one by one, travel budgets were being increased to accommodate a more appropriate one bed per athlete protocol. Meal allowances were established by each institution. I can remember clearly what the University of Pittsburgh provided daily for meals:

Breakfast $2.50

Lunch $3.50

Dinner $6.00

TOTAL $12.00

These figures matched or exceeded most of the figures provided to me by our chief competitors during those years. It became important to be able to tell recruits that our travel budget allowed us to treat our players to the best the sport had to offer during these early years. We considered it to be a significant item in our inventory of resources.

As you complete your inventory of resources, you will end up with a list that might look something like the one shown in figure 2.1.

Now select the items for action (remember, you can't do everything at once) and place them in an assignment grid that will serve as a map for all to follow. Each coach will be assigned projects for which she will be responsible. When these assignments are finalized, it is time to organize these items, along with their intended completion date, onto the three-year plan for program improvements. Table 2.3 shows a partial glimpse of what a three-year plan might look like.

Resources

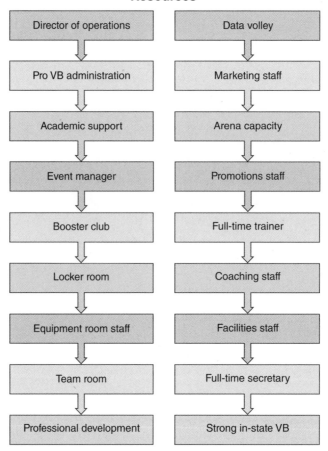

FIGURE 2.1 Resources inventory.

TABLE 2.3 Three-Year Plan

Resource	Coach	Due date
Event management	Jones	Mid-August
Recruiting budget	Smith	May*
Travel budget	Smith	May*
Locker room renovation plan	Williams	Within 6 months
Coordinate booster club chalk talks	Jones, Smith	Late August*
Game planning and presentation	Williams	Late August*
Marketing plan for season	Jones	April*
Finalize stat program	Smith	Within 16 months
Scheduling competition	Williams	Ongoing
Practice planning	Williams	Ongoing

* Refers to projects that are due on an annual basis. A complete three-year plan will, of course, be much longer and more detailed than what you see here.

Championship Manual

I was frustrated in the early years with attempting to develop a delivery system for what was becoming an unmanageable amount of information that I was expecting my players to absorb. I started by doing a stand-up teaching routine in a series of meetings with the team, but I too easily slipped into the stiff assistant professor style that I had perfected while teaching philosophy of education at the college level. Then came the Socratic years when I attempted through dialogue at meetings to lead players to discover the core principles that would serve as the underpinnings of our program culture. In the end I settled on a hybrid style that drew from both of these methods. I also created a textbook for players, called the *Championship Manual*. In it was a collection of everything I believed to be important for preparing a team to win conference and national championships. I modified and updated the contents through the years, but the message was the same. The sidebar, Table of Contents, shows the contents from a recent edition, and it will give you a feel for the scope of items that made up the infrastructure of my programs.

Allow me to share with you one of the documents from the *Championship Manual*. It is a story about an athlete who managed to become extraordinary by committing to a life of inconvenience and sacrifice. I often refer to her when I speak publically about the traits that distinguish the great athletes from the rest. She proved to me and to many others that any team that wants to win a major championship must have at least one extraordinary person on its roster. The role modeling that is supplied by this person becomes a significant part of the team's superstructure.

For some of you, these words will have little effect. Others may become motivated to pursue the goal of becoming an extraordinary player or leader. Those who wish to become extraordinary should read the account of a player who traveled this path in the sidebar "She Isn't Good Enough."

This is the challenge I place in front of each of you. It takes a special person to choose to become an extraordinary athlete. It requires more of a sacrifice than most are willing to endure. The tug of socializing, sleeping in after late nights, inefficient use of study time, and a long list of other distractions will be too much for you to overcome. This is normal. After all, not everyone can become extraordinary. Otherwise, the term would have no meaning.

But to those who want to achieve something special, both on the court and in life, I challenge you to follow the path charted by Lindsey Berg. You will encounter significant levels of frustration. In addition to the decision to spend additional time to improve your volleyball skills,

Table of Contents

choosing to become extraordinary requires that you take a significant risk. It means that you will have to live with new challenges in your life. Your new lifestyle may get you kicked out of the social web of the team. You may be accused of being the coach's favorite. Existing friendships on the team may undergo stressful modifications. You will have to live with uncertainty every day since you cannot be really sure of the rewards that may or may not be there at the end of the journey. Pursuing excellence can be a lonely experience.

Nevertheless, you will have to take the plunge. You will have to accept the risks associated with the choice to become extraordinary. Competitive greatness does not come easy.

She Isn't Good Enough

During the 2008 Olympic Games in Beijing, the U.S. women's volleyball team was on the verge of being eliminated from the medal round. They were playing inconsistently and seemed resigned to finishing out of contention. Then everything changed. Coach Lang Ping inserted setter Lindsey Berg into the lineup. With a surgeon's precision, Berg began to utilize U.S.'s middle attack, which had been conspicuously absent prior to her taking over as setter. She generated energy on the court. She pushed her teammates to a new level. The players rallied around the new life that Berg had breathed into the U.S. team. She took over as the team's starting setter and led them to the Silver Medal. She was the catalyst for the team's turnaround.

This is the same Lindsey Berg who, growing up in Honolulu, was told that she didn't have the athleticism or the body type to play volleyball. They said that she wasn't good enough to make her age group club team, but she did and became the starting setter. These same people doubted that she could make her high school team. She did, and she led her team to the state championship and was twice named the state's player of the year. Then it was time for college. These same people said that she would never play at a high level. Wrong again. She enrolled at the University of Minnesota and was named All Big Ten for three consecutive years. She is arguably the best player ever to wear the maroon and gold.

> continued

> continued

After graduating in 3 1/2 years from the Carlson School of Management, Berg decided to try professional ball. "She's not good enough," came the familiar refrain. Well, Lindsey once again silenced her critics. She not only led her team to the league title, she was also named the league's MVP!

Surely her detractors would have to now admit that they had been wrong, but no. When she announced her intention to try out for the U.S. national team, they scoffed. They said the same things. Wrong body type, can't block, too slow, and so on. She arrived at the U.S. training camp and was one of about 10 setters. Many had her ranked last among the 10 hopefuls.

Well, you are now familiar with the story. Berg made the team and eventually competed in three Olympics. She was the captain of the team in London in 2012. She also starred as the top setter in the professional Italian league. All this produced by a person who many thought would never be good enough. Has she finally silenced her critics? I doubt it, but none of that matters to Lindsey. She is too busy with her life as an extraordinary person. She found herself frequently in an underdog position, and she stood tall each time. Lindsey Berg is a winner. Her unshakeable confidence is at the center of her being. Her passion for the game shines through whenever she takes the court. She has proved beyond any doubt that she is good enough.

Lindsey didn't just decide to become extraordinary one day. She spent years learning how to prove herself in the face of doubters. Most of her confidence-building efforts took place outside the gym. Through trial and error she fashioned a persona that ultimately won over the entire volleyball community. Lindsey would have been a good volleyball player no matter what she decided to do in her spare time, but her decision to make overcoming the odds a fulltime pursuit is what separates her from the rest.

Lindsey Berg, captain of the U.S. women's volleyball team at the 2012 Olympics in London, had to overcome many detractors in her pursuit of volleyball excellence.

Jeff Roberson/Associated Press

Conclusion

I asked a lot from my players. I wanted them to join me in building a program that would command respect. I wanted them to participate in the development of a team culture that would applaud not only the accomplishments inherent in winning, but also the cooperative effort required to prepare to win. I wanted them to learn how to set goals and to live a life governed by the pursuit of goals. I wanted them to understand that excellence requires sacrifice and inconvenience. I wanted them to realize that they were being asked to do all of this in spite of the fact that they were also experiencing the normal challenges of the discovery process that confronts any young person who is trying to balance study, sport, and social life.

From the point of view of the volleyball coach, I felt it was my obligation to provide a program infrastructure that would enable players to reach their potential. I had to be a source of enlightenment and not an adversary. This is why I feel so strongly about clarifying the content of the infrastructure that guides and enriches my program. This infrastructure serves as the foundation and justification for all that we do.

As I entered the final years of my career, I realized that I was on the verge of identifying the most important element in building team success. Without it, there can be no journey to the top. No dynasties. No championships. But if you can harness its power, you will find your program on the way to levels of achievement that had been impossible before. The element I am speaking about is *trust*. It is an old-fashioned term that many have ignored, but it harbors realities that are essential to the health of a team. I will show you what I mean in chapter 8.

CHAPTER 3

Embracing
a Playing Style

In 1981, I traveled to Bucharest, Romania as an assistant coach for the U.S. World University Games team. Our opening pool match would be against Cuba. There were other highly regarded teams in the competition, such as China, Brazil, Holland, Turkey, Korea, and Japan. Armed with pencil and tablet, I watched every scrimmage, every practice session, and every match that my schedule would allow. At night I would visit with coaches from other countries to listen to them talk about how to teach the game.

The Cuban coaches were particularly instructive in this regard. The head coach, Eugenio George, is retired now, but he occasionally travels with the Cuban national teams as an administrator. I will always remember him as a very insightful man whose expertise in coaching volleyball was never limited to Xs and Os. He helped me understand the difference between teaching skills for their own sake and teaching skills within the context of a country's cultural identity.

The Cubans also helped me understand that playing volleyball was not just about the perfect execution of a skill. They told me that it was also about using the skill to express yourself. The Cuban culture is one of passion and appreciation of artistic accomplishment. This includes sport. The culture also harbors an element of pride that can easily morph into arrogance when a competitive situation presents itself. "This is why we are respected," Eugenio told me, "but not always well liked. If we were to change our personality to accommodate our critics, we would not be able to play Cuban volleyball. Every team must embrace its cultural values and learn to express them when they play. This ensures a reasonable level of trust since the team's value system will be familiar to all."

The 1981 Cuban national team featured the greatest outside hitter in the history of women's volleyball. She is 5 feet 9 inches on a good day. Her name is Mireya Luis, and she has since retired. They also featured the best and most intimidating middle blocker I have ever seen. Her name is Magaly Carvajal. She led her Cuban teammates to victory over Brazil in Sao Paulo in the final of the World Championship in 1994. In front of a sold-out soccer stadium crowd, she took on the entire Brazilian following and silenced them with one of the greatest blocking performances of all time. At one point, she stood in a defiant posture in the middle of the court and raised her fist to demonstrate her feelings toward the Brazilians. She was the quintessential Cuban volleyball player. After she and her teammates scored match point, with fists thrust skyward, they ran off the floor to the jeers of the stadium crowd. The Cubans were in their element, and they loved it.

This was the Cuban team we were preparing to play in the opening round of the 1981 Universiade tournament in Bucharest. It wasn't going to be a fair fight. The Cubans would soon be Olympic and World Champions. Our U.S. team was a collection of young college-age all-stars.

Cuban Spiking

As the two teams took the court for the opening round robin match, U.S. head coach Chuck Erbe asked me to conduct our pregame warm-up. I walked to our ball cart expecting to begin tossing balls to our setter to give our hitters a few warm-up swings. This was before warm-ups were controlled by the officials. Both teams were on the floor at the same time. Within a few seconds unofficial war had been declared. Both teams sought to annihilate the other by blasting warm-up spikes at each other's hitting lines.

The Cubans were whooping it up. Their coaches were tossing 50-50 balls (half of the ball on our side of the net and half on their side so that the toss was descending right on top of the net), which allowed them to pound away at our hitting lines with great frequency. We were completely intimidated and had no answer for the Cuban onslaught. I was hoping for the whistle to blow to end the warm-up so the match could start. When it was finally over, and the smoke had cleared, the Cubans transitioned into their famous "we will soon destroy you" glare as we shagged balls to clear the court.

They crushed us in three sets. Later, at the dining hall, they cut in front of us in line and served themselves first. Always with the glare.

The Cubans, quite literally, hit the ball harder than any women's team ever assembled. In fact, they hit the ball harder than some men's teams. They relied on their superior strength and jumping ability. They didn't use a fast, combination style of attack. Instead, they jumped straight up and blasted the ball over the top of the block. They were not overly concerned about their passing. Unlike most teams that required a perfectly located pass to execute their offense, all they had to do was get the ball airborne on the second contact and one of their gazelle-like athletes would soar skyward and drill the ball straight down for the point. They were impressive. During the Luis-Carvajal era (throughout the 1990s), the Cuban women's national team ruled the women's game. They won eight straight major titles that included the Olympic Games, the World Championships, and the World Cup.

There is a point to be made here. The Cubans' actual spiking technique differed very little from the technique utilized by many other teams. One would expect, therefore, that these teams would project a similar look. But if the Cubans are warming up on one court, and there is any other team on an adjacent court, one would easily see that the Cuban spikers do something very different than the others. The Cuban hitters display an element of intimidation every time they hit the ball. They aren't just spiking. This is spiking of a different kind. It is Cuban spiking, and it is *the* show everywhere they play. The skill-training regimen in the Cuban gym is not just about how to spike correctly. It is primarily about learning how to spike like a Cuban.

Toward the end of their incredible run as the world's best women's volleyball team, I happened to be in El Paso, Texas. The Cuban team was scheduled to play the U.S. in an exhibition at the UTEP campus. My good friend and UTEP's head coach at the time, Norm Brandl, had arranged a practice session for the Cubans on the day before the event, and he invited me to accompany him to the gym to watch. Norm and I were curious and decided to keep track of how much time was spent on each phase of practice. We were expecting to see the normal distribution of training segments present in all volleyball practices: team warm-up, individual skill training, serve and pass, team defense, team offense, scrimmage, scout team running the opponent's system in preparation for the next match, and so on.

We may as well have kept our stopwatches (this was before cell phones were used for this purpose) in our pockets. Aside from the first 10 minutes of the practice being used for a casual individual warm-up, the rest of the three-hour practice was devoted to spiking. That's right, almost 2 hours 45 minutes of jumping and hitting. Remarkably, every player in the gym pounded every set straight to the floor with incredible power. There were no wasted swings. Every attempt appeared to have the spiker's reputation riding on it. It seemed that a less than maximum effort would have scarred the hitter for life, and no one was willing to take that chance. If anything, the longer the practice lasted, the harder they hit the ball. Their singular focus on funneling every muscle, every correction in timing, and every bit of personal mastery into one explosive moment was over-the-top impressive.

The Cuban players rarely reined themselves in during matches either. They were generally given the green light by their coaches to play in an all-out aggressive style, including serving. For example, as an advisor for the U.S. women's team competing in the Cuba Cup in the late 1980s, I was asked to take statistics on serving. In the first set, the Cubans served so aggressively that they committed 25 service errors. That's right, 25 in the first set alone. Here is the kicker—they beat the U.S. in that set, 15-2 (side-out scoring). In other words, the Cubans were not worried about serving errors since their confidence in the side-out game was absolute. This allowed them to serve as aggressively as they wished. Their ability to terminate the subsequent first-ball attack rendered serving errors almost meaningless.

This was not the case with the Americans. We were forced to serve less aggressively in order to reduce our serving errors. We could not kill the ball at the same rate as the Cubans. We were forced to play a much more conservative style that emphasized fewer errors. Our conservative skill training with regard to serving was very different from the aggressive Cuban style as a result of differences in our respective abilities to kill the ball.

The Cuban Signature Style of Play

The Cubans had captured something special in the way they taught their athletes to play the game. Part of it was the fact that their players were among the best jumpers in the world. Another part came from the strength-building program taught to them through the years by the Soviet Union and East German coaches. But neither of these items accounted for the entirety of what made the Cubans so special. There was something else embedded in what they were doing.

And then it hit me. I never once saw the Cubans practice or compete without a serious effort to rehearse and maintain their style of play. I never saw them just spiking. I saw them working on how to be a *Cuban* spiker—the accelerating, all-out approach; the max-jumping on every rep; the hammer-like armswing on permanent display; the look of invincibility that accompanied every swing. These are the things I remember the most about the Cubans. To them, spiking was not just a random volleyball skill. It was an act of cultural vindication. It embodied everything the Cuban people were about. It wasn't a stale set of movements that could be repeated by just anyone. The skill of Cuban spiking was enshrined as a sacred possession among the Cuban players. It became their signature, and when they practiced Cuban spiking, it was always accompanied by the demanding performance requirements that made them one of the most recognizable teams ever to play the game.

From this experience I learned that teaching volleyball skills did not have to be limited to the acquisition of a single universally accepted list of skills and keys. In fact, I began to believe that modifying your skill-training regimen to fit your style of play made a lot of sense, but I had to feel more comfortable with the concept of styles of play. What did it mean? What did it encompass? How many different styles of play could I identify? What impact would each style have on a team's skill development?

For example, if you come from the Cuban volleyball tradition, you will play a freelance style. You will spend most of your time near the net learning how to terminate the ball with astonishing power and athleticism. This is where the hitting and blocking skills are honed. You will be expected to be among the best in the world at both. Your ability as a player will be measured by how frequently you can score by blocking and hitting. You will be introduced to the full range of volleyball skills, but you will specialize in only a few. And you will probably learn the Cuban glare.

Of all the things I learned from the Cubans, the most important was their commitment to play the game with a specific style, a style that became unmistakably their own. It was a style that intimidated opponents and transformed their own players into conquering warriors.

A signature style of play—I believe this to be something every team should strive to acquire for themselves. When a team plays with a unique, recognizable style—playing relentless defense would qualify as another example—it becomes their calling card. The team begins to play with an enhanced identity and a unified sense of purpose that is not possible without this signature in place.

Signature Styles of Play

Style of play is a phrase that I have used to suggest that teams can be differentiated according to how they play the game. There is no official listing of these varying styles, but as we cast our gaze over the volleyball universe, it is clear that at least three distinct styles have emerged at the women's international level (table 3.1).

TABLE 3.1   Comparison of Styles of Play Among Women's National Teams

Style of play	Characteristics	Sample teams
Control the net	Physically intimidating Control match by controlling net play (dominant blocking and hitting skills) Ball control is secondary to net presence	Cuba Soviet Union (now Russia) Dominican Republic
Small ball	Generally smaller in stature Great defense Accurate ball control Rely on counterattacking for points Good counter-punchers	Japan Korea China
Hybrid	Hybrid of best features of other two Players have all-around skill sets Able to play multiple styles depending on opponent	United States Brazil Italy

First are the physically intimidating teams that want to control the match by controlling play at the net through blocking and hitting. Ball control is secondary to net presence as a point of emphasis in how they play. Cuba, the Soviet Union (now Russia), and the Dominican Republic use this style of play.

Second are the teams whose players are smaller in stature and play great defense. Their ball-control ability is so accurate that they can also rely heavily on counterattacking for points. If these teams were boxers, we would say that they were good counterpunchers. Japan, Korea, and China use this style.

Third are the hybrid programs that combine the best features of the other two. These teams tend to train their players to acquire all-around skill sets. Their style is that they have no particular style. They are good at everything. The United States, Brazil, and Italy exemplify this style.

A team's skill training must reflect, both in emphasis and technical precision, this particular style. Remember, there is no universally agreed upon formula for teaching volleyball skills. The term *spiking* does not contain self-evident truths to be applied in every attempt to teach spiking. The meaning of the term *spiking* (and every other skill) is rooted in whatever movement patterns and stylistic preferences each coach brings to the table. The Cubans understood this very well.

Italy's national women's team exemplifies the hybrid type of team, one that features players with an all-around skill set.

Daniele Badolato/LaPresse/Icon SMI

Japanese Playing Style

I also spent time talking with the Japanese coaching staff. I asked the same questions of my Japanese colleagues: "What should I teach?" and "How do I teach it?" I wanted to know how they trained their players to be so tenacious on defense. I had more questions than they had time. Finally their traveling business manager, who had been eavesdropping on our conversation, entered the room. He was fluent in both Japanese and English. He was also articulate in explaining the importance of Japanese culture in training to be a skilled volleyball player.

"When a Japanese player commits to a team, she pledges loyalty to that team," he said. "In Japan the concept of single-minded hard work and loyalty to employers is an important part of our culture. The players are expected to obey the coaches at all times. They are also expected to work together as a team. No individual is more important than the team. All of these are principles of our culture."

In 1998 I arranged for my women's volleyball team from the University of Minnesota to conduct our preseason camp in the prefecture of Akita, Japan. We were nationally ranked in the AVCA preseason poll and anxious to fortify our season outlook by spending two to three weeks training with highly regarded Japanese university teams. I knew what we were getting ourselves into, but I could tell that my players had no idea what awaited them on the other side of the Pacific Ocean.

This was going to be an eye-opener. Japanese teams trained longer and harder than most, certainly more than we were allowed under NCAA rules. They were widely considered to be among the world's most highly skilled coaches and players. And we were headed straight into this extremely demanding environment.

As a result of spending several days together at the Akita training center, I was hoping to get a detailed look at how the Japanese practiced and how they played the game. I was already certain of two things. First, the Japanese players were going to perform volleyball skills at a level none of us had seen before. Second, my team was in for the shock of their volleyball lives.

Japanese Discipline

The plan was for both teams to train separately in the morning, followed by a two-hour scrimmage on selected afternoons. We arrived on the first day to begin practice at 8:30 a.m. Our players were surprised to learn that the Japanese had been training intensely since 6:00 a.m. Then came our second surprise. Thinking that we had arrived at the gym in a timely fashion to start our first morning session, we ran into an unexpected delay as we attempted to enter the building. We had our first encounter with Japanese slipper protocol. This was to be an early lesson in understanding Japanese culture.

Before stepping into the gym, we had to change from our walk-to-the-gym shoes into the first pair of slippers, which were to be worn when walking from the main gym entrance to the locker room. We then had to change from the walk-to-the-locker-room slippers to the slippers to be worn when walking from the locker room to the gym floor. In each case, there was a small changing room full of slippers. You had to leave your previously worn slippers on the changing room shelf, pick out a new pair, and start the process all over again. Slipper training on the first day caused us to be 20 minutes late for practice. You don't want to be late for practice in Japan.

When we finally entered the practice gym, our hosts immediately lined up on their baseline to acknowledge our arrival, bowed politely in our direction, and quickly resumed training. I was certain that our tardiness was seen as an unintentional cultural error. Nevertheless, our players managed to recover a degree of respect when they properly stowed their in-the-gym slippers on the shelf and changed into their in-the-gym volleyball shoes, never to be confused with the pair that would be worn when walking back to the hotel.

We put our team through a rigorous three-hour practice in a gym that featured a level of heat, humidity, and sweat found only in Japan. As we prepared to end our morning session, we wondered why the Japanese were not joining us for lunch. It was then that we found out that they were given only 10 minutes for lunch and were expected to return to practice immediately. I saw the familiar look of bewilderment spread through our team, the look that is common among those getting their first glimpse of the Japanese practice routine. Our players were exhausted and ready for a nap. The Japanese were still going full speed.

Our hosts bowed to us again as we left for lunch, and they returned immediately to their training. Our players wolfed down lunch and retired to a one-hour nap. We returned to the gym for our second practice and scrimmage. We were feeling pretty good about our improved slipper skills, but when we arrived at the practice arena, our players were again surprised to see the Japanese players still at work. While we were napping, they were going through hard-core defensive drills that really got our players' attention. Their coaches were tipping and throwing balls everywhere, and the players were expected to pursue and save every ball. It was brutal, and the coaches got more demanding as the drill continued.

One of the players, who we noticed had been crying as she struggled through the drill, suddenly stopped going for a ball. The mood in the gym immediately shifted. The sudden silence created a major contrast to the nonstop screaming of players and coaches as they went through the drill. One of the coaches walked directly toward the player and confronted her face to face. He was furious, screaming at her as loudly as he could. The player bowed to him over and over. Finally, the coach reached back and slapped her on her jaw. She continued to bow as he raised his hand to strike her again. He then walked away, poured himself a cup of coffee, lit a cigarette, and continued to scream at the player as he took a seat near her court. She returned to the drill, still crying, and decided to pursue every ball that came her way.

Our nationally ranked Minnesota team competed against four different Japanese college teams. Altogether we played 42 sets against them. Our overall record was 0-42. We scored in double figures three times (side-out scoring). After one of our double-figure outings, the coach of the Japanese team was furious. He ordered his team outside to practice on the asphalt parking lot. There were a few scrapes and bruises visible on his players when they reentered the gym an hour later.

As a gesture of kindness, the trip organizers arranged for us to play against an all-star high school team from the local Akita prefecture. We went 8-3 against the high schoolers and were fortunate to do so. They were very good. In my opinion they were better than a lot of college teams in the United States. For the record, the University of Minnesota team returned home to post a 30-4 record for the season and a number 11 national ranking.

The Japanese accomplishments were even more impressive when we compare the physical size and athleticism of the Japanese and the Americans. Table 3.2 shows the heights of the players in each position during our match against Tokai University, the defending collegiate national champion of Japan.

TABLE 3.2   Height Comparison: Minnesota and Tokai University

School	Outside hitters	Middle blockers	Opposite	Setter
Minnesota	6'2" (188 cm), 6'3" (190.5 cm)	6'3" (190.5 cm), 6'4" (193 cm)	6'3" (190.5 cm)	5'9" (175.2 cm)
Tokai University	5'6" (167.6 cm), 5'8" (172.7 cm)	5'8" (172.7 cm), 5'7" (170.2 cm)	5'9" (175.2 cm)	5'0" (152.4 cm)

Japanese Signature Style of Play

They were shorter, and they were not as athletic as our team, but they beat on us like a drum. They blocked us at will. Their offensive tempo and combination attack were the fastest we had ever encountered. They dug our most powerful spikes with ease, and they served us off the court. When their starters were taken out of the match, the second team players stomped on us in similar fashion. They were the most skilled volleyball players our team had ever seen.

Playing fast is what the Japanese bring to the world volleyball stage. They play the game in a different dimension of time. They pass fast, set fast, swing fast, block fast, serve fast, they even walk fast. Playing

Japanese teams are known for their fast, tenacious play on both offense and defense.

Kyodo via AP Images

against them can be an experience in suffocation. They are relentless in everything they do.

Eventually, we were able to evaluate what had taken place. Their skill level was phenomenal. Their training methods were superior to ours. More important, their practice and playing style were closely linked to Japanese culture. During one of our shared evening meals, our staff and players got a glimpse of what this meant.

To begin with, no Japanese player was allowed to sit at the table until the coaches had first been served their meals by the players. The players also sat politely through the entire meal until the coaches decided it was time to leave. During the course of the meal my wife, Sherry, got into a discussion with the Japanese head coach. "How often do you practice?" she asked.

"Our players practice 8 to 10 hours a day," he responded. "Last year we practiced 363 days."

"Why did you decide not to practice for two days?" Sherry asked.

"One day was national holiday," he said. "And the other day I sick of team."

Sherry pressed onward. "If your players practice 8 to 10 hours a day, when do they go to class and study?" she asked.

"This is not my problem," he answered without flinching.

This approach to volleyball works for the Japanese. It fits their culture. They are notoriously dedicated to their work. There is little room for failure. There is great attention to detail. Everything we witnessed during our visit confirmed these observations. The long hours in the gym, the elite level of skill acquisition, the tolerance of severe physical punishment following failure, and the unconditional team loyalty expressed by everyone in the program—all of this gave us a rare look into how Japanese culture shapes the way their volleyball program is designed.

One final example punctuated our stay in Japan. We arrived early for practice on the last day, and we stopped by the Japanese court to watch their scrimmage. Instead of watching them compete, my attention wandered toward a drama that was unfolding on the sideline. The coaches were using their second-string players to serve as line judges for scrimmages. The head coach seemed agitated with one of the line judges who was stationed near his bench. She had just made a call that went against the head coach's team. He got up and scolded the girl for making the wrong call. On the very next play, she called another ball out that he thought was in. With the wave of his hand, he called for two of his assistant coaches to have her removed from her position. They swooped in, lifted her up, and whisked her away. She did not make another appearance during the scrimmage. We guessed that her future as a line judge was in serious jeopardy.

We saw the incident as confirmation of all that we had come to know about Japanese culture. There simply was no room for variation. There was one way to do things. We reasoned that the Japanese style of coaching was an extension of their culture and that American players would be challenged to do well in this environment. The clash of cultures would have prevented any significant learning from taking place. The Americans and their independent style would drive the discipline-oriented Japanese crazy. The regimented style of the Japanese would not be tolerated by the Americans. No problem. We were there to observe and learn. We were not asking our players to become Japanese.

U.S. Playing Style

Americans are more reliant on positive emotion as a motivational source, not fear. If a coach were to strike an American player in the same fashion, the player would likely retaliate by swinging back. Not many Americans would agree to train 8 to 10 hours a day with only two days off per year. Nor can I envision American athletes serving dinner to their coaches and standing behind their chairs until the coaches signaled that all could begin their meals.

This does not mean that the American system is better than the Japanese or vice versa. It does suggest, however, that when cultural values and training philosophies align, this alignment can become a driving force in determining a team's identity as it shapes its style of play. For the Japanese, an all-out commitment to team defense can be seen as an expression of Japan's cultural emphasis on defending their relatively small island against all threats. Their ultrafast style of offense, including their use of highly deceptive combination attacking, might reflect the creativeness required by the Japanese to compete successfully in the global market.

The juxtaposition of the Cuban, Japanese, and American styles of skill training produces a clear contrast. The speed, precision, and deception of Japan, the deliberate, no nonsense, straight ahead power style of the Cubans, and the creative, competitive mindset of the Americans reflects an interesting and profound difference in their respective skill-training regimens.

The Japanese demand *sameness* in execution. They forbid the presence of a maverick player who insists on doing things differently than what the coach is teaching. Playing for a team from Japan will require that you have excellent ball-control skills and a willingness to play serious defense. Since your team will not be tall, your hitting and blocking skills must be developed to the highest level. You must be willing to sacrifice your life for the sport of volleyball, and you must do this with a sense of pride and loyalty.

The Cubans, on the other hand, are not concerned about sameness. They want their players to display a certain arrogance. Their players must hit and block better than any other team in the world. They want their team to embody their pride in the small, economically isolated nation they represent. Their skill training is not about technical purity. It is more about a demonstration of power and dominance.

Americans, first and foremost, are independent. They are motivated by individual challenges. Once joining a team, they have to be trained to behave as a team, where group goals are more important than individual goals. This will not come naturally. If and when they do commit to a team goal, it is sometimes done begrudgingly, and they expect to be rewarded for such a concession of individual freedom on their part. Teaching skills to an American team can be very difficult because each of the players will want to do it his way. American players often resist sameness and group discipline. It can be hard for Americans, who are so independent, to trust each other when adversity strikes. The challenge for coaches of Americans is to orchestrate a team concept in an environment that so fiercely protects a self-first mode of thinking.

While both Japan and Cuba can present a clear and consistent portrait of how volleyball is perceived in their respective domains—the highly skilled defense-oriented style of Japan and the high-flying, net-controlling style of the Cubans—the same cannot be said for the United States. The volleyball style emerging from the sport's cradle in Southern California is sometimes considerably different from the style coming out of the Midwest or the East Coast. The sheer size of the U.S. as a country leads to the evolution of regional patterns in sport. National patterns are less likely to evolve simply because of the distance between the regional areas of growth.

But if there is one thing that American players can claim as their signature style of play it would be summarized in this one word: *competitive*. From the very beginning of their birth as a culture, Americans have fought to be the very best at everything. Even though teams from the States display a diverse menu of playing styles, they are united around the desire to compete. While this characteristic may not be as visible as Japan's defense or Cuba's power, it can nevertheless affect a match in the same way.

As I pointed out earlier, skills are not self-contained entities that float in space without value or meaning. However, some coaches treat them as though they are. They teach skills the same way every season with the hope that each player will learn to execute the skills in the same fashion.

If you decide to change how you play, you likely will have to change your menu of skills. To put this another way, different styles of play require parallel adjustments in how skills should be taught. If I wish to teach the skill of spiking, I must first decide which style of spiking I want to teach. There is no one style that everyone agrees on. In fact, there are many styles, each requiring different movement patterns for execution. Allow me to illustrate by continuing to contrast the Cuban, Japanese, and American styles.

The Cubans want to rely on their power and athleticism as the basis for their offensive system. They often set a high ball to their pin hitters who routinely out-jump the opponent's blockers for a kill. Their approach mechanics emphasize straight-ahead movement using long strides and medium speed into the plant. The arm lift in jumping out of the plant features long levers (straight arms) because they are more interested in overall height of the reach than how quickly they can trigger the armswing as they reach the apex of their jump.

The Japanese, on the other hand, focus primarily on quickness, timing, accurate passing, digging, and a setter who can deliver a perfect ball even while flying through space in the attempt to track down an occasional errant pass. Their system requires perfection at all levels. All of the parts need to be in synch for their offense to be effective.

The United States has chosen to borrow from other offensive systems to create their own hybrid style that emphasizes both high-ball and quick-tempo attacking. Along the way, the Americans lived up to their reputation as agents of creative change. Led by coaches Doug Beal and Bill Neville, along with the incomparable Karch Kiraly, the U.S. introduced the two-passer, inside-out approach style of hitting that helped them win a gold medal in the 1984 Olympic Games.

Using spiking as an example, table 3.3 illustrates how the same skill can be taught in different ways. The high-ball hitting style of the Cubans, the faster-paced style of the Japanese, and the more-flexible, adaptive style of the Americans are all considered to be examples of spiking, even though each style features a different look and tactical purpose. The Cubans want to overpower you. The Japanese want to "outquick" you. And the Americans want to outthink you. One can use this same analysis to evaluate other skills in the sport, such as serving, blocking, passing, and setting.

There are no better examples of teams who had committed to playing a signature style than Cuba, Japan, and the United States. All three understood that skills come equipped with a specific meaning. The Cubans trained with a clear idea regarding how they saw spiking fit into their style of play. The Japanese trained with a different but equally clear idea regarding how their style of spiking fit into the way they play. Meanwhile the United States decided to combine the best of every style to create the hybrid style that has given their opponents fits for the last three decades. Whether we are aware of it or not, our skill training always reflects our preferences regarding how we want our team to play. Instead of training skills from the false perspective of neutrality (the belief that there is a universally agreed-upon list of skills tucked away in that bank vault), create a style of play for your team that you can control through your skill development process. Leave the practice court every day feeling as though you enhanced your team's signature style of play.

I offer the following observation to you all. Over the past 30 to 40 years, we have witnessed the evolution of differing styles of play. I believe that this process has been the inevitable outcome of historical forces from both within and outside our sport. I have cited cultural influences, anatomical differences, and predisposed beliefs regarding the appropriate way to teach volleyball skills as some of those forces. But the same forces that created these differences are now leading to the homogenization of the game. With each new wrinkle in the tactics

TABLE 3.3 Comparison of Cuba, Japan, and United States: Spiking

	Cuba	Japan	United States
Approach: starting point and angles	Positioned for a lengthy (5.5 to 6 m) straight-ahead approach. No deception intended.	Positioned for short (2.5 to 3 m), compact approach with possible change of direction into plant.	Multiple approach patterns relative to specific sets. Starting point and step length relative to set being attacked. Approach length will be in between Cuba and Japan in terms of starting location.
Degree of arm reach-back and forward thrust for jump prior to swing	Long arms on the reach-back. Long arms on the upward lift.	Bent elbows all the way through reach-back and upward lift.	Not a major point of emphasis for U.S. Similar to Japan.
Degree of core load and jump prior to swing	Always maximum core load and jump.	Combination of maximum core/jump and abbreviated core/jump (when seeking quick tempo offense).	Maximum jump and core load.
Arm length at pull through	Short levers (bent elbows) for quick sets. Long levers (straight arms) for high balls.	Create short levers for greater speed.	Create short or long levers, depending on type of set delivered.
Specialization or versatility as attacker	Primarily second tempo and high-ball hitters.	Positional specialization as a hitter.	Ability to attack all sets in the offense; versatility.
Maintenance of own skill base or conformity to coach's training	Either own or coach's approach. Must be capable of producing maximum jump to attack high ball.	Universal conformity to hitting mechanics taught by coach.	More reliance on individual player's style. Less inclination to want to change everyone's technique to achieve sameness.

Like the United States, Brazil demonstrates a hybrid style of play, with players who demonstrate all-around skill sets. Fernanda Rodrigues hits high and hard over the Japanese block in a semifinal match during the 2012 London Olympics.
Zuma Press/Icon SMI

and techniques of play, there will be counterresponses to those wrinkles aimed at neutralizing them. As this process of finding answers continues to repeat itself, there will be fewer and fewer differences in the way teams play the game. This is another reason I feel so strongly that new frontiers, such as establishing trust as a major lynchpin that holds the team together, need to be opened and explored. We may be running out of developmental room for improving technique and tactics, but the study and establishment of sound psychological principles is an as yet untapped resource by comparison.

How Values Influence Skill Training and Tactics

I began this book with the admission of my lack of preparation prior to my first practice session as a coach. I then acknowledged the importance of seeking out the keepers of the conventional wisdom by talking with the volleyball locals. I next discovered the scientific world of biomechanics and motor learning. Then, in discussing my first-hand experience with both the Cuban and the Japanese national team programs, I discovered the importance of developing a signature style of play. The Japanese, for example, were comfortable sending lower, faster free-ball passes to their setter in order to initiate their quick offense. This was compatible with Japan's cultural emphasis on efficiency and high-velocity work habits. The Cubans, at least during their 10-year reign as the world's best, preferred the dominating presence of their head-turning, super-athletic spiking machines. Any effort by the Cubans to play fast would be sent away just as quickly as an effort by the Japanese to rely on the slower power game. This was not going to happen.

The relationship between these athletes and the skill training they received from coaches within their own culture cannot be overlooked. It is one of the variables at work in deciding how to train volleyball skills. From volleyball's conventional wisdom and science to the culturally driven teams that have grown to mirror their society's values, skill training in this sport has taken on a new role. No matter how hard I tried to remove this conclusion from my observations, I couldn't make it go away. As I stated earlier, skill acquisition seems to be subject to something more than just the repeating of a benign skill. Skills are not valueless entities waiting to be replicated and taught. They are equipped with an identity that percolates to the surface whenever skill training occurs.

No doubt there will be a significant sense of irony regarding what I am about to say next, but I believe it to be an important statement, one that needs to be added to the ongoing debate over how to teach motor skills. Teaching sport-specific skills to athletes includes a value component, even if you are not aware of it. You *think* you are being neutral in your skill teaching, but no matter what you choose to do, it results in a rejection of something else. If a coach chooses to teach spikers to learn a long, high-ball approach pattern, those players will become good high-ball hitters, but it is unlikely that the same team would also become proficient at hitting lower, quicker sets required by a faster offensive style. These styles are often mutually exclusive. The coach must choose a particular style and go with it.

My recommendation would be that every coach declare her own signature style of play. Skill development will be compatible with this style. There is no right or wrong in what you choose to do. There is only compatibility or incompatibility. There is either an awareness of your team's style of play, or there is not. I believe a team will play with more purpose and with fewer distractions if a signature style can be developed.

Conclusion

When you finally decide on a style of play, make sure that you do so after having examined all possibilities. Otherwise you open the door to the type of mistake I made many years ago as a young coach. I will leave you with a brief account of this experience from the mid-1970s. I was visiting a practice session run by a good friend of mine, Joe Silipo. He was the head boys' volleyball coach at Peabody High School in Pittsburgh. As practice began to take shape, I was shocked to see that he was receiving serve with only two passers. Didn't he realize that, according to the conventional wisdom of the day, volleyball teams were supposed to line up in what was called the W formation and receive with five players? I walked over to where Joe was standing and told him about the mistake he was making. I hoped that I had reached him in time and that he would be able to avoid embarrassment by changing his passing formation back to the more popular W.

I had committed the very crime that I admonished all of you to be vigilant to avoid. Without looking properly into the matter, I hit him with the conventional wisdom argument. But to his credit, Joe realized that he could design a passing formation that made sense to him and need not listen to the critics. So in 1976 Joe created his own style of play that featured a two-man receiving pattern. How incredibly foolish I felt eight years later when the U.S. men's Olympic team won a gold medal using this same two-person receiving system. That system, the very one I told Joe to abandon because it wasn't on the Conventional Wisdom list, quickly spread to the rest of the world (modified by many to include a third passer), and even today it is the system of choice for just about every team at every level.

Before moving on, I want to share what might be my only original thought in this entire book. There are many reasons to develop a signature style of play, and I described some of them earlier in this chapter. But it occurs to me that one of the main reasons for mastering a particular playing style is to provide a safety net, a source of confidence for teams who adopt it. When it appears that all is lost, and your team is being steamrolled by a good opponent, there is a great settling effect in knowing that your team can fall back on something familiar and easily accessible. I have seen it happen so many times. Bystanders remark, "Good. They're starting to play like themselves again!" There is a tangible surge of confidence that can be detected whenever a team finds itself in trouble in a match and reverts to its signature style of play. If for no other reason than this, seeking and perfecting a signature style should be on your to-do list!

When selecting your list of skills and creating your list of keys, be sure to keep an open mind. You may be led to unfamiliar areas of inquiry. You may decide to abandon one style of play and adopt a new one. But be sure to stay vigilant. Keep grinding. And make sure that the skills you teach are in harmony with the style of play you have chosen. After all, your finished product will serve as your on-court "home" for a long time.

CHAPTER 4

Honing Vital Skills

I have no formal training as a motor learning specialist. Much of it seems unnecessarily complicated to me. If I have any insights about teaching volleyball skills, they have been formed by reading selected books and journals and by observing how successful coaches and players interact within the learning environment. This chapter documents my growth as a volleyball teacher with the hope that you can much more readily grasp what, for me, took many years to learn. And through your reading experience you might—as did I—come to appreciate aspects of the skill-training process that never seemed all that relevant before.

As I gained experience in the gym, I could feel a surge in self-confidence. But I also found that I was generating as many new questions as I was answers. Where do I begin in teaching volleyball skills to my team? Do I follow a prescribed sequence of skills, or do I pick and choose topics at will? How much individual skill training versus team training should there be in each practice? How long should each practice be? How do I know when a skill has been learned at a high enough level, allowing me to move on to new topics? How do I establish an acceptable learning rate for the players? Are penalties appropriate when players make mistakes?

I have not been able to answer all of these questions to my satisfaction, but the exploration has been fascinating.

Teaching motor skills requires knowledge, pedagogical awareness, an excellent eye for evaluating progress, a clearly defined image of the ultimate goal for each skill, and an abundant supply of patience shared by all involved. Like most coaches, I believed that there must be a universally accepted list of volleyball skills that would be accessed, learned, and taught the same way in every situation. In my case, however, what began as a search for this list led to the discovery that no such list exists. This opened the door to the realization that skills are often formed in a random fashion, depending on what the coach happens to bring to the process. Later in my career, I learned skills can be developed within the context of the playing style utilized by each team.

Cognitive and Motor Learning

Much of what I know about motor learning comes from Carl McGown, one of volleyball's most reliable and active scientists. Carl has served for many years as a faculty member at BYU, has coached internationally with U.S. teams for over 30 years, and is a founder of Gold Medal Squared, a popular coaching development program. I have attended four or five presentations by Carl in which he explained the basic principles of motor learning theory. I have done a fair amount of reading on the subject, but no one has presented the topic as clearly and with as few words as Carl. His is a voice that I find easy to tune into.

I hope I will not do him a disservice by attempting to capture the essence of what he has to say on the subject. Carl would certainly present the following topics in his own sophisticated way. He might even say that I am making a noble attempt to embrace his theoretical work but lack the intellectual accuracy to understand the whole of what he is trying to achieve. I can accept this. I would not quarrel with those who would say that I really don't thoroughly understand his views on science and motor learning. OK. But what I do know is that even my limited understanding of his work has helped me plan practices and teach skills in a more efficient fashion. I may not know the truth about every scientific articulation relevant to this discussion. But I think that my interpretation of his work has been close enough to the real thing, close enough to use it as a guiding hand as I created my view of how to teach the game of volleyball.

I do understand that all learning is, ultimately, cognitive learning. My choice to discuss the two kinds of learning as subject to different laws stems more from my desire to reshape science to meet my needs than from any commitment to legitimate scientific inquiry. I have always believed in the "close enough" approach when applying science to coaching. I never felt that I had the time to spend in a lab or to remain current as a reader of all relevant journals and books. So if I could get to the point where, for example, I felt comfortable in pursuing the teaching principles intended for coaches to follow—even if my understanding of the science was incomplete—this was OK with me. So, when you read the following discussion, remember to focus your attention on the *outcome* of my deliberation, not the shallow scientific base I may have used to justify my conclusions. As I said above, I believe my thinking is close enough.

Coaches often make the mistake of thinking that motor learning (learning a volleyball skill) proceeds along the same path as abstract cognitive learning. Instead, motor learning has been shown to be quite different.

The difference (and here is where my close-enough principle is in play) lies in the mechanisms used in processing and responding to a teaching key. Cognitive learning mechanisms are triggered when the learner receives a command that is not accompanied by complex physical movements. Motor learning mechanisms are activated when the learner receives a command that *does* require these complex patterns. The mind acts as a sorting device, sending each command to its appropriate learning mechanism. (I can see Carl flinging this book into his office trashcan in a flurry of disgust!)

Cognitive learners, for example, are able to utilize instant recall when solving a problem that requires an immediate appeal to memory. Motor learners must rehearse movements over and over for long periods of time before they can be applied in response to a particular biomechanical command. Instant recall for motor learners—some call it muscle memory—requires a much longer period of gestation. Cognitive learners can process dozens if not hundreds of variables when writing an essay or solving a mathematical equation. Motor learners are limited to a focus on one variable at a time. If you doubt this in any way, just pick up a golf club and try to hit the ball while entertaining more than one thought about your swing.

Cognitive learners can process long and complicated sets of instructions and respond in a systematic way. Motor learners can process instructions only if they are delivered in small doses, such as brief phrases or verbal keys. This is not to say that cognitive learners are using a higher level of brain function and that motor learners engage only at a simple, instinctive level. I am saying only that the two learning styles are different and require different processing mechanisms to operate.

Cognitive teachers normally do not have to worry about their instructions being too complicated. Motor learners, on the other hand, must be spoon-fed by comparison. Instructions to the learner must not assume that the learner can apply past movements in attempting to learn new movements.

For example:

Cognitive learning instruction: "When reading an offensive attack from your opponent, quickly scan the opponent movement patterns and select the one that will best enable you to make a successful play on the ball."

Motor learning instruction: "Be stopped and balanced at hitter contact."

The former is a cognitive directive asking the player to summarize, using instant recall, all of the available keys for reading an attack and then to choose the one that provides the best information. This question would have no impact on a motor learner's attempt to learn the skill of digging. The latter, on the other hand, is a directive that, when delivered clearly, provides the learner with a perfectly defined physical movement that the learner must execute.

Finally, McGown reminds us that the language used to identify movement patterns must be concise. Instruction and feedback must be short and easily understood. Athletes become overloaded when the coach's explanations become long and drawn out. It is difficult to repeat a movement pattern when "Be stopped and balanced" becomes "I want each player to first use her eyes to evaluate the ball–hitter–blocker configuration, select the correct digging lane, move with balance as she seeks her read position, be stopped and balanced at hitter contact, feet shoulder-width apart, hips low, hands and arms extended in front of the body, weight forward on the balls of her feet, and ready to push to the ball if she feels she can make a play."

Instead, motor learning theory tells us that lengthy, complex explanations of the desired movement patterns will only confuse the learner, creating a paralysis of analysis that can lead to a shut down in the learning process. Thus it's important to keep instructions simple and brief.

Identifying Skills and Creating Keys

McGown recommends that we head off this problem by creating a list of keys for each skill we wish to teach. A key is a brief phrase or a word that serves as a shorthand version of the motor pattern we want the learner to perform. He also suggests that we list these keys in a sequential fashion from the beginning of the skill to the end. Finally, he recommends that we limit the total number of keys to approximately 5 to 7 per skill. The more complicated the skill, the greater the number of keys. Table 4.1 shows a sampling of keys for spiking.

TABLE 4.1 Spiking Keys

Key for each step in spiking sequence	Meaning
1. Go posture	Basic athletic ready position. Track pass and setter.
2. Read step	Walking step, small and deliberate. Directional; moves you toward the anticipated point of contact. Timing; on-time arrival with ball (not late, not early).
3. Delay-explode	Plant step much longer than read step. Hold an extra count on your read step, then blast into plant.
4. Center the ball	Position your plant so the ball is in your midline and slightly in front of your hitting shoulder. All shots should be available (not ruled out by bad body-ball position).
5. Skate stop	Brake your horizontal drive by turning and tilting your trail- (brake-) foot in order to plant on the inside edge of your trail-shoe, perpendicular to the line of approach. Knees bend to prepare for flexion in the jump.
6. Jump coil	Jump from plant. Arms up quickly in compact position; hands lead the upward thrust and remain close to the body until separation at head level. On the way up, rotate the hips and core away to create opposition stretch. Pull hitting shoulder back and feel scapular pinch. Hitting hand faces away; hand higher than elbow, elbow higher than shoulder. Nonhitting (left) hand will naturally counterbalance the right; no need to force it into position. Knees bend (flexion) and feet kick up toward butt as back arches and rotates away.
7. Trigger the swing	When you feel the stretch is maxed out, suddenly flex (pull) your lower abs on the nonhitting side. The nonhitting elbow simultaneously pulls into the lower side of the rib cage. These two pulling movements create a forward rotation of the hips, core, and shoulder, triggering the armswing. The greater the stretch and the more powerful and quicker the pull, the faster the armswing. The armswing starts with a final end-point stretch (hips, core, shoulder); stretch to max resistance before you trigger the swing.

> continued

> continued

Key for each step in spiking sequence	Meaning
8. Hit at full extension	Crack the whip (lower ab is the handle; shoulder, elbow, loose wrist, and hand are the whip). Hitting elbow leads the hand. Feel like you are contacting the ball (throwing the whip) on the way up. Achieve full extension, a straight line from the ball to hitting shoulder and down your side to foot.
9. Swing through the ball	Full hand contact. Hit through the ball with loose-wrist snap. Pronate the wrist and hand on follow-through. Elbow above hand at finish.
10. Land on balance	Land on two feet. Cushion (bend knees to soften landing).

For most of us the list of volleyball skills includes the following:

Serving

Forearm passing

Overhand setting

Spiking

Blocking

Digging

Since spiking is considered to be the most complex of all the skills, let's take a look at the sequential breakdown of the skill of spiking using McGown's motor-learning methodology. These are my words, not his. And the selection of 10 keys is my idea, not his. Normally, the total number of keys per skill comes to 5 to 7. Through the years I have used all 10 in teaching spiking. Spiking is one of the most complicated cluster of movements in all of sport. I think it deserves all 10.

The next phase of the motor learning process calls for the athletes to learn the movement patterns represented by each key. Let's pick, at random, one of the spiking keys to illustrate the process. We will use the "swing through the ball" key. These are the four points for swinging through the ball.

1. **Make full-hand contact.** As the spiker triggers the armswing, she must be aware of the ultimate contact goal as hand meets ball. We are looking for the full hand to contact the ball so that at the moment

of contact, the palm of the hitting hand, the thumb, and all of the fingers form a slightly cupped position that will fit tightly on the surface of the ball.

2. **Hit through the ball with loose-wrist snap to create topspin.** Be sure that you trigger the swing with a loose wrist. You know your wrist is loose enough if you can hold your arm in front of your body, shake your arm up and down rapidly, and feel your wrist flapping up and down as well. As your hand moves forward to contact the ball, your swing thought should be to swing *through* with a snap of the wrist and not *stop* at the ball.

3. **Pronate the wrist and hand on follow-through.** Pronate your hitting hand on follow-through whether you are hitting angle or line.

Full extension at contact, one of the spiking keys.

This pronated follow-through of the hand forces the spiker to finish with the thumb of the hitting hand pointed downward. Some would call this the wrist-away finish. The reason for this is to maximize the power accumulation that has been stored and is ready to be inflicted as the swing unfolds. The pronated position of the hitting hand guarantees that the spiker is in prime position to attack the ball with power.

4. **Elbow above shoulder at finish.** Be sure that your elbow is above the hitting shoulder as you finish the armswing. When this occurs, it is likely that the hitting arm has executed the swing with great speed as a result of the naturally shorter and faster moving lever that is indicated by the high-elbow finish. When the hitting hand drops below the elbow at the finish, it is likely that the hitter has used a long, straight lever (the hitting arm) to swing at the ball. This results in less power (slower-moving long lever) and less control (longer and less adaptable swing path).

But all of this takes too long to explain in detail while teaching the spikers to swing through the ball in a spiking drill. Using the key system, the coach has to repeat only the appropriate key word or phrase and the players, all of whom have memorized what each key stands for, will know what to do. This shared vocabulary of keys allows practice and motor learning to proceed with greater efficiency. All the coach has to say is "Swing through the ball" and every player will know what this means and how to execute the movement patterns it requires.

Cycling the Keys

Once the coach has identified all of the skills required for functioning within the team's system of play, along with the keys for movement patterns specific to each skill, it is time to design a series of practice sessions that cycle each skill through the teaching plan until everything has been covered. When the initial cycle is complete, the coach reviews the list of keys and recycles those that need additional work. Here is McGown's suggestion for using his methodology to teach motor skills.

Step 1. Demonstrate the full skill to the learner. The learner must see the full skill performed correctly before starting the learning process. Use a coach, a player, or a video. Make sure that the demonstration mirrors the exact way in which you want the skill to be executed.

Step 2. The learner then rehearses the full skill with attention to a selected key. Coach provides feedback on each key.

Step 3. Demonstrate the full skill again with attention to the next key. Repeat this process until all the keys have been covered.

Using the keys established earlier for the skill of spiking, this learning method, when applied, would look something like this.

The coach decides to work on spiking in the afternoon practice. Specifically, the coach wants to work on swinging through the ball. The coach sets up a drill that is based on the ball being circulated in a pass–set–spike rhythm, ending with the learner performing a complete spike. This is what is meant by demonstrating and rehearsing the full skill. Repeating only a part of the skill, such as rehearsing the swing itself while standing on a box is known in motor learning circles as one phase of a progression. Motor learning theory, as taught by McGown, discourages the use of the progression concept as a theoretical foundation for teaching skills.

Let me be quick to say that I do not stand with those who advocate *only* whole teaching strategies. I believe that there are certain skills that are more efficiently taught by at least some part (or progression) training. For example, I have encountered great success by stationing hitters on a box to rehearse armswing and upper-body mechanics. It is helpful to the learner, I think, if the variable of the jump is taken out of the equation, at least until the athlete is able to sync together the top (head, hands, shoulders, arms, core) and bottom (feet, legs, core).

To be fair, McGown accepts that progressions can sometimes be useful. But he adds, "But they should be limited in number. The ones that are used should be as much like the game of volleyball as possible."

Coaches lacking enough skilled players to proficiently perform the skills required in a drill should enlist the services of players who can execute the techniques necessary for running the drill properly. Others might prefer to insert a staff member into the drill to become the passer or the setter. The point here is that players cannot learn how to spike effectively unless they are put into a drill situation that simulates movement patterns that they would encounter in competition. Using players with inadequate skills would only slow down the learning process.

One might ask, "Why run a drill that requires skills beyond the grasp of the players? Does it really help to have players outside the team demonstrate the drills and their component skills if not enough team members can perform the techniques at an acceptable level?" Actually, this would be an unusual situation. And when it occurs, the coach should have a plan to remedy the problem. Using our example of swinging through the ball, the spiker can rehearse this skill only if the set is of a sufficient quality that the spiker can get a good swing. If no player on the roster can put up a quality set, a coach usually steps in to toss the set or to set the pass. As soon as at least one player improves enough to set a quality ball, the coach is replaced.

Next, the coach reminds the learner that while performing the skill of spiking, attention has to be on the proper execution of swing through the ball alone. This is a critical link in the motor-learning chain. The coach must remain disciplined and provide feedback only on the key being taught, no matter how poorly any other key is playing out. Otherwise, confusion will reign supreme.

How long the coach remains at each stage of the drill depends on how successfully the players are learning the skill. Some players may move ahead of others in the learning process. No problem. Just make sure that you remember which keys each of your spikers are rehearsing. By rotating the skills and keys through daily practice sessions, each of the players on the team will get exposure to the proper execution of each skill. Be sure to arrange to have each key demonstrated to the learner prior to its rehearsal. Don't give in to the urge to take a shortcut by not demonstrating the full skill. It is important to keep the learning chain intact throughout.

Pathways to Motor Learning

The methodology supplied by McGown is at the heart of how to teach volleyball skills. It provides the coach with a teaching paradigm that will move the player from the beginning to the advanced stages of learning the desired skill. The job of the coach at this stage is to decide on the list of skills to be taught and to create the list of keys related to each skill. As I indicated earlier, I do not intend to build these lists here. This is an exercise for each coach to tackle.

But there is more to teaching a skill than what has been discussed so far. For example, I learned early on that most athletes differ significantly in how they learn to perform skills. Some learn best by watching a skill being executed and then mimicking the skill. These are *visual learners.* Others learn by listening to the spoken word from the coach and then performing the desired movement based on what the learner has been told. They are *auditory learners. Graphic learners* prefer to be shown a diagram of the skill. Many athletes learn from various combinations of all three—visual, auditory, and graphic.

It is important to know which pathways are the most effective for each player on your team so that you can individualize your instruction when necessary. I have observed through the years, for example, that visual learners seem to have a stronger, more natural learning response to observing skills being performed. But this doesn't mean that visual learners can't also benefit from auditory and graphic teaching methods.

Knowing how to deliver specific information to an athlete is just as important as knowing the information to be delivered.

These two approaches—the scientific method and personal observation—supplied me with a wealth of information as I crafted my own approach to teaching volleyball skills. But I also enjoyed access to the fascinating world of international volleyball. During the course of my college coaching career and various international assignments with U.S. volleyball teams, I was afforded an opportunity to observe a variety of training styles. Those vantage points allowed me to witness the subtle, and sometimes not so subtle, differences in how various regions of the world chose to practice and play volleyball. It was only after processing and evaluating this diverse variety of playing styles that I was able to understand the essence of the skill acquisition process.

I am not going to tell you, for example, that one particular stance is better than another when teaching the skill of passing. Countless books, journals, and clinics provide an excellent menu of alternative ways to pass. Instead, I am going to tell you how to *think* about building your own approach to selecting and teaching a passing stance.

Identifying Skills

"Coach, how can I hit the ball harder?" This was the first technical question ever addressed to me by a player. "Well, you just need to hit the ball harder!" That was my answer. An athlete was asking for help, and I told her to help herself. I had demonstrated to everyone my embarrassing lack of knowledge of motor learning.

It didn't stop there. I provided similar answers to subsequent questions. "Coach, how do you want me to set the ball?" My answer? "Well, like this." And I set a few balls against the wall thinking that all she had to do was watch me do it and, presto, she would be able to replicate an overhand set. At the end of that practice I had no idea why these players were having so much trouble doing things that, to me, were relatively simple. I realized that my volleyball vocabulary would have to improve now that I had been hired to coach at the University of Pittsburgh. I had to expand my boundaries to search for volleyball knowledge in new and unfamiliar places.

I had to start making progress on the skill selection front. But each time I started to identify a skill on paper I would ask myself, "How do I know this skill should be on my list, and how do I know that this is the best way to teach it? Where do I go to find out what I wanted to know?" This is what I came up with:

1. Use the conventional wisdom that grows within each of us as we find new solutions. This is sort of like a calculating a moving average in mathematics. I think that as coaches we have a tendency to eliminate information that no longer seems valid or useful, while at the same time we are always on the lookout to collect new information that serves to update our conventional wisdom.

2. Visit the Internet to check out the literature on motor learning.

3. Attend clinics and seminars, and routinely check out volleyball journals and other publications.

Ironically, my early lack of knowledge about how to teach the sport might have actually made me a better coach. Everything I learned was a result of my own investigative energy. There were clinic notes to guide me, conversations with colleagues that produced insights into how other professional volleyball coaches were teaching the game, and my own experience with the always available trial-and-error method. Although it seemed at times that there were no reliable places to go for answers, it was this early search for a skill-development paradigm that gave me insight into how to move forward. When I did stumble across an idea that I liked, I kept it on file and within reach. After a few years, I had accumulated a sizeable depository of useful information on skill training in volleyball.

One question that often surfaces is "Where do we begin in teaching skills? Is there a prescribed order that coaches should follow, or can we pick and choose as we see fit?"

Start With Posture and Footwork

I believe that every coach should start with the training of posture and footwork. These two things are in play the entire time the athlete is on the court. Either you are standing while preparing to step toward your next responsibility, or you are using your feet to move toward that responsibility. In my opinion, a volleyball player should maintain a balanced, ready posture (I call it *go posture*) and use efficient footwork whenever moving while the ball is in play. Let's take a closer look.

In go posture, the feet are shoulder-width apart. The core is engaged, and the elbows are bent with the forearms parallel to the floor. The hips are slightly flexed, and the spine is tilted slightly forward.

A player must be proficient in different types of footwork for different situations:

- Shuffle movement in both directions
- Two-count crossover move in both directions
- Three-count jab-crossover move in both directions
- Jab-and-collapse push move to floor (either foot)
- Jab in either direction for swing block or traditional block

These footwork and posture patterns will enable a player to move anywhere on the court and maintain a readiness to play the ball. If the coach introduces and trains these motor skills on the first day, they will be in place and will serve as a foundation for building the rest of the skills to follow.

Move On to Ball Control

Next, it makes sense to introduce and train all of the ball-control skills. Combination drills (pass–set–hit) cannot occur unless the players have sufficient ball-control skills to run the drill. Add these to the skills of posture and footwork:

- Forearm pass
- Overhand pass
- Digging a hard-driven ball

Finish With Point-Scoring Skills

Finally, introduce the primary point-scoring skills—serve, spike, and block—after the ball-control foundation has been laid. Your team is now ready to compete in full 6-on-6 situations.

Sameness Versus Variety in Skill Training

As I pointed out earlier, skills are not self-contained entities with permanently assigned meanings. But I have observed coaches who treat them as though they are. They teach skills the same way every season with the goal that every player will be able to repeat the skill in exactly the same fashion. This is a workable plan if the coach's intention is to recreate the exact same style of play every season. But if the coach decides to change how the team is going to play, there will likely be changes in how some skills will be taught.

Let me explain. If I wish to teach the skill of spiking, I must first decide which style of spiking I wish to teach. There is no one style

Spiking, like all volleyball skills, showcases many different styles. Reid Priddy of the U.S. Olympic Team attacks from the right side.

that everyone agrees on. In fact, there are many styles, each requiring different movement patterns for execution.

Backtrack to the 1980s. More and more teams were beginning to play signature volleyball. By signature, I mean a technically precise, separately recognizable style of play. These teams put their respective stamps on the game of volleyball. They made it look like a well-choreographed dance. I was hooked. I wanted my team to play like that, to play with a genuine look that would be unmistakably associated with my team.

As I watched more closely, I noticed that not every player played the same way. There were enormous differences in how each player executed a forearm pass. Some contacted the ball low on their platform, near the wrist hinge. Others contacted the ball much higher on the forearms. There was a time in the 1990s when the Italian men's national team coach taught his players to contact the ball on the inside of the forearms with both palms adjoining and facing up.

Some defenders dove to the floor with two arms extended to receive a ball. Others used one arm to cushion their fall and one arm to dig the ball. Some setters contacted the ball directly off the crown of the forehead at the hairline. Others contacted either higher or lower. Some servers would strike the ball from a distance of 6 meters behind the baseline. Others would run up and broad jump into the court from behind the baseline, contacting the ball at about the 8-meter line. Some servers employed deception in executing a short serve. Others boldly stared down the receivers and then tried to overpower them with a high-velocity float serve. The comparisons are endless.

This led me to conclude that skills do not need to be executed in exactly the same way by every player. Anatomical differences, for example, could account for why one player might execute the same skill differently than another: the size of the hands in setting, the length of the legs in approaching to spike, the degree of elbow flexibility in forming a passing platform, ankle flexibility in assuming a low defensive posture. I could go on. Teamwide skill execution need not be perfect or even identical. It is more important to find the right technical solution for each player on your team.

I also concluded that styles of play have and will probably continue to influence the skill-development process. I began to develop a keen awareness of this several years ago while in Havana watching the women's national teams of Cuba and China square off in a spirited final match of the Cuba Cup. I began to focus on the very different styles of attacking used by each team. The Cubans were content to hit high balls from anywhere on the court. Their approaches were lengthy, appearing to me to be around 5.5 to 6 meters. There were no quick sets in their offense, the only exception being a 2 set to their middles. Their mechanics featured long-levered arms, long steps, and maximum use of ankle, knee, hip, and neck flexion when jumping. Their goal was to jump as high as possible and swing their long arms with great force and hit over the block for a kill, and they were often successful at doing just that.

The Chinese, on the other hand, favored quickness and the element of surprise over straight power and predictability. Their pass to the setter was quick, and every one of them similar in tempo so that the hitters could develop a repeatable rhythm. Their offense featured low, fast sets to their outside hitters; quick sets to their middle attackers; a deceptive series of combination plays working off a very quick slide set to their middles; low, fast sets to back row attackers; and so on. Their approaches were short (2.5 to 3 meters) and very fast. It seemed that they wanted their attackers to hold in a neutral position for as long as possible before bolting into their approach. I remember thinking that their hitters seemed to be shot out of a cannon when they finally exploded into their approaches. Their steps into their plants were shorter and quicker than the Cubans. Their elbows were bent so that their levers would be short and move quickly. Some of their hitters used misdirection steps in their approaches to create a "suddenly appear" effect.

I also judged that the Chinese were not jumping as high as the Cubans, but I soon realized that this didn't really matter. The Chinese were about quickness, not altitude. The overall impact of this style of offense was to seriously reduce the amount of time available to the blockers to read the Chinese attack and try to do something about it. It was very impressive stuff.

Watching this unique contrast in styles left me with a series of conclusions:

- There is no one way to teach a skill. There are many adaptations to each skill that come from differing interpretations of someone's right way to do it.

- Both spiking styles were effective, but they were noticeably different, almost to the point of being distracting to a volleyball voyeur like me. I was witnessing two completely differing presentations of the skill of spiking.

- I think that instead of a right and wrong way to perform a skill, there is more likely a spectrum of samples that represents the differing ways in which that skill can be executed.

It matters not whether you refer to this process as teaching a new skill or modifying an already existing skill. I just know that the following is true: What I saw that night in Havana was either two different skills (Cuban spiking versus Chinese spiking) or two variations on the same skill (spiking). In either case, there were significant differences in the movement patterns that distinguished one from the other (table 4.2).

TABLE 4.2   Features of Cuban Spiking and Chinese Spiking

Cuban style	Chinese style
Long approach and three-count step pattern.	Short approach, usually with a two-count step rhythm.
Reach back as far as possible with both arms. Swing both arms forward and upward to maximum reach.	Abbreviated reach back with arms. Emphasis on quick transition from reach back to hitting arm ready to swing.
Use of straight arms to thrust upward out of plant.	Bent elbows at midline of pull-through. Arms and hands close to body.
Sync with maximum upward leg drive.	Emphasis on jumping quickly out of the plant. Quickness more important than max reach.
Emphasis on long levers (arms) throughout approach and swing.	Focus on short levers throughout approach and swing.
Long lever swing aimed at high contact and power.	Goal is to attack low outside sets with delay–explode armswing. Shorter levers allow for quicker adjustment to fast set.

Conclusion

It is not necessary to create a team of identical robots. If this were true, we would never have been able to enjoy Joe Frazier's peek-a-boo boxing style, Tim Wakefield's knuckleball pitching delivery, Jim Furyk's looping takeaway as he prepares to hit a golf ball, or Logan Tom's stutter-step approach to hit her jump serve.

Achieving sameness, therefore, need not function as the primary reason for determining what we teach and how we teach it. When facing that fork in the road—whether to train every player to replicate the cookie cutter mold that would produce sameness in execution or to allow differences in how each player performs a skill—the latter must at least be considered. There are just too many exceptions to the rule of sameness as the leading guideline for shaping volleyball skills.

The same analysis can be applied to the development of entire teams. Not every team can be expected to develop the same look. Different regions, different countries, and different technical and tactical preferences can lead to diverse playing styles. A team's playing style may require a set of skills that differ from a team using another style of play. This is a topic rarely visited in volleyball literature, but I would like to offer an argument for including it in this discussion of volleyball skill training.

It doesn't matter whether the Cuban and Chinese styles of spiking represent different skills or different variations on one skill. The impact on how you choose to teach spiking will be the same. My own view is that the argument can go either way. There are examples of skills that, when modified, appear to morph into a separate skill.

An example of this can be found in the teaching of emergency saves on defense. Both the forward extension move and the forward dive require that the defender push head first onto the floor with hands extended in front of the body to execute the recovery move after playing the ball. In this way they are similar. But most coaches would insist that the skills of an extension push move to the floor are very different than the dive move, so much so that they could be classified as different skills.

But whether we claim them to be separate skills or variations on the same skill, the result will be the same. If we want to play a high-ball offensive system like Cuba*, we have to teach the mechanics of hitting this type of set. And the same is true of teaching the mechanics of the faster Chinese style of offense. Playing style clearly influences skill development.

Next time you get into an argument with someone over the correct way to teach a particular skill, remember that you will need to distinguish between two modes of analysis. First, there is the discussion about how research in motor learning has led to the popularization of a theoretical teaching paradigm that emphasizes *how* to teach a skill. Second, there is the awareness of the fact that a coach's decisions about what to teach—the actual details of performing a skill—is most likely going to be tied to a coach's vision of the particular style she wants the team to play.

---

* It should be noted that the Cubans no longer restrict their offense to the high-ball option. I was on the U.S. coaching staff at the 2011 Pan American Games and spent considerable time scouting the Cuban team. They now set the ball with more pace to the pins. But their basic approach to hitting has changed very little since their glory years.

CHAPTER 5

Thinking About
Team Defense

During the seven years I coached and played volleyball in Pittsburgh, George stood out as one of the best defensive players I have ever seen. I don't think I ever knew his last name. He was one of the old guys who played in the Wednesday night game at the Allegheny YMCA on Pittsburgh's north side. He also played with a group of old country veterans who competed in the weekend tournaments in the Ohio-Pennsylvania-Indiana region. George and I rarely spoke. I was younger then and didn't have much in common with George's crowd.

The best players in the city would find their way to the Allegheny Y for what everyone agreed was the best game around. George was a regular, all 5 feet 9 of him. I figured he was in his mid-50s. His perfectly squared-off flattop led me to believe that he had left a working class life in eastern Europe to relocate to the United States. Despite his lack of height, one thing was stone cold obvious. The man could play some serious volleyball. In the 1960s and '70s, well before the concept of the libero made its appearance, George patrolled the back row of the volleyball court with the tenacity of an industrial vacuum cleaner. His defensive skills were superior to those of anyone else participating in the Wednesday night game.

Each year at the start of the tournament season, my team of mid-30-year-olds were dealt our annual lesson by George and his old guys. During the warm-up before our match, we ripped set after set straight down with the thundering kaboom that accompanies every big-time swing. On the other hand, George and the boys would spend their warm-up time pushing soft tips down the line into the deep corners. Some even relaxed on the bench waiting for the match to start. Ours was a physically gifted, talented team. We attracted attention wherever we played. George's team, on the other hand, averaged slightly over 55 years of age. The prevailing winds of age had robbed them of their once formidable power game, and they were now seen as the underdog whenever they competed. People enjoy watching teams jump high and pound on the ball like sledge hammers during warm-up drills, but few understood the brilliance of the old guys and their subtly efficient game.

Over the years they managed to defeat us on several occasions. Every time this happened, I was reminded that these old guys knew something about the game that we didn't. I was determined to figure out what it was.

Defensive Reading

As a team they passed every serve, every free ball, and every out-of-system ball perfectly, allowing their setter to deliver the ball accurately within their low-risk offense. It seemed that George would dig everything, no matter how hard the ball would be attacked. He was a magician, and he was fearless. He seemed to know where the ball was going before the hitter did. He would move into position to dig the ball and simply wait for it to arrive. It always seemed to me that he could have moved to his digging position, sipped on a cup of coffee while waiting, and then dig the ball.

I also noticed that he rarely used the same defensive move each time he went after the ball. Sometimes he would pull his platform back into his body in an attempt to cushion the hard-driven ball. At other times he would extend fully to the floor to reach a ball far out in front of him. Sometimes he would run after a ball with the speed of a gazelle and save it back to the court where a teammate could play the next contact. At other times he would just stick out one arm to intercept a ball. And then there were the incredible tumbling moves, never the same one twice, that left me shaking my head.

I once asked him during a break in play, "George, where did you learn those skills, and what do you call them?" I asked the question in this form because within the skill paradigm of American volleyball, we refer to skills as the dive, the roll, the collapse move, the overhand dig, and so on. Everything had to have a formal name, so I was surprised by his answer. "What?" He looked at me the way a genius would look at a beginner. "I don't know what you mean. I learned to play volleyball in Poland and we learn only one thing: make sure ball goes to setter." He finished his cup of water and walked back to the court. Twenty minutes later he and his all-flattop team had done it again. They defeated us by a score of 15-7. This meant that, once again, our team had to pay for the Wednesday night beers.

I was mesmerized by George's abilities. He knew where the ball was going before anyone else did. I wanted to find out how he did it. If I could fill in the missing blanks, maybe I could teach it to my players.

I had been a good, but not great, defensive player on the beach at UCSB. I understood the geometry of the game. There were only two guys to worry about when playing defense, and only certain angles were available to each hitter. A decent job of reading the attacker combined with a reasonable level of effort means defense on the sand becomes a manageable, though never an easy, task.

The phrase "a decent job of reading" had begun to pique my interest. I was sitting with Bruno Krsul, the acknowledged godfather of the Wednesday night game, when the light suddenly came on for me. I asked him what made George such a great defender. "He reads the hitters really well," Bruno explained in one of his all-time understatements.

A perfect storm was beginning to form for me around the concept of reading. I began to connect the dots. Was this the missing link for me? I was learning to appreciate the value of reading by watching George play. Other veteran players I respected, like Bruno, were united in encouraging me to learn how to teach the concepts of reading. As my own playing career was winding down, I was able to experiment with many of the concepts embedded in the reading process. This allowed me to talk to my team about reading from the point of view of having done it. I believed that I had discovered the final, missing step in teaching team defense.

Reading the hitter is a critical skill if you want to play the sand game well. Two people have to cover the entire court on defense. Their ability as readers would usually determine whether or not they would be able to dig the ball. Athletic ability and accurate ball-control skills were important, but reading and moving to the right spot to dig the ball may stand as the most important skill of all if you wanted to be a good defender on the beach.

Was it the same for the indoor game? Were there too many players moving simultaneously in too many directions around the court? Could an indoor player learn to read and anticipate the probable point of attack with the same level of confidence as outdoor players? To answer these questions, I needed to know what percentage of the time for each game

Reading is crucial to good defense. Here Nicole Davis and Jordan Larson position themselves to dig a spike during the semifinal between the United States and Korea at the 2012 Olympics in London.

Zuma Press/Icon SMI

(sand and indoor) the ball landed in the defensive court for a point. The formula seemed to be a simple one:

$$\text{kill points} / \text{total attack attempts} = \text{scoring \% by kill}$$

I decided that I would rifle through my boxes of videotapes of both indoor and outdoor matches to find out if such a comparison could be established. I recorded the total number of attack attempts followed by the total number of attempts that scored. I reasoned that the game with the higher digs per attempt percentage would be the better reading game, since I had already come to believe that good reading leads to good digging. I realized that, at best, my research would yield only a highly informal comparison between the outdoor and indoor games, but that was enough for me.

Once the results were calculated, I was mildly surprised to find that the digging percentages for both the sand and indoor games were approximately the same. I thought that reading in the indoor game, because of the significantly higher number of movement patterns and set options, would be a much more challenging task than the less complicated, but no less difficult, outdoor game, but I was wrong. Reading in the indoor game may have looked more complicated, but players were using their reading skills to dig the ball at the same rate as their beach volleyball counterparts. My next task was to learn how they were doing it, and devise a way to teach it.*

Teaching Players How to Read

I wanted to walk into the local volleyball superstore and purchase a user manual to teach reading. I quickly found out nothing like that existed: neither the store nor the manual. Without any professional literature on the topic, it seemed that a trip back to the reliable conventional wisdom was in order, but this would have been asking a lot from players and coaches in those early days. Remember, this was Pittsburgh in the 1970s. Not many were proficient in teaching or learning the subtleties of reading, so there was no accumulated conventional wisdom to retrieve. I then decided that learning, through trial and error, how to break it down and teach reading to my college players would be the place for me to start.

As I huddled with my assistant coach to begin planning for the upcoming season, I had already decided to launch my defensive training segment by teaching the skills of reading. It seemed to be, chronologically at least, the first in a sequential chain of skills that a player must acquire in order to become a good defender. If you don't know where the ball is going, I reasoned, then you are going to have a difficult time playing defense. All of the individual defensive skill training in the world would be for naught unless the defender knew, first, how to read.

The more I watched George play, the more I began to understand the importance of reading in defense. As I said earlier, sometimes he seemed to beat the ball to the right spot and pop the ball up for an easy dig. On other occasions he would sprint away from the court to pursue a teammate's wayward dig attempt and return it to play. His eyes were never stuck on the set ball. He was always watching people on the other side of the net in an attempt to anticipate what they would likely do next.

During my final years at Pitt and my early years at New Mexico, I established reading as my skill du jour. By the time I arrived in Illinois in 1983, I was confident that I could teach the concepts of reading well

---

*Note: The data to calculate a game's kill percentage is readily available today by checking the box score of the match. It will list the total number of attack attempts and the total number of kills. There was no such thing at the time I was seeking data. The NCAA box score, along with universal Internet access to it, made its appearance in the mid-1980s.

enough to make a run at conference and national prominence. Here, in its remarkably simple form, is the outline I used to teach reading to my players.

Reading

Reading is the use of a defender's (blocker or digger) visual acuity to anticipate the opponent's attack and to move to a position on the court that will provide him the best opportunity to block, channel, or dig the ball. Reading involves two distinct phases. The first phase I call the preliminary read (figure 5.1).

During the preliminary read, the defending team moves into its defensive base position. Base position is determined by the type of quickly

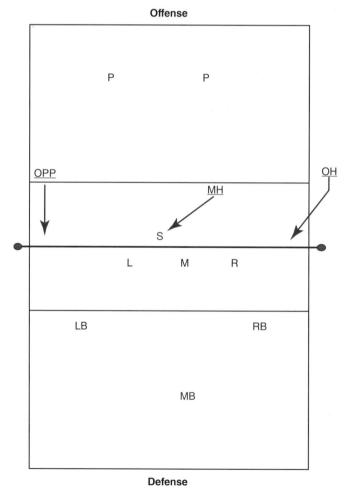

FIGURE 5.1 Base position and the preliminary read.

developing offensive situations that a defensive team must face every time the opponent executes an in-system pass or dig. A typical base position would deploy its personnel to track the pass and be prepared to defend against an overpass (see figure 5.1). If there is no overpass, the players' eyes immediately focus on the setter to rule out or confirm a second-contact setter attack or a third-contact quick attack. If none of these options occur, the defensive team moves to the final read position, which is the defensive response to the possibilities that remain after the base position options have been ruled out. This is known as base-to-read movement.

The final read occurs between the setter's release of the ball and the hitter's contact (average elapsed time is 1.4 seconds or less*). The defenders' eyes stay on the setter to determine the upcoming offensive pattern. Defenders assess the remaining third contact possibilities by tracking and reacting to the pass/setter convergence point (P/SCP). This information will dictate which third contact possibilities are possible in that situation.

Does the P/SCP eliminate certain offensive possibilities? Yes. A common example is a pass that forces the setter too far off the net to be able to run a quick set. The quick set, therefore, is one offensive option that the defense no longer has to worry about. The same could be said about a pass that is too far left or right, a pass that is too low, or a pass that is too fast. But if the pass is perfect, all offensive options are still on the table.

With each touch of the ball by the offensive team, the defenders are eliminating or calculating the offensive team's options. At this point, players visually evaluate the offensive approaches and move to achieve optimal position to defend all third-contact possibilities. All blockers and floor defenders are now responsible for verbally calling out the approach patterns being run by the offense. I call this pattern identification (PID), and we verbalize what we see because it reinforces our ability to know what we are reading.

As the ball is set, defenders watch the set trajectory briefly in order to identify who the intended attacker will be. As soon as the blockers and defenders know where the set is going, all eyes turn away from the setter to focus on the attacker. This is a critical point in the reading process. *It is essential that defenders' eyes move off the set ball and onto the attacker.* There is simply too much information available at that moment to ignore it. As the blockers move into position, the floor defenders read the evolving hitter-ball-blocker (HBB) configuration (figure 5.2). This tells the floor defenders where the ball is likely to be attacked, and they make their

---

*Ulmer, K. Nov. 2011. The swing block. *AVCA 2.0*. 15-19.

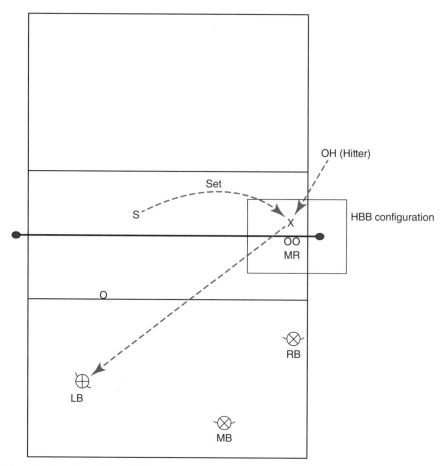

FIGURE 5.2 Final read and the HBB configuration.

final movement into the digging lane. This is, as noted earlier, called base-to-read movement.

The HBB configuration is the central component of the reading process. The speed and location of the set tells the digger how much time is available to make the base-to-read move into the digging lane created by the blockers. The depth of the set tells the digger how shallow or how deep the attack will be. By watching the hitter's approach, you can see if she has either overrun the set (producing a deep or off-speed save) or underrun the set (producing a late, flat shot deep in the court).

Your teammates who are setting the block will provide you with even more information. Their hands appear above the net at the point of attack. They take away angles of attack and tell the digger where to line up in relation to the attacker's approach. Diggers square up to the approach angle and body line of the attacker, but they must be careful to stay in the digging lane and not drift into the block shadow (figure 5.3). The HBB configuration can also provide a glimpse of the depth of the set. Jump early to block tight sets, and defenders look for the tip. Delay the jump against a deep set, and defenders prepare for high hands and deep angle shots.

At this point, the diggers zoom in visually to get a final view of the hitter prior to contact. Assume a full swing by the hitter unless a tip or off-speed shot is signaled by the hitter's arm-lift pattern. I have found that when a hitter lifts the hitting hand and pulls it behind the head, no matter how briefly, the full swing can be expected. If the hand remains visible throughout the arm lift and swing preparation, expect the tip or off-speed shot.

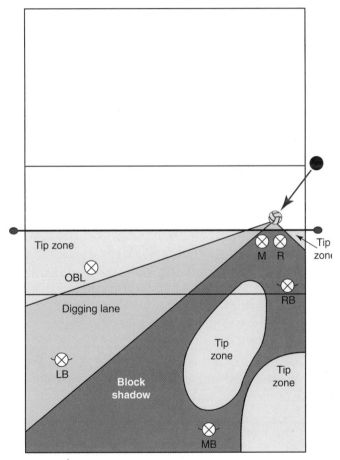

FIGURE 5.3 Block shadow and digging lanes.

Learning to read requires rehearsal, just like any other part of the game. Knowing how to read is one of those difference-making skills that need to be kept finely tuned. Above all else, remember these observations:

- When *they* have the ball, we are watching (reading) people. When *we* have the ball, we are watching the ball.
- The pass determines what is possible. Patterns and approach angles announce hitter intentions.

Effort

I often become confused by coaches who call for more effort from their players. For example, a player might attempt to dig a hard-driven ball but unintentionally send the ball out of play. My confusion stems from what happens next. The player made a good read but misplayed the ball. The next thing I hear is the standard incantation asking the player to give more effort. Did the coach want her to expend more effort as an analyzer of variables? More effort as a person standing in athletic posture waiting for the ball? Perhaps a coach could yell at the player to think with more effort! No. These examples do not warrant the coach's demand for more effort. Quiet reminders regarding what to look for when reading are probably more effective.

The player who is pursuing a ball at less than maximum speed, for example, is a player who can justifiably be told to give more effort. But the in-place defender mentioned here must be evaluated according to the accuracy of his read and the quality of his play on the ball, not according to his effort level.

These are two different categories, reading and effort. Most observers, especially the coaches who would raise their voices to demand more effort from their players, are talking essentially about defenders who would suddenly see a carom or deflection and then pursue the ball either to create an additional contact for their team or to send it over the net to the opponent as the final allowable contact. This would be an example of effort. Moving to the correct spot and digging a hard-driven ball, on the other hand, is a matter of multivariable analysis. We call it *reading*. For me, teaching volleyball defense would henceforth be separated into two training categories: reading and effort. Together they form a powerful duo.

At this point one might legitimately ask the question, "What about technique?" Technique seems to be missing from my foundation of defensive principles. Players need to learn how to roll, sprawl, or dive in order to prevent injury when hitting the floor; manipulate platform angles to dig balls out of their midline; cushion hard spikes; and use a collapse move to push their platform under balls driven hard toward their feet. Shouldn't technique be added to the teaching formula so that it reads like this: reading, effort, and technique? Perhaps it should, but I was usually satisfied if I could get my team to execute the first two. Technical training for individual defense seemed to work its way into the practice plan on its own, but reading and effort, these things had to be singled out and taught.

Has there ever been a coach who has *not* demanded more effort from athletes? I don't think so. Extracting maximum effort levels is one of the primary responsibilities of the coach. But there is no magic formula or series of drills that can make this happen. Instead—and this observation is confirmed by what I have seen throughout my 50-year career in volleyball—the coach must decide to impose his will on the team. It is a matter of forcing players out of their comfort zone on a daily basis. To reiterate, effort is associated with drills that require an all-out approach to run down, dive after, or reach for balls on defense. Technique is the skill that is applied to each attempt to play the ball. Effort is not a skill. Rather, it is a state of mind, an expectation that engulfs the program. Usually effort is the result of the presence of a particular coach or coaches who are willing to establish an unyielding presence as enforcers of the team's effort standards.

Practices can become testy. Players can be driven hard, physically and mentally. This commitment to a daily effort standard will either fortify a positive gym culture while motivating players to give great effort, or it will result in the opposite. It depends on the skills and style of the lead defensive coach and must be monitored constantly.

When things are going well in this regard, players feel challenged, not abused. When things go south, players become less motivated. They lose respect for the coaching staff, and they feel abused. They begin to feel that practices are often more about the coaches' release of stored-up anger than about improving the team's level of effort. Practice must be viewed by all as a welcome challenge and not as abusive victimization by an angry coach.

Reminders about effort can never disappear from the practice environment. Players must be kept aware of the effort requirement at all times. More than any other phase of play, the effort level of a team is a direct reflection of the coach's level of insistence on this important ingredient.

How important is effort? Think about it. Would you rather compete against a team that plays with an unbelievable defensive attitude but lacks a high-level defensive skill base? Or would you rather compete against a team with a good skill base but does not play with great effort?

Which team presents more of a challenge, all else being roughly equal? I would bet that most coaches would choose to play the team with good skills but not much in the effort department. The display of team-wide effort is infectious and can intimidate most opponents.

Technique

There are several approaches to the teaching of defensive technique. I firmly believe, however, that technical purity takes a back seat to a team's all-out mentality when preparing a team to play defense. Don't get me wrong; a team must possess a reasonable technical base. But the widespread availability of what and how to teach individual defensive technique leads me to recommend that you visit your favorite coaching manual for details. There you will find strategies for training individual defensive skills such as digging balls hit directly at the defender, floor moves to dig and avoid injury, run-through techniques to impart back-spin on the ball, platform manipulation to control the direction of the dig, and a long list of additional techniques. Coaches can evaluate each skill and decide which will fit their specific needs as they build their defensive systems.

But before leaving the topic of defensive technique I would like to point out some of the common errors associated with learning to play defense that will provide you with some important checkpoints as you train your team.

If this sounds like a cop-out, so be it. But coaches must pick their battles as they plan a training segment. As I look back through the years, it strikes me that players showed up to my early practices with fewer skill deficiencies in individual defense than in any other phase of the game. I always felt that we could leap right into our defensive preparation without having to teach defensive technique from the ground up.

Although their individual technical abilities may have allowed a more advanced starting point than other skills, it is also true that the mistakes that were made seemed to be the same ones. It was uncanny how players from such diverse backgrounds could arrive with virtually the same list of execution shortcomings. My contribution to the discussion of defensive technique will be limited to identifying what I believe are universal bad habits (see table 5.1) for which each player should be screened early in the training cycle.

These mistakes are so widespread that all coaches are bound to see them gain a foothold in their respective gyms. It would be prudent for coaches at any level to identify and eliminate these behaviors as soon as possible.

TABLE 5.1 Common Violations of Defensive Principles

Violation
Creeping into the block shadow
Not being stopped and balanced at the moment of contact by the hitter
Watching the wrong things; eyes stuck on the ball
Poor first-step mechanics (false-stepping)
Breaking posture throughout base-to-read movement (leaning, jumping, or any other unnecessary or inefficient movement prior to hitter contact)
Poor platform mechanics (such as swiveling, telescoping, hands together too early)
Leaning back to dig or receive ball
Sluggish recovery after play on ball (get up quickly!)
Creating unnecessarily dramatic dig by being out of position or utilizing poor timing
Turning the head away from a hard-driven ball
Allowing the eyes to bounce with the head (need eyes level while moving)

Making Decisions

As in any other phase of the game, designing a defensive system requires that coaches make a series of key decisions that will eventually shape how their team will play defense. One of the first decisions a coach should consider is whether to play a gambling, scheming type of defense or take a more conservative, low-risk approach. My nature has always been to play the role of the riverboat gambler and look for the high-risk, high-reward potential in every situation. I routinely hired more conservative assistants whose job was to make sure that I would keep my high-risk decisions from blowing up our team. Most of my head coach colleagues, however, maintained a conservative, predictable profile when it came to the tactical presentation of their teams. They were much more comfortable in the role of protector of the traditional, old school approach and could not understand why I orchestrated so many unusual tactics at crucial times during matches.

The essence of these differing styles of play was captured in a critical NCAA playoff match against Ohio State in 2004. We did two things in that match that not many coaches would ever contemplate. Ohio State's All-American outside hitter, Stacy Gordon, was shredding our defense. We had no answer for her. We were behind 2 sets to 1, and I was pondering my moves. If we didn't do something significantly different in the fourth set, we were headed for defeat. So I called on a freshman middle blocker, Jessy Jones, who had played very little that season. In fact, I am not sure that she had played at all. But she was hungry and could block with the best of them. So in she went, pausing at the edge of the court as if her eyes were searching for her prey. She sprinted to the net to take her position as a middle blocker. "Game on," she must have been thinking, because she went on to make me look like a genius. We won the fourth set to tie the match at 2 to 2, and went on to win in five sets.

Jessy was a big reason we won the match. I never forgot a suggestion Doug Beal made to me during one of the many coaching clinics he conducted. "If you want to have a chance to win at an elite level," he said, "you have to reserve a spot on your roster for a player who can step in and immediately make your team better." I remember repeating that suggestion to myself as I decided to insert Jessy into the match. Indeed she made us better right away. I owe that one to Doug.

That turned out to be the second gamble—inserting an inexperienced freshman to perform a miracle in the toughest match of our season in front of an overflow crowd of nearly 6,000 fans. The first gamble was even more edgy. Prior to the match, our staff had spent the entire week looking for a way to scheme our blocking system so that we would create some doubt or perhaps distract their staff and players.

I had never been shy about releasing a blocker early to form a double team against an opponent's hot hitter, or to commit jump with their quick hitter, or to switch blockers at the point of attack. But in our staff preparations for this match, I agreed to do something I had never done before. Our plan was to commit two blockers to Gordon at all times, even if it meant that one of their other hitters would be swinging on an open net. And by open I mean no one was going to be even close. No one would be chasing after the open hitter even if the set went to her. We would have to dig the ball on the open net if we wanted to stay in the rally. But we were *always* going to have at least two blockers up against their top hitter.

We devoted much of our preparation time to rehearsing this blocking system, but things didn't go all that well. The B side kept pounding on the open net for points and were beginning to frustrate the starters. "How are we supposed to win the match doing this?" had to be the thought forming in everyone's mind. We stuck to the plan and sent the troops into battle. The worst thing that could happen would be that we go back to our normal blocking system, a system that had helped us to a top 10 ranking in the national poll.

Ohio State discovered immediately what our strategy was going to be. Their setter locked into our release-blocking tactic on our first attempt to use it. She delivered a perfect set to their 6'3" opposite who buried the ball straight down for a memorable kill. Right then, at the very moment that ball was crushed for such a dramatic point, everything I had ever believed about coaching was suddenly frozen in time. Was I really a risk-taker, or was I just a talker? Was I a leader, prepared to march up the hill when everyone else, including my own players, were probably thinking about retreating? I knew my next move would have to be decisive. So I did nothing, and this was probably the most decisive thing I could do.

In the few seconds it took for me to process what had just happened, I realized that *nothing* had happened. They scored a point by hitting on an open net. We were expecting that to happen. And the set didn't go to Gordon, which we also had predicted. It was just that moment, when a good player pounds the ball to the floor with no blocker in sight that stands out as something you rarely see. For a brief second it scared us. Then, as everyone scanned the collective expressions on each of our faces and realized that we were OK, we went back to work, and we did so without changing our dangerous blocking plan.

They kept setting the same player, the one who was matched up with the open net, and the most amazing thing happened. After scoring five or six straight points with her impressive hitting, she finally made an error. With that error came a slight but noticeable loss of confidence. Since we were doing a reasonable job of blocking Gordon, making her change her shot, and even popping up some of her mighty swings for a control block, their setter kept going to the opposite. After all, this was the player who was open. But the deeper we got into the match, the less reliable the opposite hitter became. She started hitting a few balls out and into the net. She simply wasn't the point scorer that she had been earlier in the match. In our staff huddle during a late time out, we suddenly realized, at least in our minds, what was happening.

Our game plan had forced them into a situation that they either had not or had rarely encountered up to that time. We were taking away their traditional go-to offensive option, which was to set to Gordon at every opportunity, front or back row. To her credit, when she did receive the set, she racked up enough kills to keep them in the lead in what was a highly competitive match. "Mixed results," would be how I would describe the success level of our blocking game plan through three sets.

When I inserted Jones into the match for the fourth set, her performance lifted our team to a new level of confidence. She reenergized our players. Our block started controlling Gordon in a way that frustrated her. Their setter began to set the opposite more frequently, freezing Gordon out of the offense. The problem for our opponent was that the opposite had never, or rarely, been in the role of closer for that team. She was unaccustomed to carrying that kind of load, and we knew that. We had succeeded in disrupting their team chemistry by forcing them into new and unfamiliar roles. For this to work, Jones had to play well, and she did.

Standing courtside at the start of the match, watching their opposite bury that first set for a jack hammer kill, I was not certain that I had made the right decision to leave such an explosive hitter on an open net, but I did know that our game plan had merit. The question would be, did I have the patience to get behind the plan and support it during the match? With the help of my assistant coaches who crowded around me every time my confidence faltered, I was able to witness one of the great coaching lessons of my career. Sometimes you have to take risks, and no matter how shaky the early returns on that decision, you have to stick with the plan.

Not all decision-making, however, need apply to such a high-risk level of play. Many decisions are directed toward the basic mechanical, system-related aspects of blocking. One such decision is whether or not your team should even *attempt* to block.

Should We Block?

This is a decision that usually occurs when coaching young, developing players. At what point does a player begin to block? I have asked many coaches this same question, and the consensus seems to be: as soon as she can reach high enough to create a control block. Teams that do not feature any players who can jump high enough to control block should be confined to playing a defensive system that utilizes digging formations that resemble serve-receive patterns. Later, as team rosters begin to fill out with players who can pass the control-block test, the development of defensive systems that include blocking can be designed.

What Blocking System Should We Use?

Should you decide to block, you will be confronted immediately with the need to design a system of blocking for your team. First you have to decide what, for you, constitutes a successful block. Here are some possibilities:

- Maximize terminal blocks per set
- Maximize control blocks per set
- Channel the attack to our best defenders
- Train to achieve superior technique and timing
- On-time arrival at point of attack

Which of these is at the top or your list? Or are they *all* important? You must decide.

The Bunch-Read System

This system has dominated the game in recent years. It is a system designed to protect the middle of the net, yet be flexible enough to chase the outside sets and get two blockers up at the pins. Various offshoots of the bunch-read system, such as the spread read, bunch front, and the 4-2 matchup, are less popular.

Swing blocking (see table 5.2) is a term that is misused by many coaches today. It is not a separate system of blocking. Rather, it refers to a style of movement within the bunch-read system. It refers to the dynamic movement of the blocker who must move quickly from base

TABLE 5.2 Swing Blocking

Points of emphasis	It's a footwork technique used in the bunch-read system. All blockers react to the set ball as it leaves the setter's hands. Blocker stays coiled and balanced while reading. If no quick attack, blocker executes efficient push to wide point of attack. Body turns to face direction of point of attack. Blocker completes approach and plants feet at approximately 45-degree angle to net to execute maximum jump. Arms fully lengthen and swing from outside in to highest reach (hence, swing blocking). Timing element (delay-explode) is crucial. Must learn to execute in tandem.
Significant advantages	Touch higher than traditional block jump (42 mm or 1.67 inches).* Block time is longer above net (.04 seconds). Unleashes blocker's athleticism; engaged in full commitment to dynamic movement. Designed to stop or slow down inside attack and still get two up versus pins.
Potential problems	Blocking platform still moving (sweeping motion) at contact; creates problem for diggers. Timing of blocking must be precise. Approach coordination between two blockers must be perfect. Involves lots of moving parts; hard to eliminate inefficient movements. Digging lanes harder to identify. Timing errors more costly. Achieving balanced landing less likely. Swing blockers move faster but lose 7 inches in distance.

*Ulmer, K. Nov. 2011. The swing block. *AVCA 2.0*. 15-19.

position to the point of attack, using an approach and upward arm swing to gain greater height and increased reach into the attacking zone. But this is not a system. It is merely a technique used within the bunch-read system. It encourages speed and athleticism by blockers who have to guard against a particular set and release to another if the earlier set is not made.

The current debate over swing blocking is actually about which style of movement—the dynamic, swing-blocking style or the more conservative, traditional crossover, stay-square-to-the-net-while-moving, style—produces better results. Advocates claim that swing blockers can stand and read in a stationary base position and sprint to the final point of attack in time to execute a block. Opponents maintain that some of the distances a blocker must travel are too far, and execution is impossible. The most common of these situations occurs when defending the opponent's 2H rotations that feature the go-slide split. In this play the ball can be set low and fast to either pin, and very few middle blockers are fast enough to arrive on time to block both. The points of attack are simply too far apart.

So it is decision time again. Should bunch-swing blocking be used to defend against the go-slide? Do the advantages of bunch-swing blocking outweigh the disadvantages? How efficiently can we read and react? Let's say, for the purpose of argument, that swing blocking cannot stop the go-slide because blockers are not fast enough to arrive at the ball in time. Are you willing to consider an alternative system for dealing with this type of attack?

The 4-2 Matchup System Using Release Blocking

The prevailing alternative to swing blocking is what I call the 4-2 matchup system. The system emphasizes early releases by blockers to establish a solid block against the opponent's most effective hitters, while settling for a one-on-one block against the other hitters. The system requires that you make three decisions. First, are you going to ask your MB to read block, or are you going to release your MB early to one of the wide points of attack (go or slide)? In other words, are your MBs fast enough to read and execute an on-time arrival at *both* sets?

Second, if you decide that your MBs are unable to do this, are you prepared to dump the bunch-read concept and accept that, by design, you will be one-on-one with at least one hitter?

Third, are you prepared to accept that you might have to defend the second-contact (setter) attack with your wing diggers with no blocker up? There may or may not be a blocker available to get up against the setter, depending on the pass location and the hitter patterns.

Your overall decision must be to either defend the front-row setter (4-2) rotations using the orthodox bunch-read, or create a hybrid system that addresses the realities of the front-row setter rotations in a more specific way. We call it a hybrid system since blockers are asked sometimes to read and sometimes to commit. The choice also exists for blockers to use dynamic swing-blocking footwork in selected situations.

The most frequent 4-2 (two-hitter rotation) play to prepare for is go-slide (figure 5.4). Here is how that play is defended using this system.

Either through prematch or in-match scouting, your team must know in which direction your MB is going to release during each defensive opportunity. The coach can signal from the bench, or blockers can determine this during the flow of play. It must also be decided whether the release stays throughout the rally or just during the serve-reception sequence.

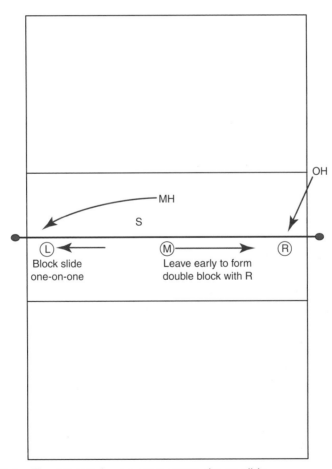

FIGURE 5.4   The 4-2 match-up system versus the go-slide.

This system employs a more traditional style of footwork for blockers (see table 5.3 for more on traditional blocking), and is a blend of swing and traditional. The blocker moving the longer distance (in this case the MB closing to the opponent's OH) may use swing footwork, especially if she is delaying her move to give the setter a false read. But if the blocker elects to release early to the OH, there is no need for swing footwork. Traditional blocking footwork such as push-crossover-plant with the upper body square to the net during the move will suffice.

Left-side blockers (L) must be very athletic and capable of blocking the slide one-on-one. They must jump commit with the slide hitter even if she does not receive the set because we want her to stay airborne and in control of her blocking platform against the fast slide. During matches we will probably release to their OH more than the slide hitter. The left-side blocker's footwork will usually resemble the swing-blocker dynamic footwork since she will not have help from her MB very often. We don't want any distractions clouding the open space needed by the left-side blocker to execute her most uninhibited, bold move. Finally, when we do release our MB to the slide, we must also be able to play one-blocker team defense against the opponent's OH. The blocker (L) must be able to go to her right to commit jump with the 1. MB and R will double-team the OH. If the MH stays in front of the setter (and no back-row swing from the OPP), L should commit jump on both the slide and the 1, and also on the setter dump in obvious tight pass situations. Blockers, especially MBs, are encouraged to fake in one direction and release to another when they realize the opponent setter is reading the release.

TABLE 5.3 Traditional Blocking

Significant advantages	No shift from lateral to square movement along net is required; traditional footwork is preferred. No need for long arm swinging to maximum read; arms thrusting straight up from plant is preferred. Hands are in blocking zone earlier. Timing requirements are not as precise. There are cleaner digging lanes for back-row players. There are fewer out-of-balance landings from straight-up jump.
Potential problems	Can't reach over the net as far. Can't hang in the air as long. Opponent's set speed may be faster than our MB can close. Reach blocking: Lower jumping style may not be enough for lateral reach.

Finally, make adjustments to account for a back-row swing by the opponent. Keep one of the wing blockers close to the point of attack in order to assist in forming the block against the back-row swing.

Here is your first decision. Are you going to ask your MB to read block or are you going to release your MB early to one of the wide points of attack (go and wide slide)? Are your MBs fast enough to read and execute an on-time arrival at *both* sets? Which system (bunch-read or 4-2 matchup) are you going to use?

Second decision: If you decide that your MBs are unable to get to both points of attack, are you prepared to dump the bunch-swing concept and accept that, by design, your defense will be one-on-one with at least one hitter (yes or no)?

Third decision: Are you prepared to accept that you might have to defend the second-contact (setter) attack with your wing diggers (yes or no)? Depending on the pass location and the hitter patterns, there may or may not be a blocker available to get up against the setter.

Fourth decision: If your opponent sets the one-on-one option, are you comfortable playing defense behind one blocker (yes or no)?

Note: I use the term *slide* to refer to the low in-system, one-foot-take-off back set, but the principles of the defense can apply to a nonslide, two-foot regular approach from area 2 or 1 as well.

Standard Package Defense

The perceived need to design separate defensive alignments for each opponent invites yet another major decision. For years, when preparing our defensive game plans, I would engage in unnecessary repetition by drawing each rotation's offensive patterns on my scouting sheet. I was locked into the routine—draw the offensive play the opponent will likely run in each situation, then create our defensive response to each of those plays—of deciding match by match how a particular team should be defended. After too many years, I finally realized that most teams were running the same plays. Instead of separate preparation to defend each opponent, I concluded, we should learn how to defend the six common plays that all teams tend to run.

Those six plays, I believed, would account for approximately 80 percent of the opponent's in-system offense. We needed to be very good against that 80 percent. I wouldn't mind slippage against the other 20 percent. These were usually a handful of special plays that each opponent kept in their offensive scheme. We always believed that we could leave these plays unscouted and still have success. I was happy with the

80 percent versus 20 percent focus. It was comforting, knowing that we were always prepared to defend at least 80 percent of everything the opponent could generate in their in-system offense.

Here are the commonly run plays that should go on the 80 percent list:

3H: three-hitter (opponent setter back row)

Go-1-R

Go-3-R

Go-S-2

2H: two-hitter (opponent setter front row)

Go-S

Go-S-Bic

Go-3/1

For purposes of this discussion, it does not matter how these commonly run plays are defended. This can be done in a variety of ways. What matters is that the team is able to recognize when they are being run and can respond immediately with a planned defensive alignment. This poses another decision. Do you treat each of your opponent's offensive opportunities as separate entities, or do you establish a standard package defense that automatically addresses 80 percent of the offense being generated? When necessary, the coach can deviate from the standard package and create specific defensive adjustments to address atypical features of an opponent's offense. But designing and teaching a standard package approach to playing defense seems to be the most sensible way to trigger team defense.

Defensive Alignments

Some of you may have noticed that I am many pages into a chapter on defense, and I have yet to reference the popular predetermined defensive schemes such as *perimeter* and *rotation*. This is because both of these defenses come prepackaged and tend to discourage creative thinking. They seem to be tied more to the principle of memorizing where to stand and less to the principle of reading and reacting situationally to what is happening on the other side of the net. A defense is not a chart that a coach superimposes over the court like a plastic overlay. Rather, it is a coordinated set of movements and adjustments triggered by what the players see.

Let me provide an example of what I mean. I had the pleasure of coaching a terrific libero, Paula Gentil, back in early 2000s. She taught me that there was no point in forcing players into the restricted movement patterns that were the hallmark of predetermined defensive alignments. In fact, she taught me just the opposite. She played the game without a map to tell her where to go on the court. She allowed intuition and great visual acuity to govern her decisions, and she moved around the court without hesitation of any kind. She lined up officially as our left back defender, but she was allowed to go anywhere on the court that would enable her to make a play on the ball. I designated her the green-light defender, which authorized her to go anywhere she needed to go and do anything she needed to do. I didn't want her to become confined by a rigid system of defensive assignments. I wanted her to be spontaneous. I wanted her to make plays.

The challenge for the coaches was to make sure that her teammates, all of whom had been schooled in the traditional predetermined defensive systems, would be able to learn how to play with her. I can remember her often digging a ball in area 5, running to cover in area 2, and chasing a deflection into deep area 6 before winning the rally. It took a while for her teammates to learn how to stay out of her way! In the beginning they felt like she was poaching on their territory, but in time her style of play became our signature, our brand as a defensive team.

Conclusion

I never worried that my players may have strayed from the perimeter defense placement chart. I expected my team to instead to follow their reads and position themselves in relation to what they *saw* and not where the chart told them to go. Defense is the creative, calculated response to the offensive tactics of the opponent and should always be viewed as such. It should never be viewed as a prescribed, unwavering set of locations for each defender. When floor defenders read the offensive attack, they should follow basic keys in determining where to go to receive the attack. Here are some of those keys:

- Move into the digging lane created by your read of the HBB configuration.
- Evaluate the depth of the set (distance from net) in order to move to either a shallow or deep read.
- Evaluate the hitter's hand location to read full swing or off-speed shot.

In my estimation, this is what George was doing every Wednesday night at the Allegheny Y in Pittsburgh. It took me a while, but I think I finally figured out how he could be in the right spot at the right time to dig the ball. I had moved away from Pittsburgh by the time I understood why George was such a great defender. I never got the chance to thank him. To this day, although he never knew it, I count him as one of my chief mentors. He taught me how to play and coach defense, and he did it without ever saying a word.

Wait! He did speak to me that one time. "Make sure ball goes to setter."

CHAPTER 6

Drawing a Blueprint
for Offense

Throughout my career, I spoke to thousands of coaches at a variety of clinics, covering hundreds of topics, but there is one clinic that stands out from the rest. My assignment was to provide the coaches in attendance with ways to think about creating an offensive system for their respective teams. I opened the presentation with a series of questions.

"How do you measure the performance of your offense?" No one said a word. "How about calculating the kill efficiency (KEff) recorded by your team?" The formula for calculating KEff is (Kills - Errors) / Total Attempts. They all thought this would be a good idea.

"How many of you have ever established a KEff goal for your team?" Again, silence. "How many of you know the KEff of last season's championship team in your conference?" Not surprisingly, no one raised a hand.

I pressed on. "Let's assume that each of you in the room wants to win your conference championship next season. Would it be helpful to know approximately how efficient your offensive system would have to be in order to win the conference?" They all agreed that it would.

The point here is that if you wish to catch and pass the previous conference champion, it is helpful to establish specific performance goals for your team. For example, if the defending champion posts a .265 KEff for the season, you probably have to perform at a similar level if you wish to contend for the title. The same could be said for any statistical category you wish to name, using the same reasoning process to establish performance goals.

Limited Offensive Systems

Let's stay with the KEff example, since it is widely believed to be the statistic that most often correlates to winning in volleyball. With the help of the participating clinic coaches, we managed to create this piece of logic:

Premise 1: If the former conference champion won by hitting at a .265 clip, it would seem to follow that any team wishing to contend for the conference title must perform at a similar level.

Premise 2: In order to attack at a .265 team efficiency in a match, a team must be able to do this in practice. We will record and monitor each player's hitting efficiency in practice throughout the season.

Premise 3: In order to post a team efficiency of .265 in practice, there must be at least one player who can attack higher than .265. Otherwise, the goal would be mathematically impossible to attain.

Therefore: We will funnel our offense to those who demonstrate, in practice and in matches, the ability to attack at .265 or above.

I then provided a clinic handout (table 6.1) that listed each player from a hypothetical team (the Washington Generals) along with each player's KEff accumulated up to that point in the season. I instructed the coaches to create an offensive system based only on the small amount of information given to them in the handout.

TABLE 6.1　Statistics for the Washington Generals

Name	Position	KEff	Total attacks
Peg	Setter	.155	28
DeSandra	Middle hitter	.202	62
Sheila	Outside hitter	.147	199
Celeste	Defensive specialist	-.333	3
Julia	Outside hitter/Middle hitter/Opposite hitter	.386	256
Sarah	Outside hitter	.176	245
Chaka	Middle hitter	.188	44
Leslie	Setter	.000	2
Cemile	Opposite hitter (L)	.132	71
Paula	Libero	.000	0
Gwen	Outside hitter/Middle hitter	.500	2

One-Hitter Offense

It didn't take them long to come up with a solution: the one-hitter offense.

- Set the ball to Julie every time we get a chance to do so, whether she is in the front or back row. There is no reason to set anyone else intentionally, since no one else has demonstrated the ability to hit at a .265 level or higher. Gwen's .500 KEff is based on too small of a sample to warrant consideration as a primary attacker in the offense.

- Julie should audible her set choice (where and what to hit) to Peg every time an offensive opportunity occurs, both in serve-receive offense and in transition.

- Julie will switch to block and defend any position she wishes or is assigned from the bench and will call her audibles from her switched position.

- The rest of the team will work on accurate passing, setting, and spiker coverage.

- Julie should be aware of every cover situation and create a transition approach that will take her away from the original, congested point of attack.

- Julie must be superbly conditioned in order to embrace the physical demands placed on her. She probably will need extra rest throughout the season.

- The box score from each of her matches will show that Julie will take at least 80 percent of the team's swings. This is her job in this type of system.

The rest of the team will have to understand this, and if they want to be more involved in the offense, they will have to improve enough in practice so that they are hitting at the .265 standard or better. This is a necessary condition if the team is to reach its goal of winning a conference championship.

This one-hitter offense may be unorthodox, but there is no escaping the reality that you can't set the ball to sub-.265 hitters and expect to win the conference title with a KEff of .265 or above. In this example, it is essential that the ball circulate through the offensive system and end up on the hand of the one hitter who can achieve success.

Some of the clinic coaches stayed in contact to tell me that they had attempted to install an offensive system that, as a result of roster shortages, could not field a full complement of offensive attackers. All of them invented offensive systems that featured only one or two primary attackers and experienced what was to them a surprising level of success. But they also reported a universal psychological response. They said that as soon as the announcement was made to emphasize only one or two hitters in the offense, the rest of the hitters began to sulk. They seemed to take the decision personally.

This reaction should not have surprised anyone. For almost every player, volleyball offense includes a setter, two middle attackers, two outside hitters, and an opposite. Each player assumes that he will receive a fair share of sets within the flow of the offense. This is what all of them were trained to expect as they worked their way up through the age-group club system, the high school system, and into the college level.

I counseled each coach to do two things. First remind your players that one of the basic principles of offense in any sport is to put your best offensive players in a position to score. Punters in football don't sulk if the quarterback doesn't throw passes to them. Their job is to punt. Centers in basketball don't sulk if the coach doesn't ask them to dribble through the opponent's full-court press and distribute the ball to begin an offensive sequence. Their job is to rebound and score in the post. Weak-hitting relief pitchers don't sulk if they are not asked to pinch hit and drive in the winning run in the bottom of the ninth inning. Their job is to be ready to pitch if called upon. Golfers at the high school and college levels play qualifying rounds before each competition in order to determine who will be in the lineup. They know what they must do to be named to the starting team, and they accept the results of the qualifying rounds. So why do nonqualifying spikers in volleyball sulk when their role in the offense is either eliminated or greatly reduced? Their job is to hit .265. Instead of sulking, they need to improve their hitting efficiency in practice so they can qualify to receive sets in the offense.

Second, remind them also that even though they are not a go-to hitter in the offense, they still have assignments to carry out. Challenge them to become better blockers and defenders. Challenge them to improve their serve. Challenge them to improve their ball-control skills. Challenge them!

Standing Roll-Shot Offense

Later on, at this same clinic, one of the attending high school coaches asked me if she could present an idea to the other participants. I was more than agreeable. That evening she became the teacher, and the rest of us became her pupils. She began by describing her unique situation.

It turns out that there were no players on her roster who stood taller than 5'8", and none of them were good jumpers. In her estimation, no one on her team could become an effective offensive player. "What am I supposed to do?" she asked. "I still have to come up with an offensive system!" Then she recalled a ball-control drill that she had been running in practice recently. With two players on each side of the net, the coach enters a ball to one side. The receiving team must return the ball using a dig-set-hit sequence. When the ball crosses the net, the other team must do the same. It is a simple warm-up drill that tests a player's ability to control the ball as a receiver, a setter, and an offensive shot-maker.

In the course of the drill she noticed that two of her players, both of them 5'5", were on the winning side more often than any other players. In particular, they both had a knack for winding up and ripping standing roll shots into the opponent's court. They attacked the ball with great confidence and rarely missed. In fact, both of the kids were so good as standing roll-shot artists they began to pile up impressive offensive numbers. They were hitting the ball with great speed and with great accuracy. Both of them could direct the ball at will to the deep corners, to the baseline, and to anywhere else they felt gave them a chance to score.

In a moment of genuine creativity, the coach developed the following offensive system:

- There would be no sets near the net. Every set would go to one of the two roll-shot hitters who would be splitting the court at about 4 to 5 meters.

- Since these two players had demonstrated in practice and matches that both of them could attack with standing roll shots at about a .250 KEff, and no one else could come close to this number, it became clear that they should receive all the sets in both first-ball attack and transition.

- The rest of the team would be assigned to improve their defensive, setting, serving, and coverage skills in order to solidify the rest of their game.

This was a case of a young coach being willing to think for herself and not be trapped by the conventional wisdom. She understood that her personnel were not a good fit for the traditional offensive style of play employed by virtually every team in the nation. She was confident enough to strike out on her own to create a system that *would* fit her athletes. What a remarkably courageous thing for her to do.

By the way, her high school team won the state title the following season using her adapted offensive system!

Full Offense

The reason this clinic stood out from the rest must be obvious by now. The participants were not there to obey my instructions about how to play offense. They were there to learn how to *think* about designing their *own* offenses. Unfortunately, we ran out of time. The coaches wanted to move beyond offense and apply the same method of inquiry to the full slate of topics embedded in creating a system of play, such as defense, serving strategies, coverage systems, and serve-receive tactics. This wasn't possible, of course, but to this day, whenever I randomly encounter one of the clinic's participants, we stop to recall how special the experience was for all of us. They all felt the excitement and regenerative enthusiasm that accompanies the discovery of solutions through thoughtful inquiry.

Here are the questions they listed as needing answers in order to create an offensive system:

- What KEff does your offense have to produce in order to meet team goals?
- Do you have the personnel capable of achieving this KEff level?
- How would you deploy your personnel to achieve this KEff level?

These same concepts can be applied to building any offensive system and are always the place to start. The earlier examples provide a basic look at how offensive systems can evolve from a limited availability of traditional offensive weapons. Now let's accelerate our creative thinking to design an offense that features +.265 attackers at every position. While the first two examples focused more on the abilities—or limitations—of the hitters as a starting point, these more sophisticated examples will be shaped less by the hitters' talents and more by the characteristics of today's defensive systems. In other words, at the higher levels of play where no shortage of offensive weapons exists, the primary motivation for creating an offense is to design patterns that can successfully attack today's sophisticated defensive systems. Here are the issues that will need to be addressed in order to build the foundation for such an offense.

Players Adapt to System Versus System Adapts to Players

This will be the coach's first major decision. Does she create an offensive system commensurate with the talent level of the players, or does she attempt to train players to execute a system that may be beyond their capabilities? The tugging feeling from behind will be the urge to copy what everyone else seems to be doing. The conventional wisdom in volleyball can be a strong magnet. I understand why this is so. It is often the case that popular strategies are popular because they work.

Here are the fundamental concepts of the current conventional wisdom with regard to offense:

- The 5-1 (one-setter system) is, by far, the system of choice.
- Outside hitters and middle hitters line up opposite each other in the rotational pattern, with an outside hitter following the setter.
- The opposite player lines up opposite the setter.

Figure 6.1 shows the normal placement of attackers in rotation 1.

In 2004 the University of Minnesota squared off against Stanford University in the finals of the NCAA Championship. In an era when most teams were trying to speed up their offense, Stanford coach John Dunning sent his All-American outside hitter, Ogonna Nnamani, to the court to attack a steady menu of higher-than-normal sets. Even though this allowed the Minnesota block enough time to set up against Nnamani, she was hitting over the block and scoring at will. This was clearly the case of an astute coach who recognized the value in designing a system of offense based on the skill set of the players. Nnamani was

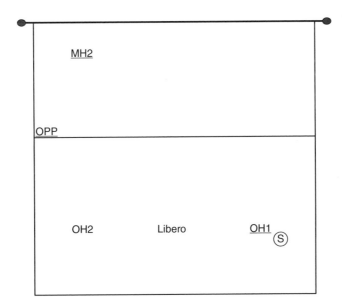

FIGURE 6.1 Common attacker placement in rotation 1. Front-row attackers are underlined.

Lauren Gibbemeyer and Megan Wilson trying to stop All-American Destinee Hooker in the semifinals against Texas at the 2009 NCAA Women's Volleyball tournament.
Cliff Welch/Icon SMI

unstoppable as a high-ball hitter, but she sometimes struggled with the faster tempo style. Stanford went on to win the title, with Nnamani piling up incredible offensive numbers hitting high balls.

Five years later Minnesota faced Texas in another Final Four. Texas was loaded with quick, powerful athletes. Their coach, Jerritt Elliot, decided early on that he would assemble this group of mostly raw athletes and develop a system of offense that would feature their speed and athleticism. The sets were lower and quicker. Their hitters displayed fast, powerful approaches. Leading the way for Texas was their splendid outside hitter Destinee Hooker, who became a fixture for the U.S. in its silver medal run in the London Olympics. Here was a case of a coach saying, "I have the athletes to play fast, and that's just what we are going to do." He trained them to play the system he wanted. And they were formidable.

Deciding on Set Options

Every offense in volleyball features a series of sets that function much like plays in football. Like a quarterback, the setter often calls a play using hand signals or verbal communication to direct each member of the offensive team to run an assigned approach pattern. Some coaches prefer that the setter remain silent, giving way to spontaneous audible calls by each attacker. The setter will deliver the set to the hitter that she believes has the best chance to score. In order to run offense, whether it is setter-directed or attacker-generated, everyone on the team must be familiar with all of the possible sets in the offensive system. Figure 6.2 is a set chart that I used at Minnesota during my final season.

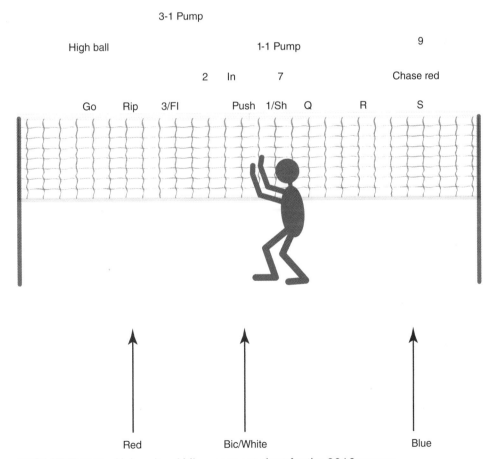

FIGURE 6.2   University of Minnesota set chart for the 2010 season.

Here is the key for figure 6.2:

Go: Second tempo set to the left pin

High ball: Safety high set to the left pin

Rip: Second tempo lob set to inside zone

3: Low, first tempo, quick set to the gap, approximately 2.5 meters in front of setter

Flare: Same set as 3, but hitter approaches off one foot

2: Second tempo lob set 1.5 meters high and 1 meter in front of setter

1: Zero tempo quick set directly off setter's forehead

Push: Similar to a 1 but pushed slightly further

3-1 pump: Fake approach to 3, step in to 1

1-1 pump: Fake jump to 1, regather and hit a high 1

Shake: Same set as 1, but hitter approaches off one foot

Q: Tight slide

R: Medium slide

S: Wide slide

In: Same as 2, but set in out-of-system situations

7: Second tempo lob set 2 meters behind setter

Chase: Wide slide set against the flow, setter running left

9: Safety high set to right pin

Red: Second tempo back-row set to area 2

White: Second tempo back-row set to area 3

Bic: Lower-back-row set to area 3

Blue: Second tempo back-row set to area 1

Using the Set Chart

The set chart supplies a common language that allows coaches and players to communicate efficiently and quickly with one another. Time and space prohibit me from laying out all of the offensive combinations that could derive from the menu of set selections described here, but the following account will provide insight into how shared access to a common language can facilitate in-game adjustments.

I have always emphasized the importance of playing with increased awareness and an improved volleyball IQ. I never passed up the chance to remind teams that they, the players, would make most of the important decisions that would come up in a match. I didn't want them always looking at me for guidance from the bench. I wanted them to trust themselves to do the right thing.

They responded. They often made adjustments on their own during matches. They knew who to serve to, who to double-team as blockers, and what digging lanes to occupy against each hitter. They knew how to make changes in these tactics when our opponent began to show different tendencies.

Most importantly, they embraced the offensive principles that guided our system of counterattacking. It was an audible system that required two very different skills. First, our hitters were required to be extremely disciplined as they evaluated the opponent's blocking tactics. They had to know how each of our sets was being blocked. Where were the gaps? Where did help come from? Were they committing against our quick attackers?

Second, they had to quickly create a sequence of counterattack audible calls that would fit each offensive opportunity. For a play to be a good fit, it had to attack the opponent's block vulnerabilities. For example, calling a set that would take you directly into a blocker would not be a good fit, but calling a set that would take you into a gap between two blockers would. This required that each hitter employ some serious creativity as the match developed. There could be no ruts. We didn't want hitters calling the same set over and over because they had achieved early success. Instead, we wanted hitters who could catalogue the results of the various sets they called and learn how to diversify their calls so that automatic kills would be there when needed. We felt that we had to stay ahead of our opponent with our counterattack decisions.

Our hitters had to become very disciplined, sharpening their awareness of the game. At the same time, they had to be creative. The combination of these two skills would produce an offense that would prove to be hard to contain.

It was clear to me that the players enjoyed this style of play. They felt empowered to make decisions during matches. Sometimes they would show up early before practice to work out some new wrinkles in the offense. They were always trying to find ways to improve.

Our Final Four match with Hawaii in 1988 started horribly. We were behind 1-0, and down 10-6 (side-out scoring) in the second set. Hawaii was handing us our lunch. Their confidence soared with each point they scored. They positioned their great All-American left-side hitter Teee Williams to block our slide attack, and she was doing just that. She was single-handedly shutting down our highly respected slide hitters. We had relied heavily on this weapon all season, and now it was gone, taken away. The life had been sucked out of our team. I had run out of things to say. Nothing I dialed up had any impact on what was happening in the match.

Then, out of the blue, came one of the most gratifying moments of my coaching career. I looked up to see our All-American middle, Mary Eggers, take off on yet another slide approach. Teee Williams was poised and ready to jump-commit and push her long arms over the net to stuff yet another slide attempt by us. But wait a minute! As Mary and Teee rose together to contest the ball, the set took on a different trajectory than all the previous slide sets. This one flew faster and further than the rest, past the anticipated point of attack. To my great surprise, Laura Bush came running from behind Mary on her own delayed slide approach, aimed at jumping past Mary to hit a wider slide set. As both Mary and Teee descended from their respective jumps, the set flew directly into the wheelhouse of Laura's arm swing and—with no blocker even close—she crushed it to the floor.

Our team and the crowd went berserk. We had just executed the first double slide ever witnessed. At least that was what everyone was saying at the time.

Before running the play, our setter Barb Winsett, Mary, and Laura had huddled briefly on the court. They knew something had to be done to change the momentum of the match. Allowing Teee to continue her incredible commit blocking against our slide meant certain defeat for us.

It was at that moment that the three of them created their response to Williams. On their own, these three players drew upon their confidence and their volleyball IQ. They invented the double slide. The first slide hitter ran a Q, and the second slide hitter ran an S. Now Williams was forced to stay on the floor and read. She and her teammates never knew whether we were going to run one or two slide hitters behind the setter. This slight change in tactics was just enough to disrupt Hawaii's confidence and begin to solidify ours.

Illinois ended up losing 3-1, but the final three sets were each decided by only a two-point margin. We came close to pulling off a major upset, all due to the availability of a common set language and the players' sudden creation of the double slide.

First-Ball Attack Versus Counterattack

Two types of offensive possessions are possible in volleyball. The first is initiated with the reception of serve and is called first-ball attack (FBA). The second is initiated with the reception of any ball, subsequent to the serve, that is sent into the defensive court. This phase of offense is called counterattack (CA). At most levels of play, a team is in FBA mode around 60 percent of the time, and in CA mode for the remainder of the time (40 percent).

Passing Formations and FBA

Success in FBA is determined by how well a team can pass the ball to their desired setter target point. All teams designate where they want their setter to receive the pass. Normally, this point is near the net and approximately 3 to 4 meters from the right sideline. The more accurate the pass is, the more efficient the offense will be. It is no wonder that teams spend an enormous amount of time practicing their passing game. Good passing begets good offense, and good offense begets winning.

Passing formations and the rise of passing specialists have been well documented over the past 25 to 30 years. There is no need to replicate this material here. But there is one dimension of the passing game that I would like to bring to your attention.

The most common passing formation in today's game uses three primary passers spread out in a balanced fashion across the court in a straight line at approximately 6 meters (figure 6.3). The gaps between

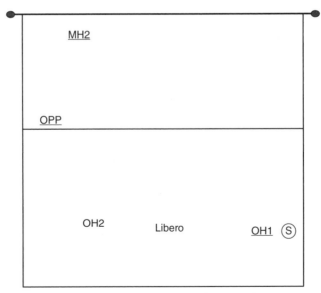

FIGURE 6.3 Common FBA passing formation (balanced). Passers are OH2, Libero, and <u>OH1</u>.

the passers are roughly equal in distance. Nonpassers are hidden at the net, the baseline, or near a sideline to discourage the opponent from serving at them.

The balanced formation is useful when a team presents three passers who are equal in ability and who possess the same level of efficient movement in any direction. Each of these passers would achieve similar levels of success, but this would be a rare and unlikely circumstance. I have never seen a team that can put three equally skilled passers on the floor.

My observation is that every team uses passers who demonstrate a pattern of strengths and weaknesses. Some passers are better moving from right to left or from left to right. Others might be more comfortable lining up in a deep position and moving forward to receive a short serve, while others prefer lining up in a shallow position and moving backward to receive the deep ball. If this is true—and I believe it to be so—why not design serve-receive patterns to entice the server to attack your passers' strengths and to protect their weaknesses? You can discover each passer's strength and weakness profile by testing each of them early in the season. Specific patterns emerge in a very short time.

For example, passers OH2 and Libero in figure 6.3 are much more efficient when they move from left to right to pass a ball outside the body line. I would ask them to shift their receiving position to the left, leaving a large area of court to the right (figure 6.4). Servers will usually serve into unprotected zones, but in this case passers OH2 and Libero *want* the ball to be served to their right. They feel more comfortable and confident moving in this direction and are more likely to pass a good ball. I call this dictating the serve. Each of the passers has the freedom to reposition herself in the passing formation in order to dictate where she wants the ball to be served. Passing formations can be squeezed, spread out, and manipulated in so many ways that it is common to see teams line up in a different formation in every rotation.

Once the ball is successfully passed to the setter, the FBA sequence is carried out. Typically, the setter has communicated, either verbally or through hand signals, which set each of the attackers should expect to hit. These sets are among the set options listed on the team's set chart (figure 6.2). Most coaches feel that a team's FBA efficiency should be near the .300 mark. After all, the receiving team has been given plenty of dead-ball time to position itself to receive the serve. The setter has had time to evaluate the opponent's defense and call the right sets, and the attackers have had enough time to process their respective attack assignments. It is now the job of the setter to select and execute the correct set in order to have a chance to score a point.

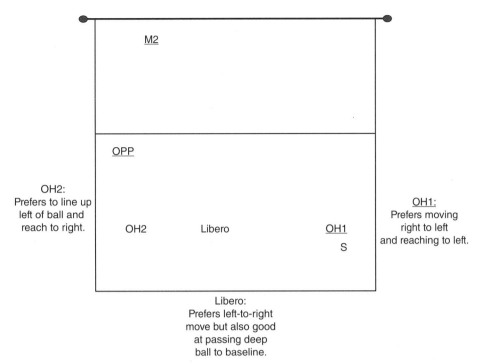

FIGURE 6.4 Sample FBA passing formation (unbalanced). Passers are OH2, Libero, and OH1.

Counterattack and the Use of Audibles

Once the serving team controls the ball returned by the FBA team, both teams switch to CA mode, and things become very different. The average time between a dead-ball whistle and the whistle to serve is approximately 8 to 12 seconds. This allows the receiving (FBA) team plenty of time to organize their attack. However, there is usually a much smaller window of opportunity for the CA team to organize and execute a counterattack. Counterattacking occurs during the flow of play and requires a quick, well-rehearsed response by the attacking team. This can be difficult since the ball is often attacked into the defense with power and velocity, making it much more difficult to control the ball to the setter.

Three things distinguish CA from FBA. First, the transition from defense to offense by the CA team is more complicated than FBA transition. FBA court positioning in a passing formation enables an easier transition to attack. It is a much more predictable and controlled situation. Teams in a counterattacking phase, however, must scramble to recover from a variety of unpredictable defensive positions and reset for an offensive attempt.

Second, there is no time for a counterattacking team's setter to call sets or to use hand signals to communicate the offensive assignment for each hitter. Instead, hitters must call audibles spontaneously during the flow of play. The setter, while moving to get under the pass, must listen to and process all of the audibles and decide which hitter to set.

Finally, unlike FBA where the serving team is already in their defensive base position at the time of service, the CA team must reset on the fly. Since both teams are moving back and forth from defense to offense and back again, each team has the option of trying to out-quick the other and trigger the counterattack before the defense has regrouped.

In-System Versus Out-of-System Offense

In both instances, whether it is a FBA or a CA situation, the pass (or dig) is intended to land directly on the crown of the setter's head. This is called an in-system pass (or dig), and the offensive possession is referred to as being in-system (I/S). One of the first obligations a hitter faces in either an I/S or an out-of-system (O/S) situation is to evaluate the quality of the team's reception. Is it an I/S or O/S pass? If it is I/S, then all of the hitters run their assigned patterns and prepare to receive the set. If it is an O/S pass, then everyone—the receiver, the setter, and the hitters—has just enough time to assess the situation and audible an appropriate O/S set.

When the pass or dig brings the setter out of the setter target zone so that the setter is unable to deliver all of the set options that were called for during that possession, the offense is referred to as being out-of-system (O/S). The more often a team can remain I/S, the greater the probability of winning the match. Teams work tirelessly on their ball control (passing and digging) in order to maximize the number of I/S offensive opportunities they will be able to create in competition. But there are often times when, for example, the opponent delivers a very difficult ball to control such as a hard-driven spike. In this situation the digger is not asked to send the ball to the setter at the net. Instead, the digging target changes to a location I refer to as the well, located in the center of the court near the 3-meter line. This is a safer target for the digger to aim for because it reduces the chance that the ball will be sent over the net. It is better to deliberately create an O/S offensive opportunity than risk losing the ball back to the opponent.

In every I/S opportunity, the middle hitter (MH) triggers the offense. She selects the set she wishes to attack. It will always be a zero or first tempo set. She will choose from the quick set options in the set chart (3, flare, push, 1, shake, Q, R, or S). Her selection is based on finding a seam to attack, attacking a short or poor blocker on the slide, attacking against one blocker when there is no help coming, and on the availability of scouting information on the opponent. The MH audibles the set choice and is usually the first option to receive the set.

As the MH drives to attack, the opposite (in back-row setter rotations) or the back-row hitter (in front-row setter rotations) listens to the audible and calls a complementary set. A complementary set is one that, in combination with the MH call, stresses the opponent's block. An example would be the MH calling 3, and the opposite calling red. There is no way that the opponent's middle blocker (MB) could read the situation and get to both points of attack. The 3-red audible spreads the points of attack so wide that the offense creates an advantage over the defense. The outside hitters are on a steady diet of gos and do not need to use an audible.

This type of CA offense is dependent on the following:

- The MH is available in every I/S opportunity. Being available means jumping for the quick set or calling for a fast, wide slide on every I/S pass. Staying down is never an option.

- The second audible attacker must quickly assess the MH's intentions and calculate a complementary audible that will have a reasonable chance to score. She must become skilled at hearing, processing, and making the correct audible call.

- The MH must make an early call so that the second call can be conveyed to the setter in time.

- The audibles are always in sequence: first the MH, then the second call.

- When the setter digs, the ball is sent to the well. The libero will set to either pin hitter unless also trained to set to back-row hitters.

- If the setter ever senses any hint of trouble (such as confusion, traffic jams, hitter too early or too late), she sets a high ball to an outlet hitter. Never risk losing a possession because of an attack coordination error.

Adjusting to New Defensive Developments

There is an additional set of variables that can be important in establishing an offensive system. These variables come from the coach's ability to anticipate any new trends in the game that should be addressed and accounted for when mapping out an offensive system. Consider table 6.2. It illustrates a series of possible trends that need to be a part of the planning process.

TABLE 6.2   Responses to Defensive Trends

Defensive trends	Offensive response
Bigger, smarter MBs who can read	Accelerated quick-attack tempo Combination attack to confuse MBs Spread points of attack to force MB movement
Better closing speed to outside by blockers	Faster set to pins, fast enough to beat the blockers to the point of attack Pin hitters who can approach quickly and hit a low, fast set Faster slide approaches Setting back-row hitters to keep blockers honest
Good commit blocking	Pump plants and misdirection approaches to counter the commit jump
Disguise block scheming tactics well	Development of reading skills and audible system to counter schemes

Next, a series of decisions must be made regarding the final touches to be installed in the offensive system. Here are some of the more important features requiring attention.

First, establish the tempo of the pass (or dig). Should the pass be low and fast, or should it be high and slow? A fast pass places more pressure on the opponent's block and defense, but it is a high-risk tactic. A higher pass is a low-risk tactic, but it gives the opponent more time to organize its block and defense. Establish the location (point of attack along the net) for each set. Establish a quick set tempo. Use audible sequencing and decide which hitter calls first and second. It is essential that a coach review all of these principles, making decisions about each of them, before any formal competition.

The system features four tempos:

1. Tempo 0: Hitter jumps before setter touch: push, 1, Q.
2. Tempo 1: Hitter jumps as setter touches: 3, flare, shake, R, S, bic
3. Tempo 2: Read step as setter touches: go, rip, 2, 7, in, red, gap, white, alley, blue, 9
4. Tempo 3: Wait and drive: high ball, chase

For the first-ball attack (FBA), the setter hand-signals with the occasional audible option counterattack (from defense, free ball, coverage). In an all-audible system, these are the options:

Three-Hitter

MH first call

Opp second call (complementary to MH call)

OH constant (no calls except rip)

Back row constant (no calls except BIC)

Two-Hitter

MH first call

OH second call (complementary to MH call)

Back row constant (no calls except bic)

My philosophy has always been that the MHs are the initiators of each counterattack. They decide which call to make, and everyone else adjusts their call to them. We want to set the MHs at every opportunity. They have to be prepared to carry a heavy load. They have to be intelligent students of the game in order to know what call to make in each situation. They must work their butts off to be available on every offensive opportunity.

Let's also review some of the important features of the system. The passed or dug ball should reach its apex just above the top of the pin. If we pass too low, we lose the setter dump. We would like the setter to receive the ball approximately 1 meter off the net in the traditional right-of-center zone. Overpasses and digs usually result in a point for the opponent. If you are going to miss, miss *off* the net. When the setter digs, we will direct the dig to the well so that our libero can set the next contact. A high dig to the well should be the target in any difficult situation such as a hard-driven ball, tough serve, emergency pursuit, or unexpected block deflection.

Conclusion

Our offensive goals will be specific. We will be a hand-signal team in FBA and an audible team in CA. We want to play fast but not recklessly. We want to hit second-tempo sets to our OHs, back row, and opposite (both S and blue). Our OHs have to be able to hit both line and angle. Our opposite has to be able to hit the blue set; this will be a key to our offense. We want to score with our quick attack and slide as often as possible. I want our setter to always look for these options first. Everything else is established as a result of a successful quick slide attack. This will require that our setters deliver an accurate first- or second-tempo set from anywhere. Our hitters must learn to approach with speed and to trigger a very quick armswing. We want to use rip-gap-S-white as a base play in three-hitter rotations. We should train our MHs to come down from the block against their OHs and get to the gap; this will require fast footwork.

In addition to standard three-hitter options, we would like to execute the following:

Slide-2

3-inside 2

Double slide

Double quick

We want to play fast in two-hitter rotations as well. I want our setter to be a constant offensive threat; our setter will have to learn to be deceptive when second contact opportunities arise. We want to use rip-dump, slide (plus all back-row options, especially white) as our base play in two-hitter.

Finally, we want to be a very fast transition team that constantly looks for opportunities to get a swing. This requires fast footwork in order to become available. This also means our MBs must evaluate and make a call as early as possible. We will become a good risk-management team, never trying to do too much and never settling for too little. We want to hit hard when it is available. We want to choose the appropriate shot when the hard swing is taken away from us. We must score on every free ball (if they give it to us, they must pay!). We will play a low-error offensive game (no more than 13 percent attack errors because most elite teams keep their errors at 13 percent or less).

Make sure your hitters look at the opponent blockers before each FBA opportunity. Look for helpful information. Are they bunched or spread? Do we attack gaps or pins? Is there a small blocker to exploit? If so, how do we exploit? How are their MBs reacting to situations? Are their MBs ball-watchers, pass-fronters, or read blockers? Do their MBs front our quick attacker? Are they fronting the 1 and 3, or are they neutral and reading the setter? Do their MBs jump (commit) with quick sets? Do their MBs release early against two-hitter rotations? If so, how do we find out, and what is our response? Do their MBs possess good balance and a quick first step, or are they sluggish in their reaction to an outside set?

How are their wing blockers reacting to situations? Who helps on different plays? Are they focused on stopping the OH or the MH? As the blockers move inside out against the go, S, or 9, do they overrun the set and open up an angle shot? Do they reach outward toward the ball? Does their blocking style encourage rip and 7?

How does their MB react to an O/S situation? Release to the left-side hitter? Stay neutral and read? Do they front our setter on a tight pass in two-hitter situations, or are they open for the setter dump?

Finally, look at the blockers every time after the opponent blocks for a point. How did they react to the set you just made? Were they in good, solid position? This would indicate that their defensive alignment worked very well against that set. Or was there only one blocker descending and out of balance? This would be an invitation to repeat that set later since the opponent would likely deploy the same defense against that same set. You can learn a lot by evaluating what happens after the whistle has blown.

CHAPTER 7

Promoting a Positive Gym Culture

Many years ago, while sitting on a plane for almost two hours readying for takeoff from Istanbul, Turkey (I had spoken at a volleyball clinic arranged by my friend and former graduate school roommate Umit Kesim), I was becoming fidgety and looking for something to do. I took out my calculator and started adding up the number of hours I spent annually in the gym as a college coach. This included practices at home and on the road; conditioning; team meetings for scouting and other matters of internal concern; team meals; meetings with auxiliary personnel such as equipment managers, athletic trainers, and facilities coordinators; and the hours spent running camps and clinics. That number turned out to be close to 1,600 hours per year and 4.5 hours per day, based on a seven-day work week. Considering that I might average around nine hours per day on the job, this meant that I was spending at least 50 percent of my workday in the gym.

I had never thought about it that way. I was spending over half of my professional life in a gym. After letting those numbers sink in, I was left with the uneasy realization that I had never addressed this very important question: If I, along with my staff and players, were going to be sequestered in a gym for half of our volleyball-related lives, shouldn't that environment be structured so that we all felt good about being there?

Knowing that I was facing a minimum of 10 uninterrupted hours of work time, I decided to step back and take a good look at the atmosphere in my gym and determine if there were any changes to be made. I wanted to be sure that I was creating a positive, efficient gym culture.

This defining moment for me occurred while high above the Adriatic Sea sometime in the mid-1980s, well before the term *gym culture* became one of volleyball's buzz phrases. No matter what level of competition a player is considering as a participant in today's volleyball world, he is going to want to know something about the program's gym culture. He is going to want to know about how people behave when they are around each other and about the value system that governs their interactions. Some of what he wants to know is already outlined in other chapters of this book. The program's infrastructure, team goals, and the lesson plan to nurture team trust are all laden with directives intended to shape the athlete in the image of the program's value system or culture.

Think about gym culture as the application of the program's value structure as it applies to activities occurring in the gym. This includes practice, competition, and team meetings. I will attempt to catalogue each item that I used in piecing together the elements of a gym culture that I believed would succeed. I will also let you know which items were significant in their presence and which were not.

Positive and Efficient Gym Culture

Let's take care of one possible misunderstanding right away. For as many of you who will respond favorably to the term "positive" (as in positive gym culture), there are just as many who will respond unfavorably. This latter group can sometimes equate positive with soft or non-demanding. This would be a mistake and would deflect attention from the intended meaning of positive, which I will clarify right now.

It's OK to get mad at your team. It's OK to penalize your players following a poor performance. It's OK to withhold praise when it isn't deserved. My mind races to the often-repeated scene where a coach, whose highly favored team has just defeated an opponent of lesser skill in a sloppy match, and the first thing out of the coach's mouth is, "Nice job. Great win!"

This is not positive coaching! It is deceptive coaching, and it doesn't belong in a gym where positive coaching is the order of the day. Positive coaching is not the absence of intense emotion. It is not the absence of the iron will of the coach. It is not the absence of significant and sometimes dramatic confrontations between player and coach. Positive coaching encourages the coach to tell the truth to players and then teach them how to listen and deal with its consequences. Tim Crothers, in his 2010 book *The Man Watching*, tells us how Anson Dorrance, coach of the NCAA champion University of North Carolina women's soccer team, described this from the perspective of coaching females:

> [We are] fighting against a sociology that discourages most women from being competitive. So much of what girls have been taught growing up is about cooperation and acquiescence. Women have the superior understanding that friendships are more important than winning the game, and there's really nothing in their culture that encourages them to be competitive. Girls who compete are considered bitches. Girls would rather be accepted and liked than be competitive and respected. We want girls in our system to understand that we don't want you to be popular, we want you to be respected. My job is to change their natural course.*

Of course, the coach must be attentive to the emotional and physical welfare of the athlete, but resorting to worn-out, sugar-coated, and ill-deserved phrases like "Good job, Mary" to simply make the athlete feel good does not capture the essence of what I mean when I talk about positive gym culture. For me, a positive gym culture closely resembles the atmosphere I describe in chapter 8 of this book, where mutual trust is the common goal, and the term positive stands for a coach's character and not for a coach's inability to convey the truth.

You will also notice that I used the term *efficient* when announcing my intention to create a positive and efficient gym culture. I am going to assume that we can all agree that the definition of an efficient gym culture goes something like this: Participants in this culture, functioning under the guidance of competent supervisors and in the best possible manner with the least waste of time, join together to accomplish a specific social task; in this case, conference and national championships.

---

*Tim Crothers, *The Man Watching: A Biography of Anson Dorrance, the Unlikely Architect of the Greatest College Sports Dynasty Ever* (New York: St. Martin's, 2010), 94.

The Gym

The gym is the gathering point for the team's players and coaches. Almost everything of significance occurs within its four walls. Here players learn how to play, people learn how to trust and, yes, coaches learn how to coach. It all takes place within the confines of the gym culture that evolves to envelop the program. It would seem at least prudent, therefore, for the coach to build the proper foundation on which the program's gym culture will stand.

In chapter 8, I will provide a map that a trusting team must follow. I stand by my claim that the building of team-wide trust is the single most important thing a coach can provide her team, but other things are also important. In this chapter I would like to review many of the features of what I would call a positive, efficient gym culture.

The centerpiece of life in the gym is practice. Practice serves as a vehicle for change. It is a testing ground for developing a trusting heart. It is a training ground for honing competitive instincts and mental toughness. Most of all, it is where every aspect of the program intersects daily. It is where the seeds of success or failure are sown. It is where the team's gym culture appears in full bloom. Practice, it would seem, deserves serious attention.

The Underlying Principles of Practice

Practice is the theater within which volleyball players rehearse their physical and mental skills in order to prepare for competition. Designing an efficient practice should be the first thing that captures the coach's attention. Let's begin by identifying the guiding principles upon which I believe a practice should be built.

Competition and the Cauldron

The goal of the journey is to compete and to win. Can there be any more appropriate element of preparation to be rehearsed in practice than competition? Score should be kept. There should be consequences to winning or losing. This makes everything more meaningful and makes everyone better. The recent popularizing of the competitive cauldron has created widespread interest in the idea that competing in practice should be a staple in volleyball practice gyms throughout the U.S. The cauldron has become the mechanism of choice for tracking the competitive success of each player on the roster.

Some coaches use the results of the daily cauldron to determine the starting lineup for the next match. I do not agree that this should be done. In fact, the father of the cauldron, Anson Dorrance, doesn't believe it either. In a personal conversation in 2011, he told me that cauldron results did not necessarily play a role in selecting a starting lineup. The cauldron, he explained, was "mainly for parents and a few players" who enjoyed keeping up with competitive results.

There was a time in my career when I believed that there was value in pursuing the idea of the cauldron. In 2002 I worked closely with Dennis Amundson, one of my assistant coaches, to streamline the concept of the cauldron in the Minnesota program. We had embraced the idea that competing in practice and recording the results would enhance our players' focus on learning how to compete. We also believed that player evaluation should not be confined to winning or losing. We believed that players could and should compete at several different levels. So Amundson and I decided to take a closer look at the existing cauldron model with the idea that it could be expanded to include competitive situations that more closely fit our needs.

In the spring of 2002, we developed our own version of the competitive cauldron. The purpose of our cauldron was to identify which players were doing the things that were necessary to help us win a championship. This cauldron, after calculating all the results that had been entered over a period of time, produced a single number that represented that player's ability to compete. The ingredients of this cauldron were skill execution, win/loss records in various forms of competition, error control, physical training, and academics.

In order to make sure that we compared apples to apples, a form of decathlon scoring was used. In our version of decathlon scoring, a score of 100 was given when a predetermined standard was met. A best standard was determined for each test. The best standard for passing might be 2.4, and the best academic standard would be 4.0. If an athlete matched a best score, her score was 100. If her grade was below the best score, she received a score proportionally lower than 100, and the opposite was true if her grade exceeded the best standard.

Each of the competitive situations was also assigned a relative value to be factored into the athlete's score. A passing competition in practice might be weighted a 3, whereas a 6-on-6 scrimmage might be assigned a 5. In other words, receiving a score of 100 in the passing competition would be worth 300 cauldron points (3 x 100), while the same score of 100 in the 6-on-6 scrimmage would be worth 500 Cauldron points (5 x 100). Therefore, if a player dug 65 percent (65 percent being the best score in this performance category) in a 6-on-6 scrimmage, she would receive 500 cauldron points (100 x 5).

Athletes could expect to engage in several cauldron activities each week in practice. As a result, their scores would change daily. To prevent good but old scores from ranking a slumping player too highly, a moving average was used. That means that each time a new score was added, the oldest score was dropped. The only way to improve your cauldron score was to work on improving your skills every day and winning the competitions.

After each cauldron event, so went our plan, players would receive an updated spreadsheet. The first sheet was a summary sheet where they could check their standings. The elements of the cauldron would be listed across the top with the weighted factor below it. Players would find their current totals in the second column.

The third column was to be the academic component. The player's most current semester GPA was used, and 4.0 was the best score. Physical testing was in the fourth column. It was a composite of the vertical jump, dot drill, beep test, push-up test, sit-up test, flexibility test, core test, spike velocity, and body composition.

Columns 5 through 9 contained skill scores. The best scores for serving (2.0), passing (2.4), digging (65 percent), attacking (.300), and blocking (stuff blocking 10 percent of all balls attacked at a particular player) were all graded. The number of skills that were graded depended on the number of coaches available for stat work. Skill scores were generated in skill drills such as pass versus serve, small-group competitions (any competition less than 6-on-6 that requires all the players to perform all the skills), and 6-on-6 scrimmages that were game-like situations. Since some players specialized only in game scrimmages, the cauldron didn't lower their scores if they didn't participate in all the skills during the competition. A defensive specialist (DS), for example, would have a score that might include only serve, pass, and defend (no block or attack). Her score, using the decathlon system outlined here, would reflect the efficiency with which she executed *her* skills. Her overall score and ranking would not be penalized because she did not participate in hitting and blocking.

Columns 10 and 11 were for competition scores. They were the percentage of games won and lost in practice and were again broken down by small-group games and 6-on-6 scrimmages. A best competition score of 100 equaled a win/loss percentage of 100 percent. The best way to improve this score is to win games in practice.

Column 12 quantified error control. It measured how well an athlete controlled her errors by not giving points to the opponent. Under the error-control column, a player received a best score of 100 by keeping hitting errors below 15 percent and service errors below 10 percent. A player also lost 10 points for a net violation, a ball-handling violation, or a rotation violation.

One incentive for players was that they could be awarded 10 points for making a big play. The players involved in the competition identified the big plays. There had to be a general consensus. The player making the play could nominate the play, or teammates could initiate the nomination. The cauldron spreadsheet would provide the data that would allow each player to follow her progress and the progress of her teammates as the cauldron unfolded.

But we never got that far. We never developed the cauldron summary sheet. Here is what happened.

We carried the cauldron principle into practice in the fall of 2002. It took an army of assistant coaches, managers, and statisticians to make this happen. It gobbled up resources, both in the accumulation of data and in the interpretation and recording of the data. It created an enormous drain on our time. Very quickly we identified three basic reasons for discontinuing the cauldron:

1. Stats do not reveal intangibles. They provide no information, for example, on how successfully the player has learned how to trust and be trusted.

2. The results are not worth the time spent. We were suffocating under the strain of cauldron deadlines.

3. We were not getting new information. We asked ourselves the question: What is the cauldron providing that we couldn't accomplish on our own? The answer kept coming back, "Not much!" It seemed to everyone that for the limited information we received about the competitive level of our team, we were devoting an indefensible amount of time to the maintenance of the competitive cauldron.

After three weeks we junked the project. Our staff was exhausted from having to do cauldron calculations under the pressure of daily deadlines. We collectively felt, as a staff, that while the data we collected was interesting, it did not warrant the time and energy drain on the program's resources.

The final nail in the cauldron's coffin occurred when I set up an informal experiment. I directed each of the coaches to select a starting line-up, but without referencing any statistical information we had collected up to that point. We would then compare our line-ups to the line-up that the cauldron would have selected. Not surprisingly, all of us wrote down the same line-up, but the knockout blow was delivered when the cauldron's line-up was exactly the same as ours.

I recognize that the elaborate record keeping required by the cauldron system could be a source of motivation for some players, but its limited motivational appeal still did not justify the drain on resources. Nor did my personal observation that high scores in the cauldron did not necessarily correlate with performance in matches. I also questioned the absence of any mechanism for measuring the team chemistry aspects of a player's contribution to team success.

Coach Dorrance's comment about his minimal use of the cauldron convinced me to return to the shorthand version of record keeping that I had used for most of my career. I paid great attention to how well each player understood and accepted her role in our pursuit of championship level volleyball. I trusted my observational powers more than the collection of numbers after each player's name. I reserved my appreciation for statistics primarily for the realm of team and rotation-specific analyses that, I felt, provided me with a more reliable basis for making important team decisions.

I don't disapprove of the cauldron's popularity. I just think that there is more than one way to measure an athlete's competitive nature. Competing in practice is an essential quality of a program's gym culture. It is up to each coach to decide what form of evaluation will provide the most reliable mechanism for testing competitiveness.

Coaching as Behavior Modification

Behavior modification is the use of behavior change techniques to increase or decrease the frequency of behaviors, such as altering an individual's behaviors and reactions to stimuli through positive and negative reinforcement. In other words, coaches are teachers and, as such, need to understand and apply the principles of positive reinforcement.

The importance of positive feedback will be discussed in chapter 8 of this book. Without positive feedback, teams cannot achieve goals of any kind. For many years I didn't understand this. I simply provided the positive feedback (you remember the "Good win!" example) that I thought was expected of me. As the months and years went by, I began to notice that my positive feedback to players was having less of an impact, but I still didn't understand why this was happening.

I decided to take a closer look at the issue. I wanted to put myself into a situation where I was being coached to execute a difficult skill set and during which my ability to process feedback would play a major role in whether or not I would be successful in learning this new skill. I wanted to feel what my athletes must have been feeling. I wanted to experience their level of frustration so that I could develop a clearer understanding of how to tailor my feedback patterns to them.

I chose golf as the skill set that I would try to learn. There can be no more difficult skill set in the world, no skill set accompanied by as many unnecessarily intricate and often conflicting teaching cues, as the one required for golf. I traveled to Florida where I met longtime friend and excellent volleyball coach Shelton Collier. We were there for the same reason. We wanted to improve our own game. We also wanted to return to our practice gyms with a deeper understanding of how to use feedback patterns in coaching.

For three full days, Shelton and I pounded, putted, and chipped golf balls while listening to Marty (our instructor) fire corrections, evaluations, suggestions, and criticisms at us in rapid fashion. I would sneak off during breaks to make notes about the experience. By the end of the three days, it seemed as if I had enough notes to fill a briefcase.

When I returned home I poured over the notes intending to select the most meaningful points and apply them to my approach to giving feedback to my own athletes in the gym. Take a look at my original stab at creating a summary of my experience:

Coaching transfer from golf school

- It was very hard to remember the learning keys during the lesson. I had to be reminded regularly. I need to be patient with the learning process among my own athletes.
- Calm reminders are better than impatient, condescending attacks.
- It is much more important to teach rather than to show impatience.
- Changing a volleyball player's hitting mechanics is like trying to change my golf swing—virtually impossible. (This is a big one!)
- The frustration level I felt must be similar to what my players feel while I am trying to coach them. Somehow I have to adapt to this reality.
- The highs and lows I felt must be similar to what my players feel.
- You might have it for a moment, then lose it. This one surprised me, and I know that it occurs in my gym.
- Positive feedback is very comforting. It's OK to overdo it; there can never be too much.

- Actual game pressure can wipe the screen clear of all newly taught keys and cause a complete return to old habits. I thought I was prepared to go to the golf course to apply all that I had learned, but I choked on the first tee. I forgot everything I had been told and was reduced to a quivering idiot. I learned that you have to encourage the learner to remember the cues and to trust them. Tell her to feel reckless and unconcerned about failure as she prepares to play.

- I also remember how important it is for the learner to be motivated to learn so that the instructor remains motivated.

- Resist the temptation to talk too much (such as telling irrelevant stories). Keep the learner at center stage! I was a violator of this one, as are a lot of coaches.

My golf game has never improved. Fortunately for me and for my program, the lessons learned in Florida had a positive impact on how I managed feedback patterns with my athletes. For the remainder of my career I held on tightly to the memory of what it was like to be the learner. This, coupled with the recommendations set forth in the section on learned optimism in chapter 8, will provide an excellent foundation for establishing your own feedback patterns. Make no mistake about it; feedback patterns—the things that are said to the team by the coaches as the learning is taking place—are a major factor in shaping a program's gym culture.

USA Volleyball Axioms

My time working with U.S. volleyball prior to the London Olympics gave me the opportunity to get up close and personal with the program and how it functioned under head coach Hugh McCutcheon. Hugh is not one to overstate a point. He prefers to provide brief, succinct responses. When I asked him to share with me his list of underlying principles, here is what he provided.

Repeatability (Simplicity)

Simple is easier to execute than complex. The aim is to make the game, its techniques, and its systems as efficient as possible.

Variance Reduction

It is important to achieve consistency of results, a smaller range of error, and the elimination of unnecessary movements in motor patterns.

Hugh McCutcheon, former head coach of the U.S. men's and women's national teams and current head coach at the University of Minnesota, motivates players through basic principles that focus on players and performance.
Ray Grabowski/Icon SMI

Risk Management

Players must learn to reduce errors by making good decisions regarding the degree of difficulty to be attempted while executing a skill. For example, when spiking, know when to hit a difficult shot and when to keep the ball safely in the court in order to preserve another chance to win a point.

In a November 2012 interview reported in *The Minnesota Daily* following a conference win, McCutcheon explained, "We . . . talked about trying to make good plays. Not trying to force it, to make the whole thing happen in one swing."

I should add that McCutcheon was not the only U.S. coach with whom I had the pleasure of spending long hours in conversation about volleyball. Doug Beal, Terry Liskevych, Ari Selinger, Lang Ping, Mick Haley, Toshi Yoshida, Jim Iams, Shelton Collier, Debbie Brown, Chuck Erbe, Fred Sturm, Kevin Hambly, Karch Kiraly, Carl McGown, Jim

Karch Kiraly, U.S. women's team coach, with Kristin Hildebrand at the 2013 USA Volleyball Cup.

Stan Liu/Icon SMI

McLaughlin, Dave Shoji, Bill Neville, Terry Pettit, Arnie Ball, and many others form the long list of coaches with whom I shared the U.S. coaching lineage; they all played a significant role in helping me understand how to teach this game.

Specificity in Teaching Volleyball Skills

Players learn a particular skill by rehearsing that exact skill. To the extent that the skill is modified for training purposes, the efficiency of the learning process has been compromised. As Bill Neville (former collegiate and U.S. Olympic team coach) put it: You don't *drill* volleyball, you *play* volleyball.

The dependent nature of each contact in volleyball (each contact, except for the contact to initiate the serve, is preceded by a prior contact) makes the creation of drill mechanics difficult. The science of motor learning requires that the skill being taught must be presented within the specific context of the skill's execution. The skill of setting occurs *after* the ball has been directed (passed or dug) toward the setter, who then delivers the set to an attacker. This is very specific.

But where does the concept of specificity end? The passer (or digger) had to receive the ball from another source in order to pass it to the setter. The contact prior to that contact had to have occurred, and so on, until every contact is traced back to the serve that initiated play. This is, to me, is the definition of specificity in coaching volleyball. Since all of the contacts following the serve are linked together, any drill to rehearse one of the skills must include all of the preceding and succeeding contacts.

This would be impossible to recapture in a drill situation. We have to cut the chain of events on both the front and back end of the single skill repetition. Otherwise, skill development drills would go on forever, and the total number of reps per player would be minimal. It forces a decision on how much of the specificity criterion must be compromised in order to provide a sufficient volume of reps, while maximizing the specificity criterion. One of the purest examples of high-volume repetition drilling can be seen prior to most volleyball matches around the world. Hitting lines and digging lines, used to provide a maximum number of contacts per player in a limited amount of time, are a part of everyone's prematch warm-up.

Where the volume principle collides with the specificity principle, as is always the case, the need to compromise the specificity principle requires some deliberation by the coach. So far, there seems to be some agreement that a specific volleyball skill can be learned within the three-contact pass-set-hit configuration, but should drills also include the earlier contacts specific to that particular repetition? The logical result of this line of thought leads to actually playing 6-on-6 volleyball. Would this provide an appropriate number of contacts for each player to improve the selected skill? Or is the pass-set-hit format needed to increase contact volume? Or are there drill formats that lie somewhere between pass-set-hit and 6-on-6?

It would seem that anything less than 6-on-6 would fail to satisfy the specificity principle, but would the resulting reduction in volume of contacts per player offset any gains that would be made by adhering strictly to the specificity principle? This is one of those decisions each coach has to make. How literally do you want to interpret the specificity concept? The answer will determine the paradigm that is used to structure rehearsals.

Player-Centered Practice

Where the appropriate level of skill exists, it is better to assign players, not coaches, to run drills. Motor learning theory tells us that skill acquisition occurs more efficiently when players increase the number of game-like contacts they execute in the course of a drill. A coach standing on the floor hitting balls at a line of diggers, for example, is unlikely to improve the team's digging skills as efficiently as if a skilled player is hitting the ball over the net with blockers up. When the player is hitting the ball over a net at the defender as part of the pass-set-hit chain, the defender's learning rate is even greater.

Life on the Plateau

In his book *Mastery: The Keys to Success and Long-Term Fulfillment* (Plume 1992), George Leonard talks about the nature of the learning process, and what we have to know about it if we are to achieve mastery. Learning a new skill involves moments of progress followed by sustained periods of repetitive rehearsal until the next moment of progress appears. I call these periods of repetitive rehearsal the *plateau*. Athletes spend most of their time on the plateau as they wait patiently for the next moment of progress in their skill development to appear.

These moments can be exhilarating and tend to provide motivation for the athletes to want to continue training. But the hours, days, and weeks spent on the plateau—without moments of progress—present a different challenge. Coaches need to provide an atmosphere where athletes are motivated to practice even when they seem to be getting nowhere. Leonard's point is that mastery can be achieved only if athletes commit to the concept of practice for the sake of practice itself. Athletes must learn to accept the day-to-day grind. They must be willing to do whatever it takes, for as long as it takes, to reach an elite level. They must learn to appreciate life on the plateau.

The elite performers I coached through the years found a way to appreciate this fact and showed up every day with an awareness of its importance. Passion. This is what players such as Mary Eggers, Disa Johnson, Nancy Brookhart, Erin Borske, Laura Bush, Kirsten Gleis, and Chris Schwarz gave me at Illinois, and what Katrien DeDecker, Becky Bauer, Lindsey Berg, Paula Gentil, Erin Martin, Jessy Jones, Cassie Busse, Marci Peniata, Jess Granquist, Meredith Nelson, Steph Hagen, Christine Tan, Kelly Bowman, Jess Byrnes, and Lauren Gibbemeyer, plus so many others, gave me at Minnesota: passion for the program, for teammates, and for the journey. They understood what it took to remain committed to life on the plateau. This is what separates the great from the good.

Identifying and Maximizing Player Strengths

We must understand that we cannot change the essence of people. We can improve their skills, but we cannot change them as people. Our focus should be on enhancing what they *can* do and not what they *struggle* to do. We don't ask defensive tackles to play quarterback. We shouldn't ask slower, shorter, not-very-jumpy athletes to play the middle blocker position.

These basic principles have been at the foundation of my thinking about practice for many years. Before moving on, I should offer a word of caution to any players within earshot of the ideas presented in this chapter.

You need to realize that your desire to appreciate these principles and allow them to guide your approach to practice collides with the prevailing winds of today's culture. These principles demand patience, discipline, an awareness of the big picture, and an uncommon love of practice and preparation (passion). We live in an age of the quick fix; fast, temporary relief; cell phones; texting: all designed to discourage you from the time-consuming, labor-intensive, and rigorous commitment that awaits those who choose to pursue excellence. Even as you learn to appreciate your journey, you will be confronted by a cultural tug-of-war. Your nonathlete friends will question your sanity. You will feel left out when others pursue the social scene, and you are joining teammates for a meeting or a video session. You might even question your own commitment. One minute you feel motivated to keep practicing and go the extra mile. The next minute you feel like rejoining the human race where all the fun takes place.

This tug-of-war is normal. Just know that if you want to be an elite player on an elite team, you will have to make many sacrifices. Learning to appreciate these practice principles is one of these sacrifices. But don't look at it as a sacrifice. Learn to perceive it as your life's passion.

As far as coaches are concerned, identify each player's strengths. Attempt to leverage each of these strengths and use them as a focus. Understand that we cannot change the essence of players, but we can improve their skills and help them communicate better. Our coaching strategy must accept who the players are and ignore trying to change them.

Practice Content

On to the next set of decisions. Before you walk onto the gym floor, you should know exactly what you want to cover in practice. Where does one find the information needed to inform the practice plan? Here are some places to start.

Outline of Skills Required to Execute the Team's System and Style of Play

Every team performs within a system of play. Every system of play requires specific skills for its execution. This is often the first place that coaches go to find practice content.

Here is an example. Your team's system of play includes the following 2H offensive combination:

OH = Fast tempo ball to the left pin

MH = Wide slide to the right pin

Middle back = Bic

Setter = Second contact attack

Here are the skills required to execute it:

- Perfect pass
- Setter who can set all options
- OH who can approach to attack fast tempo
- MH who can execute slide approach
- Setter who can attack the second contact
- Middle back who can approach to attack second tempo bic

The same analysis can be applied to any phase of the team's system of play. Obviously, this process begins to yield considerable overlap as the number of required skills accumulates. In other words, the skill of passing will not have to be treated as a new skill every time it is listed as an ingredient in the system of play. Instead, passing becomes a standard item on the list of daily skills to be rehearsed. Some of these skills will be unique to your system of play, and their rehearsal must be planned for in a specific way. Learning to set a hittable fast tempo ball to the OH could be an example of one of the skills that would be unique to your own system.

Scouting and Game Plan Preparation

The game plan provides a wealth of information that can be converted to practice content. Drills can be designed to rehearse exactly how your team will serve, block, attack, and defend your next opponent. This type of preparation should be a standard part of your practice content.

Eliminate Common Errors

Many of these execution errors are common among young volleyball players, and it is important to retrain the offending player as soon as possible. Here are some examples:

- Moving early or charging forward when attempting to read and defend the opponent's attack. Instead, the defender should be stopped, neutral, and balanced at contact by the attacker.

- Blocking with hands straight up from shoulders without ever penetrating the plane of the net. Instead, the blocker should lead with the hands and thrust them as far as possible into the opponent's air space.

- Rising (standing) up to position oneself to receive a serve with the forearms, thereby allowing the serve to handcuff the passer if it comes in high. Instead, maintain good passing posture (weight forward) throughout the passing stroke.

These are only a few items on a long list of common errors that you will encounter. There is no need to delay in eliminating them and to begin the retraining process.

Statistical Information

Another valuable resource for helping the coach determine the content to be selected for practice comes from the data contained in whatever statistics a coach decides to keep. A common example would be the use of statistics that would identify the number of net points won and lost in each rotation. Table 7.1 is a rotational comparison that would lead to the formation of a practice item.

TABLE 7.1   Rotational Comparison

Rotation	Net points scored
1	+6, -5 = +1
6	+3, -2 = +1
5	0, -4 = - 4
4	+7, -3 = +4
3	+5, -1 = +4
2	+4, -3 = +1
Total	+25, -15 = +10

Your team wins the set 25-15. All of your rotations, except one, seem balanced, scoring and yielding points in a patterned fashion. Rotation 5 reveals a specific problem; that is, this rotation failed to score any service points. It gave up 4 reception points, but this was not too far out of line from the other rotations in terms of yielding points. This would suggest that the issue is not a reception or FBA problem; but the inability to score even one serving point in the same rotation suggests there is a problem with the point-scoring mechanics in rotation 5. By reviewing the full range of statistics used to evaluate each rotation's performance, the coach can quickly locate the exact problem. The point-scoring mechanisms in each rotation are serving, blocking, and counterattacking. The statistical review of rotation 5 reveals the comparisons shown in table 7.2.

The data show that the problem is not the inability to counterattack. This rotation is keeping up with the other rotations. But the serving and blocking numbers are noticeably below the team averages. Two practice items are suddenly born from this analysis. Either our server in this rotation must improve, or we must find a replacement (substitute) server who can perform at an acceptable level.

TABLE 7.2 Statistical Review of Rotation 5

	Rotation 5 average	Team average
Serve average	.7	1.79
Ace:error	0:3	1.6:1.8
Blocks per set	.03	2.4
Counterattack KEff	.255	.268

Coaching the Little Things

These are not really little (as in unimportant) things. I found myself on many occasions asking a player to do something in a match that I had not covered thoroughly in practice. An example would be something like this: "Katie, we're going to set you a high ball on the outside, and it's going to be tight into the block," I would say. "And then I want you to swing hard on a line wipe-off shot!"

Katie knew what a line wipe-off shot was, but I also knew that she didn't possess the skill to hit that shot. Not many players can invent that shot on their own. They need to be trained. There are dozens of little things that escape our teaching paradigm because we assume that any real volleyball player can do them, but many cannot. They climb to the top level of play without knowing how to execute even the most common skills.

Other examples of little things:

- Block lower and tighter to the net against this small hitter.
- Aim for high hands and hit over the baseline digger.
- Use a tip or roll shot to area 3.
- Delay your block move against this big jumper.
- Jump early when you commit against the slide hitter.
- Use the show-and-take move against their middle blocker.

All of these are samples of directives that coaches use frequently but are rarely rehearsed. They are part of the long list of little things that players are supposed to know. I recommend that coaches make their own list and spend practice time learning to execute the little things.

Prepractice Decisions

Now that practice content has been declared, it is time to decide on an additional number of issues that also should be resolved prior to your walking into your first practice.

Atmosphere in the Gym

The atmosphere in a practice gym is usually a by-product of a huge number of decisions a coach will make regarding how the gym will be configured. It is this atmosphere that a visitor will notice first. Like many coaches, I endured a period of being an over-the-top disciplinarian. It was fascinating to see coaches try to outduel each other when it came to running a tight ship and cultivating the profile of a disciplinarian.

When I started coaching, I had not given much thought as to how I wanted my gym to be perceived. Then, as I traveled to more competitions, I started to notice some of the things that other coaches were doing. One coach made his players line up their gym bags neatly against the wall in numerical order. Another coach made his players stand at attention in a straight line until he finished his prewarm-up remarks. Warm-up jackets were not thrown randomly at the bench; the players had to walk to the bench area and carefully drape the garments over one of the chairs. Prematch warm-up drills were carefully choreographed, and any player not in sync with the drill would be waved off the court.

For a relatively brief period of time, I was fascinated with the atmosphere this approach could produce. The head coach seemed to be the maestro in charge of every note that would be played by his musicians (athletes). I loved the clarity and efficiency this approach created. I could sense it as soon as I entered any gym where this type of atmosphere prevailed. I believed that if I were to replicate this strictly disciplined environment, I would somehow become a better coach.

I was wrong. Under the austerity program that I briefly sought to install in my practice gym, the program's personality was stifled. Players were discouraged from playing an active role in the formation of their own practice atmosphere. For many, the gym had become a torture chamber. It had not evolved toward the relaxed environment that would encourage the critical thinking or questioning that I was looking for. Nor would there be room for trial and error on the court. Everything would be dictated from the top.

This type of gym would create a feeling of stiffness among the players. This environment was far from the open universe of mutual trust that I was seeking. Plus, this type of atmosphere was not *me*. I was never effective as a power coach. After a short period of experimenting with it, I abandoned my quest. What I thought was an expression of airtight leadership and mental supremacy was really, in my opinion, a cover-up for the coach's inability or unwillingness to forge trusting relationships with his players. In fact, *trust* is not a word that fits into the mosaic of the austere approach.

Setter Training

It has long been accepted that the setter requires additional training beyond time spent in practice with the rest of the team. The setter handles the ball more than any other player, and the quality of the setter's touches often determines who wins and who loses. The decision is not whether to provide setter training sessions, but *when* to provide them. The basic options boil down to this: either you train your setter during practice (training sessions on a separate court when not needed on main court), or you train her outside of the normal practice time. Many coaches elect to combine both approaches.

Use of Video

The use of video to capture practice and match performances has been with us for decades. There is no reason to suspect that the use of modern technology will die away. Since it is here to stay, a coach should have a plan for how to collect data and use it to enhance the team's performance. Today's software programs are lightning fast and can generate complex video reports at the push of a button. The challenge in this area of coaching is choosing how to select, from all that is available, that which will provide the information you seek. All too often coaches get it backward, choosing to use a piece of equipment or software solely because it can generate a seemingly endless array of video clips, scouting reports, and statistical analyses. The video function in the gym can be used efficiently, or it can become a runaway train. Be sure to plan carefully.

Use of Penalties

Should practice include the use of penalties? All coaches ask this question at least once in their careers. We become so frustrated with our players in practice that we turn to individual and team punishment as a penalty. There was a time when I actually made a list of different kinds of penalties so that my team could experience variety in how they were being punished.

I have witnessed the full range of punishment drills. On the one end of the spectrum, I would place the North Korean women's national team. After his team lost to the U.S. team I was coaching in the World University Games in the former Yugoslavia, the North Korean coach kept his players on the floor for a full three hours after the match was over. He and his assistants put the team through a brutal defensive workout. They pounded balls at their players with intent to harm, or so it seemed to me. It was hard to watch. I felt as though the purpose of the punishment was to provide an opportunity for the coaches to fully express their dislike of the team rather than make their team play better.

On the other end of the spectrum lies the 2012 U.S. Olympic team under Hugh McCutcheon. I was often present in their practice gym during the months leading up to the London Olympic games. The only penalties I witnessed occurred when one team lost to another in a competition. The losing team's players were each asked to do a five-and-five. This meant that each loser had to do, on her own, five push-ups and five sit-ups. My impression was that this penalty was intended more as a psychological reminder that winning is better than losing and not as a demeaning, physically demanding punishment.

If asked whether punishment should be employed in practices, I would say yes, it should. The reasons for using penalties are the following:

- Sometimes teams need to be shocked back to life after a poor performance in a drill.
- Players occasionally need to be reminded that their coach can be tough.
- Some athletes respond to the whip more than they respond to reasonable requests to provide more effort.

But there appear to be just as many reasons *not* to use punishment:

- Punishment takes away from technical and tactical training time.
- It causes unnecessary wear and tear on players' bodies.
- While some athletes respond to the whip, others respond to reasonable requests to provide more effort and need not be punished into following the wishes of the coach.

Whatever one's choice, it can set off criticism. The coach, along with the gym culture that features an extensive amount of punishment drills, will be labeled as extra harsh. Conversely, the coach who limits the use of punishment drills will be labeled as soft and nondemanding. In the center lies the compromise approach. Whichever path you select, make sure that you are prepared to defend your choices.

Should you decide to use penalties and punishment in practice, be sure that it is done for the right reasons. Using them as an outlet for expressing anger never produces a good result. Using them as a form of attitude correction, making a major statement to the team that their practice performance must improve, or trying to get the team's attention are all legitimate reasons to send the team through the punishment gauntlet. It has to be done for the right reasons. Your team can tell the difference.

Finally, you might consider the possibility that punishment can be replaced by the use of correction and exaggeration drills. A correction drill is used when players commit the same mistake over and over. The players are put through corrective repetitions of the skill in question. Exaggeration drills are similar, except they require the player to exaggerate the movement patterns of the skill. An example would be to ask players to set the ball a distance of 30 feet, then return to the drill which had required them to set a 20-foot ball. This functions very much like the overload principle in lifting or physical conditioning. In both cases punishment is replaced by skill repetition as a response to poor performance.

All coaches can think up punishment drills, but what is the objective? Is it to improve a skill, to assert power, or to change a player's attitude? This is worth thinking through!

Injured Player Ruled Out of Practice

Injuries often occur, and the injured player is sometimes prohibited from practicing until the injury heals sufficiently to return to activity. What should this player be doing during practice? Here are some suggestions.

Write out an exercise plan that can be done courtside in the practice gym. The plan should not be limited to injury-specific rehabilitation exercises. The player can also use this time to increase range of motion, strength, and sport-specific movement patterns. Make sure that the player is located close enough to the practice court so that the coaches' instructions can be heard. If the injury allows, have the player assist in shagging, drill scoring, ball entry, officiating, recording competition results, and so on.

It is vital that the player stay connected to the team in every way possible while the injury heals. Being a sideline-injury player is not an invitation to engage in casual conversation with everyone who happens to walk through the practice gym. Injured players are still on the clock!

Communication System

Communication issues on the court spring from the fact that the sport of volleyball features the smallest area of play per player than any other sport. Officially, the space to player ratio is 13.5 square meters per player (81 square meters for 6 players). This is a relatively small area for absorbing the rapid and spontaneous movement patterns required to play volleyball. Teams must therefore consider developing a communication system that will streamline the team's ability to play efficiently within this contracted space. Here are some of the situations that require an efficient system of communication.

No one is excused from the commitment to LOUD and timely communication responsibilities! We often faced resistance from players who were bashful, naturally soft-spoken, or who claimed that loud, aggressive talking was not within the scope of their personality. On a few occasions, I sent players to a speech therapist to develop a more powerful vocal delivery. No one had the luxury of staying quiet.

Clean air is a term I use to describe the quiet atmosphere existing between the whistle that starts and ends play. The clean air concept is important if our players were going to be able to hear each of the calls and respond correctly. Clean air breaks down if, for example, a quick hitter approaches to hit a quick set, yelling repeatedly and loudly that she wants to hit a 1. Her domination (sometimes I think it can become contamination) of the air space in the vicinity of our counterattack sequence can drown out the secondary set call that is being made by one of the complementary hitters. We need clean air to play our style of volleyball.

For example, here are some situations that, if not verbally clarified during the flow of play, can lead to unnecessary team mistakes. Two players begin moving to set an out-of-system pass. It is not obvious who should set the ball. It is one of volleyball's grey areas. If no one identifies which of the two players should set, it is likely that the ball could fall harmlessly to the floor due to the hesitancy on the part of the two players. This situation requires an early, firm call by one of the potential setters.

In fact, each time a ball is to be contacted there must be an accompanying call that coincides with that particular touch. The receiver of the first contact is asked to say "Ball." The setter clarifies all second contacts with either "Got it" or the teammate's name and the word "Set." The person setting the ball then calls out the name of the teammate receiving the set. In O/S situations, the communication sequence is the same. The first contact person identifies the second contact person, who then identifies the third contact person. In FBA situations, the play call is passed to everyone through hand signals from the setter, combined with setter-hitter verbal communication while waiting for the whistle to initiate play.

When we serve to our opponent, a separate set of communication rules are triggered. Our players are asked to evaluate the quality of the opponent's pass. All players announce (together) if the pass is good ("on"), bad ("off"), or over ("over"). This alerts the defense to ready themselves in anticipation of the approach patterns of the hitters. We call this pattern identification (PID). Next our blockers call out the set choice of the opponent's setter. Finally the players are responsible for identifying the type of attack being executed by the hitter, especially if the hitter goes to an offspeed, tip, or roll shot. This information is based on watching the approach starting point and early movement.

FBA and CA opportunities differ from each other in significant ways. Unlike FBA play calling by hand signals, our counterattack (CA) sequences are audible. Hitters deploy to their CA position as soon as it is clear that we will be receiving the ball. Each hitter evaluates the opponent's blocking patterns and then audibles the set that will give her a good chance to score.

I believe that by seeing and verbalizing actions during the flow of the game, a player learns how to observe and anticipate what the opponent is doing much more quickly than if there is no verbalizing. Players are also able to maintain a greater awareness of where teammates are on the court when they are forced by the communication rules to identify the location and movement intentions of teammates. Developing a system of communication is an essential, and often ignored, phase of building a system of play. Make sure that you include it as you finalize your plan.

Self-Control and Freedom From Emotional Distraction

A widespread misconception about athletic competition is that participants must drive themselves into an emotional frenzy in order to compete. Each sport correlates with a particular arousal level that fits that sport's needs. A linebacker in football requires a very high arousal level, whereas a professional golfer requires a much lower level. Volleyball, most agree, requires a medium level of arousal. Listen to some of the experts on this topic.

> In *The Art of War,* Sun-Tzu identifies unnecessary emotions as fundamental causes of turmoil and defeat. Becoming outwardly angry, frustrated, or upset is a sure indication of your loss of control and an admission that the opponent is getting in your head.*

Instead of expressing emotions that distract you from playing your game, focus on the things you can control, such as your passing, hitting, commitment to defense, and so on. Your confidence in doing what you can control leads to empowerment. You can now remain relaxed and in control of your emotions. You can avoid emotional distractions.

In *Wooden on Leadership,* coauthored with Steve Jamison, John Wooden also weighs in on the role of emotions and consistency of performance:

> Peaks and valleys belong in the Alps, not in the temperament . . . of a leader. . . . Emotionalism destroys consistency. A leader who is ruled by emotions . . . produces a team whose trademark is the roller coaster—ups and downs in performance; unpredictability and undependability in effort and concentration. . . . This is a pattern I sought to avoid at all costs. Consequently I never gave rah speeches or contrived pep talks. There is no need for ranting or raving, histrionics, or theatrics before, during, or after practice and matches. For every artificial emotional peak they might create, a subsequent valley, a letdown, is produced.**

And to put a cap on this highly sensitive and important topic, I borrow again from Lynch and Huang (2006; pages 72 and 73) and Wooden (2005; pages 112 to 114). Their voices rise in unison in identifying lack of emotional control as something to be avoided. Control of self is essential for consistency, and consistency is the trademark of the true competitor. The team must understand that self-control is highly prized; loss of control will not be tolerated. Learning to control small things (foul language,

---

*Jerry Lynch with Chungliang Al Huang, *The Way of the Champion: Lessons from Sun Tzu's* The Art of War *and Other Tao Wisdom for Sports & Life* (North Clarendon, VT: Tuttle, 2006), 57.

**John Wooden and Steve Jamison, *Wooden on Leadership* (New York: McGraw-Hill, 2005), 107.

whining, lying, and so on) will provide you with the foundation for controlling the bigger, more important things.

Allow me to again offer a brief warning. It is very likely that some of your players will interpret the request for emotional control as an attempt to change them as human beings. You may incur resentment. In my case, these were the players who would initiate a major celebration when the opponent served into the net. They couldn't understand why I would attempt to reign in this type of misplaced emotion. It would be wise to monitor player reaction to this particular request.

Practice Protocol

One of the most visible features of any practice gym is the manner in which practice is run by the coach. I always started practice by meeting my players on the baseline. They would line up in numerical order, facing me. I would then ask the line-up leader, a player I assigned to that position, if any players were unable to practice or would be late for practice. Players had been told that if anyone was going to have a problem with showing up on time, she had to call the line-up leader, who then reported to me at the start of practice. This worked very well, and we rarely had to spend time tracking down a missing person.

I also made sure that any staff or player announcements were delivered at the end of practice, not the beginning. I didn't want the players to be distracted by whatever the announcement was about.

The practice plan would be discussed with the players prior to warming up. The warm-up is not something that warrants long discussion. It is simply a warm-up. My preference would have been to ask players to warm up on their own, but the culture of women's volleyball in the United States simply would not allow a warm-up to be conducted without the elaborately choreographed movements that provided them valuable social interaction time.

My interest in practice would return once the warm-up was complete. At this point, with the start of planned drill work and competition, several procedural rules would kick in.

Balls in: Medium jog by all players to shag all the balls. No walking or throwing balls into carts from a significant distance.

Gather in: All players run to wherever I was standing in the gym, forming a semicircle around me so that I could speak to the team.

Tight: When players are engaged in net play (hitting and blocking), and unintentional tight set may create a dangerous situation. Net players can descend from an approach or block jump, land on a teammate's foot, and injure an ankle or knee. The tight set rule defends against this type of accident. Rather than allowing play to continue, anyone in the gym who sees this situation about to unfold is obligated to yell out "tight." After hearing this call, all players must stand down and discontinue play. Once the danger is removed, practice continues.

Don't jump: While players are involved in a drill or scrimmage, a stray ball from another court can fly or bounce into their area without the players noticing, creating the risk of injury. After recognizing this situation, players yell "don't jump" to prevent a possible injury to a player who might jump and land on the stray ball. Play continues once the stray ball is removed.

Water: All players go to the water cooler for mandatory hydration. I would also allow my players to drink whenever they felt the need as long as their trip to the water cooler did not disrupt practice in any way. Denying water to an athlete is not among the safest or medically justifiable practices in the world.

During practice I would ask my physical-training leader, another appointee, to give me a report on the health of the team. Her job was to ask around and provide me with a summary. If, for instance, a lower-body workout in the weight room that morning was causing lower-body pain at practice, I would adjust the practice reps to emphasize upper-body work. I kept a close watch on this situation through constant communication with the athlete in charge. I made many critical decisions over the years based on the reported health of our team.

Practice ended each day with an individual and team stretch. This was followed by another line up so announcements could be made. I also asked selected players to evaluate each day's practice. These discussions were brief, but they provided significant opportunities for staff and players to interact about a variety of relevant topics such as physical conditioning, understanding of the game plan, progress on trust-building behaviors, and learning to incorporate optimism into the skill acquisition process.

Gym Rules

Every gym I have ever wandered into over the past four or five decades has a set of rules. I do not object to this. In fact, I appreciate the structure these rules provide. The tight set rule and the don't jump rule are two that are common to most practice gyms. Gym rules are another ingredient of the overall atmosphere that affects gym culture. Here are some common situations that arise from normal activity before, during, and after practice. I will tee up the situation, and you make the decision.

- **Bad language:** What is your position on the use of bad language, however you might define it, in your gym?

- **Male practice players:** Coaches of women's collegiate teams in the United States must be careful to follow all of the rules surrounding the eligibility of male practice players. They can often raise the level of play in your gym. For those of you who coach females, are you willing to invite the guys into the gym?

- **Keeping score:** On every team there is at least one player who knows the score of every competitive drill and every scrimmage. This person is a human scoreboard, and the team begins to rely on him to keep track of the score. The good news is that you will always have the correct score available. The bad news is that the rest of the team is not building an awareness of the score at all times. Is this all right with you, or do you want to make everyone develop this score awareness skill?

- **Staff division of labor:** Is there a division of labor plan for your staff? Who will coach the second team in practice? Who will write out and post the practice plan? Who will be the main voice in the gym? Who will plan and execute the stat or video program for each practice? Who will work with which positions?

- **Disciplined ball-handling tempo:** Do you believe that players should establish and maintain a specific pass tempo, location, and height so that your team can play in the same rhythm together? What about overhand setting, defensive retrieval, and all other forms of ball control?

- **Hitting drills and blocking:** Motor learning theory says that practice must mirror gamelike movement patterns. Do you agree that every spiking opportunity in practice must be contested by a block? Or are hitting lines with no block acceptable to you?

- **Player mentality:** Do you want players to become critical thinkers or obedient soldiers?

- **Pepper:** Will you assign partners or allow players to choose? Do you prefer a full-on chili pepper style or cooperative control?

- **Team keys:** Is there value in using team keys when playing 6-on-6? An example is to focus on a *team* key instead of an individual key. One such team key could be "Base-to-Read Movement." During this scrimmage, we will improve our movement from base-to-read position when the ball is attacked into our court.

- **Practice gear:** Do you want your players dressed identically for practice except for their respective numerals on their tops? Will you allow players to wear gear from another team or school?

- **Practice length:** How long will your practice go? Will you use timed segments? Will you let drills run to completion regardless of elapsed time? Will you taper your practice length as you near the end of your competitive season?

- **Practice flow:** How much time will you devote to individual skill development versus team play?

- **Balanced landings:** Will you demand that your athletes, when descending from a jump, execute a balanced landing to avoid injury?

- **Role of athletic trainer:** If you are fortunate enough to have an athletic trainer on your staff, you should articulate her role to everyone as soon as possible. Will there be consequences for missing rehab appointments? What level of staff seniority will the trainer carry?

Conclusion

I recommend that coaches take time to monitor everything that goes into the creation of the program's gym culture. It takes all of the items discussed in this chapter and more: the personalities of the players and coaches, the work ethic evident in the gym, the communication level, the day-to-day effort to solidify teamwide trust, the commitment to life on the plateau.

Like a beeping transmission signal from a radio tower, the gym sends its own signal to everyone in the program. This signal serves as a constant reminder of how things are done here and what is expected from each person. Of one thing I am certain. It is better to control the content of the values and behaviors upon which your gym culture will rest than to allow the process to develop in a random fashion. Remember: A gym culture will emerge whether you are aware of its ingredients or not. The process is a lot easier to embrace if the coach controls its content.

CHAPTER 8

Strengthening Team Trust

Team chemistry is an elusive thing with as many definitions as there are coaches. "Let's all pull on the same end of the rope" and "Let's have some fun out there" are examples of appeals to team members that play with chemistry. What do we mean when we say these things? What are we asking our players to do? Here is what I think: Team chemistry is a commitment by each player to the daily cultivation of a common set of behaviors that maximize a team's ability to achieve their goals. I know. That's a mouthful. But I believe firmly in the contention that the better the team chemistry, the better the team's chance to reach its goals.

The ingredients of chemistry can differ from team to team, but I suspect that there is an overlapping set of principles that lies at the core. These principles have the common goal of overcoming any psychological obstacles that might keep a team from succeeding. These principles become the heart of the team, and they flow through the team's arteries to each player, coach, and staff member. They pump life into the team's mission. For a team to achieve its goals, these arteries must remain clear.

If the team's ultimate goal is to rid itself of the obstacles that can clog these arteries and block the emergence of team chemistry, then I use the word *trust* to describe the process by which this chemistry is achieved. Chemistry is the noun. Trust is the verb. Almost anything can become a roadblock to the development of team chemistry, and I have seen it all over the years. My response to each episode has been uniquely related to the circumstances of that particular moment and that particular team.

However, there are some generalizations that emerged over time as I accumulated more and more of these defining moments. Here are three of the more important ones:

1. Team chemistry lies at the very core of successful team performance. It is more important than the skill base of a team.

2. Every athlete brings to the table a uniquely different personality. It is impossible to cram everyone into one generic personality style. Each player deals with frustration differently, each player responds optimally to different motivational techniques, and each player sees a different path to resolving interpersonal conflicts. Every coach must tirelessly attempt to acquire the skills to identify these differences and to unify everyone around a common set of ground rules.

3. Conflict-resolution skills must be taught and rehearsed on a regular basis by every player and staff member. This is not always a popular team activity, but it is essential to team success.

I have learned that the process of cultivating the skills required to resolve conflicts actually draws a team together, even if a total solution is never reached. Extracting a full commitment to the process is generally enough. Achieving full solutions to problems can often result, but the process itself is what keeps everyone committed to the maxim that team goals always supersede individual goals. The active allegiance by all players and staff to this process is what I refer to as trust.

Creating Team Trust

The trusting person does the right thing even when no one is watching. Trust means doing what you are supposed to do even when you don't want to do it. Underneath the search for trust in team sports lies a nucleus of trust-enabling behaviors.

Each time you act in a trusting way, two good things happen. First, you exercise the trust muscle, and it gradually becomes stronger. Second, you invest in the same things your teammates are investing in. When you invest in a group, you achieve ownership. When you achieve ownership, you develop a passion for the group and its goals.

Creating individual and team trust ultimately comes down to practicing a small set of principles over a long period of time. It is more about embracing common sense with uncommon levels of discipline and persistence.

Said in another way, trust is to an athlete what scales are to a musician. Mastering the scales is what allows the musician to perform music.

Mastering the skills of trust is what enables a team to play with great chemistry.

What exactly is trust? I am going to enlist the help of Patrick Lencioni and his thought-provoking book, *The Five Dysfunctions of a Team*. His concise and articulate treatment of the concept of trust is essential to understanding its role in my approach to building a team.

> The kind of trust that is characteristic of a great team . . . requires team members to make themselves vulnerable to one another, and be confident that their vulnerabilities will not be used against them. . . . It is only when team members are truly comfortable being exposed to one another that they begin to act without concern for protecting themselves. It is a challenge for [team members] to turn those selfish instincts off for the good of the team, but that is exactly what is required.*

When everyone in the program can rise above the fray, when everyone accepts that contributing to a winning team is more important than protecting personal turf, only then can a team can be in a position to succeed.

My way of making sure that we never lose sight of this process is to conduct regular artery check-ups. It might occur before or after practice, before or after competition, on a bus, in an airport lobby, or at a hotel meeting. I provide ample opportunities for players and staff to identify any blockages that might prevent those arteries from pumping valuable life to every corner of our team environment. If we find a blockage, we examine it, suggest a strategy for treating it, and work hard to make sure that the blockage is minimized, keeping the arteries clear. This has become a staple in my list of coaching principles.

I once had a team that was cruising along quite well. We were winning at a high level. But beneath the surface, an issue was percolating that would soon begin to clog the team's artery system. The issue had its roots in the simple notion of communication on the court. All coaches are keenly aware of the need for teamwide verbal communication during practice and competition. This communication is vital to the team's ability to clarify uncertain situations, declare intentions, elevate confidence levels, provide positive reinforcement to each other, rescue a player who makes a mistake, and so on.

Producing consistent and relevant communication requires energy. Some players are naturally better at it, or perhaps work harder at it. Some players are naturally quiet and rely on the more outgoing players

---

*Patrick Lencioni, *The Five Dysfunctions of a Team: A Leadership Fable* (San Francisco: Jossey-Bass, 2002), 195-196.

to supply all the energy. These players are either naturally quiet, or they are less confident of their verbal skills than their physical skills. They exist on every roster.

Even though we were winning, only two players consistently provided the energy required for an adequate verbal communication system. The other four players were selfishly relying on the two energy-providers to shoulder the entire burden. This worked for a while, but about six weeks into the season, the signs of frustration were beginning to appear. The energy-providers were becoming more and more impatient when a serve would drop between two of the silent types. Even worse, the energy-providers were beginning to resent the fact that they had to carry the communication load. Their own performances were beginning to suffer, and they wanted help.

Left unchecked, this issue would turn a potentially successful season into an underachieving one. It was clear that something had to be done.

Practicing Trust

I conducted a series of meetings with the team. I asked a consultant to sit in. He was a proven facilitator who specialized in values clarification and had a good track record helping groups resolve conflicts and move forward. He guided us through some complex and sometimes difficult discussions. This is what we learned.

If we do not wish to remain the same, we must do things differently. The world of elite athletics creates a stressful environment, requiring that players and coaches operate in a stressful range of human interaction. It requires that all participants develop advanced communication and conflict resolution skills. It requires the development of relationships strong enough to survive the stress.

The absence of conflict does not mean that a team is doing well. The depth of conflict usually is parallel with the depth of the relationships within the group. If we don't have the ability to deal with conflict, we won't be able to deal with the stresses of the season.

All teams face the following challenges. When little things go wrong, the offended party takes a little step away from the group. When this response is repeated often enough, the players pull apart from each other. Dealing with each of the little things is a quality of groups that achieve long-range success.

Impulse control (frustration management) is the single most powerful quality for succeeding in a group. Learn how to manage yourself in the present and deal with the issue after the impulses have lessened.

The rule of reciprocity must be in place. This rule states that if you want to be critical of others, you must be willing to take criticism from others.

In our case we had a dilemma. Everyone wanted the team to be energetic on the court, but only two players had been providing it on a consistent basis. Should their teammates trust that these two would never be sick or injured, never fatigued, and never in a bad mood, and therefore rely on them to supply energy at all times? Or should we work on developing additional energy-providers from among others on the team, even though they might not be naturals for this role?

The reality of this dilemma was driven home during a brief exercise at one of the meetings. The facilitator asked the players, on the count of three, to point to the person who supplied the most energy and initiated the most communication on the court. On the count of three, every finger pointed in the direction of one player. The same occurred when they were asked to point to the player who was second in line as a supplier of energy and communication. Again, all fingers pointed at one player.

Then he asked the players to point to the person with the third best skills in this area. Not one player raised a finger to point to anyone. In this one moment, several things became clear. The top two energy-providers quite obviously stood out from the others, and it was just as obvious that there were no other energy-providers.

For our team, this was a defining moment. They realized immediately that a solution was needed. They could no longer rely on mere chance. What if one or both of their energy titans were to become unavailable? Others would have to step up. From that day forward, other players made a conscious effort to help out. None of them became nonstop talking machines, but their efforts were enough to render the issue sufficiently benign and allow the team to complete a highly successful season.

As I look back at this episode, it is clear to me that all of us had benefitted from our earlier work together with the concept of trust. They were learning to trust each other when taking on issues. They were freeing themselves of the fear of retaliation that often accompanies such intimate discussions. We were able to arrive at a full awareness of both the problem and a solution without having to waste time tiptoeing around the issue. We trusted each other to refrain from unfairly exposing each other to ridicule. We trusted each other to leave individual agendas behind and to contribute to the dialogue in an open and unselfish fashion. All of this was possible only because sufficient levels of trust were in place.

Trust is one of those words found embedded in just about every book written about athletes and sport. "You have to trust yourself" and "You have to trust each other" are axioms that are repeated to athletes from an early age. Trust stands alongside loyalty, sacrifice, commitment, and accountability as words meant to describe the attributes necessary for a team to achieve chemistry, another word that shows up frequently. When I am asked to reveal the secret to my past success, I could answer that I was an exceptional skill trainer, a tactical genius, a thorough game planner, and a great motivational speaker, but I don't. Instead, I tell them the truth: I spent most of my time trying to get people to learn how to trust. All of the other elements are important, but trust is the one variable without which the entire program-building effort would collapse.

Yes, you heard me correctly. I am saying that the most important variable in building a program, whether you are coaching men or women, is the cultivation of teamwide trust. No matter how skilled your players, and no matter how sophisticated your system of play, if your team cannot function according to the principles of trust, you are going to experience failure. As Lencioni put it, "Trust lies at the heart of a functioning, cohesive team. Without it, teamwork is all but impossible" (195).

When talking with other coaches about this subject, I often lead with the following question. What kind of team would you rather not play against: A team of fearless, unheralded, marginally gifted athletes who play with relentless determination, confidence, and pride, or a team of thoroughbred athletes who can physically dominate an opponent, but who are undermined by moments of inconsistency?

Nearly all coaches choose the first option. No one wants to play against the army of dedicated, nothing-to-lose attitudes that the first team brings to the court. The coaches would rather take their chances against the greyhounds who have trouble generating the gritty style of play seen in the first team. My unofficial poll on the topic would reveal a 10:1 ratio against playing the first group. When I ask why, coaches all respond with something like this. Those scrappy ball-control teams are very difficult to play against. If you have a vulnerability, they will find and exploit it. If you are not prepared to match their commitment to defense, they will intimidate you and force you into mental lapses. If you fall behind to this team early in the match, you will quickly find out all you need to know about the importance of team trust.

Discovering Trust

Why should this be so universally true? Why are coaches so apprehensive about playing against these no-name scrappy teams? I will give you the answer. These teams have discovered the power of trust. It binds them together, uniting them in their common quest for excellence. They refuse to allow nontrusting behaviors to stand between them and their goals.

During my career as a player, I became aware of the special feeling that would sometimes envelop the court during a match. On those nights, it felt as though nothing could go wrong. My teammates would all gravitate toward a common euphoric frame of mind that usually accompanied these moments. The game itself seemed to slow down. This suddenly enhanced awareness of each other and of each competitive moment in the match made it much easier to anticipate and execute. It was evident for all to see. It was indeed special. Even then, I realized that I had been experiencing moments of great team chemistry.

Later, as a coach, I was driven to replicate this environment. As I searched for a way to re-create it in my program, all of my efforts led me to the same conclusion. I began to realize that the key ingredient in achieving team chemistry was team trust. I knew what it was when I saw it, but for many years I couldn't explain it. Nor could I produce it on demand in my teams. Trust seemed to be an elusive item that floated in and out of our locker room in a completely random fashion. Instinctively, I knew that it was important. I knew that if I could harness the power of trust, I would enjoy the luxury of coaching teams that would lead with their hearts whenever they took the floor.

Most importantly, I realized that for me, success would be determined by the extent to which I could teach teams to trust. I could learn how to teach volleyball skills and how to create a system of play. That was the easy part. Getting a team to learn how to trust was going to be an enormous challenge.

As I said earlier, my first up-close encounter with the psychology of team chemistry occurred while I was a player. Later, during the early years of my coaching career, I continued to experience frequent brushes with it. At this point I was only beginning to understand the link between team trust, team chemistry, and team success. During my tenures at both Pitt and New Mexico, I was constantly searching for answers. I knew that my teams often played with special team chemistry, but I still didn't know why.

As the seasons rolled by, however, my focus on the issue of chemistry began to sharpen. In 1987, the University of Illinois squared off against top-seeded Western Michigan in the semifinals of the NCAA Midwest Regional Tournament. It was an epic match that lasted 3 hours and 20 minutes. In the fifth and deciding set, Illinois was behind 9-5 (side-out scoring). I called my second and final timeout. Western Michigan's athletes were putting a hurt on us. All I said during the time out was, "It's in your hands, team. All I ask is that you give your best effort." As I turned to take my seat on the bench, I heard our All-American middle blocker Mary Eggers say to me in a low voice, "What's the matter, Coach? Don't you trust us?"

In the next 20-minute stretch, Illinois outscored the Broncos 10-1 to win the fifth set going away (15-10). Illinois then went on to win the regional championship the next night against Nebraska and qualified for its first-ever Final Four.

Mary Eggers was a competitor of the highest order. She could not fathom the prospect of losing at anything. As a child, when she found herself losing at Monopoly, she would reach out and bat the Monopoly board off the table. One summer during her teenage years, Mary was lounging at the home, bored, with nothing to do. She saw an ad in the paper stating that the tennis tournament at the country club was open to the public. So she signed up and rode her bike every day for a week to play in the tournament. It didn't matter to her that she had never played tennis before. For the record, Mary went undefeated, beating the defending club champion in the finals. She knew a thing or two about winning.

I tended to pay close attention to anything she said in the heat of battle, no matter how sarcastic, no matter how impatient her tone. If she wanted to know whether I trusted the team during the 9-5 timeout against Western Michigan, there had to be a reason for it. In my mind, it was Mary's way of saying that I needed to display more trust in my team.

I continued to notice player references to the concept of trust as the seasons unfolded. One such episode was played out in 2004 at the University of Minnesota. We were hosting an NCAA Tournament Regional Championship, and we were competing in the finals.

The night before we had played in the regional semifinal against Georgia Tech. That match included a fourth set loss (46-48, still an NCAA record for total points scored in a set), that forced us to play a deciding fifth set. Georgia Tech had every reason to be confident. They had just ripped the momentum of the match away from us by winning the fourth set. We, on the other hand, were reeling. We would now have to reenergize and reclaim our favored status in the match. Both teams were exhausted. In the midst of all this, my setter and captain Lindsey Taatjes walked over to me and said, "You can trust us."

There was that word again: trust. Minnesota went on to win the fifth set (15-9) and the match (3-2).

This night would be much more difficult. We would be playing in the NCAA Regional Final against Big Ten Conference rival Ohio State. They featured Canadian transplant Stacy Gordon, who had recently been named Big Ten Conference Player of the Year. They came out blasting. We knew that we had to do something to slow their momentum. We couldn't stop Gordon, and we couldn't establish any kind of foothold in the match. Ohio State was outplaying us.

Down two sets to one, I made a surprising personnel move. Remember Jessy Jones? I decided to insert the freshman middle blocker into the line-up, even though she had played only sparingly throughout the season. Now I was asking her to enter an NCAA playoff match with a trip to the Final Four on the line, but I felt something had to change, and Jessy had shown us all season in practice that if nothing else, things would not be the same after she stepped on the court.

Jessy never lacked confidence. She didn't need to be comforted or reassured. She ran onto the court looking for anyone to slap hands with. She was almost out of control. "Oh yeah," I said to myself. "That's what I'm talkin' about!" Jessy and her teammates immediately embraced the challenge. They began playing with the kind of chemistry only witnessed in championship playoff situations. With each touch on the block, Jessy was gaining confidence. She was beginning to figure out Ohio State's offensive rhythm and was started to put the clamps on Gordon. The blocking war began to turn in our favor.

Jessy was phenomenal in our fourth set win. Her blocking against Gordon allowed us to climb back into the match at 2-2. Bedlam reigned during the break between sets. Everyone in the arena was primed and ready to explode, knowing that the winner of this fifth and final set would receive a bid to the Final Four. In the midst of all the chaos, Jessy managed to find me sitting on the bench getting ready to fill out my line-up card. She sat down next to me, wanting to tell me something. But the overflow crowd of 6,000 wasn't making it easy for coaches and players to have conversations on the bench. You couldn't hear yourself think. All I could make out of what she said to me was something like "You can trust me," followed by "Don't worry, we'll win this."

Jessy played inspired volleyball in that fifth set, blocking Gordon at key moments. We won the set 15-9 and qualified for our second straight Final Four. As I drove home from the matches that night, I found myself mulling over what had happened. Just as Lindsey Taatjes had done the night before, Jessy had sought me out in order to ask me to trust the team. Was this a mere coincidence? Or was it a signal to me that I needed to find out more about the trust factor? What, exactly, did it mean? How could I teach all of my players to acquire it? Is trust just a matter of predictability based on past performance? Or is it a deeper, more complicated feeling of security that allowed teams to perform at their best once the obstacles to security had been or were in the process of being removed? If the latter is true, then I am talking about a sense of security that can only come from the daily effort to rid the team culture of the limitations that frequently seem to infest team dynamics. This is not the kind of trust that simply pops into your head, available for immediate use.

I suspected that it was the latter. As I evaluated my past performance as a coach, I began to realize that, without knowing it, I had already been practicing the laws of team trust. I reasoned that I had always been committed to the cultivation of team trust. I just didn't realize it until my final years in coaching.

On the last home weekend of the 2010 season, my last as a head coach, Minnesota hosted Penn State. The Nittany Lions had just won four consecutive national championships. Many believed they would win again in 2010. An energetic crowd of more than 5,000 spectators settled in at the Sports Pavilion in Minneapolis to watch Minnesota take on Penn State.

No one except my family knew that I had already made my decision to retire at the end of the season. It was in a self-imposed silence on the topic that I prepared to face my long-time friend and colleague, Penn State's remarkable coach Russ Rose. I knew this would be our last confrontation in a rivalry that started in 1976, but nobody else did. The

Until my final years as a coach, I didn't realize that I'd been building team trust all along.

Cliff Welch/Icon SMI

evening was already going to be special, requiring that all of my coaching skills remain intact. Harboring the retirement issue throughout the evening was going to be challenging.

The first two sets went according to everyone's expectations. Penn State jumped out to a 2-0 lead, and we headed to our locker room for the midmatch break. I found myself calm and self-assured. I told the team that they were very close to performing at a winning level and not to slip into a defeatist mentality. Outside the door were our fans, our arena, and our time. I told them that I trusted them to come back in the match.

Why was I so calm and self-assured? During my remarks to the team, I kept my eye on our phenomenal All-American middle blocker and captain, Lauren Gibbemeyer. She sat there during the entire meeting staring straight ahead. Her pressure gauge was reading in red numbers. She was about to explode. As I was leaving to return to the floor, Lauren called the team together. With the look and tone of someone about to take over a match, she told the team to trust each other. Just trust each other.

That moment alone would have been enough to validate, at least for me, my entire career. One of my players had decided, during one of the most pressure-packed moments of her career, to invoke the concept of team trust. What happened next made the evening even more memorable. Minnesota came back to win the match 3-2, outscoring Penn State in the fifth set, 23-21. Fittingly, Gibby pounded an overpass to register match point. It was a nice retirement present.

Coaches often see and remember events much differently than spectators. I suspect that very few, if any, spectators were thinking what I was thinking after the match. Most of them were wildly celebrating a major win for the program. I stayed in the postmatch shadows. I didn't want to be interrupted as I replayed the match in my mind. It was clear that a different team took the floor for the third set. Was it coincidence? Or was it the result of previous years of training that equipped Gibby and me with the confidence to pick the same moment to appeal to team trust? I believe it was the latter. Here is why.

Team Sports and the Central Paradox

The absolute most important enabler in team sports is teamwide, unconditional trust. It is the lynch pin that holds a team together. For most, if not all of us, trust is not part of our nature. Instead, we walk into any new setting equipped with a natural desire to protect our own turf. I consider this protectiveness to be an expression of our human nature.

Volleyball depends on individual execution of skills in a team setting. Players must work together and trust each other to be successful. Russia controlling the net versus Brazil at the London Olympics in 2012.

We can begin to drop the curtain of protectiveness only if we trust that no harm will come to us.

This is not always possible. Players today are well-equipped with the skills to skirt around the responsibilities inherent in teamwide trust. They are able to reach back into their past to reclaim behaviors that in previous situations had kept them from having to change their ways in order to learn to trust.

Some time ago, after the 2005 season was over, I received a phone call from one of my players. She told me that she felt guilty about how the team had mismanaged the trust issue. She revealed to me that the team was living a double life, one that was manufactured to be played out in front of me, and another that was unknown to me and fiercely protected by the players.

She provided me with a list of behaviors by teammates that basically added up to be the opposite of what I was trying to accomplish. I wanted trust, but I was getting deceit. She knew that I felt good about the team's performance, but she could also tell that I was frustrated with my inability to understand and connect with the players. She took it upon herself to fill in the blanks. Basically, no one on that team trusted anyone. The outcome of our NCAA Tournament run in 2005, which ended with a bitter second-round loss to host Tennessee, was clearly affected in a negative fashion.

I call this the central paradox of team sports. On the one hand, there is the self-evident need for a team to be able to cooperate in an open and trusting fashion to achieve its collective goals. On the other side of the paradox lies the equally self-evident need for team members to squelch their desire to trust and to instead protect their vulnerabilities. Since trust is not possible in an environment where selfish (protective) agendas exist, as coaches of a team sport we are faced with the challenge of teaching people how to trust each other. We must resolve the central paradox. We must battle for the hearts and minds of our players.

Trust Enablers

The daily rehearsal of trust building behaviors can take many forms. Some of these behavioral expectations are embedded in the program's infrastructure (described in chapter 2). They include adherence to policies and guidelines, pursuing team goals, accepting the tenets of Mike's coaching philosophy, living up to the principles of competitive greatness, and adopting the expectations outlined in the championship manual. Most fall under the category of what I call trust enablers. These enablers are specific behaviors that, when taken as a whole, prepare players to embrace the pursuit of becoming a trusting team.

I began each spring with the same exercise. I felt it was important that the players play a major role in identifying what we called the laws of building trust. We started by conducting open-ended discussions to determine the trust-building behaviors that this team believed to be essential. When the team decided that the list had been sufficiently trimmed down, we had it printed using their language, and everyone received a copy. We all agreed to live by its principles. Here is an example taken from one of my teams at Minnesota.

Laws of Building Trust

- Teams cannot manage manipulation and lying. Tell the truth at all times. Tell the complete truth. Half truths are lies. Face up to it.
- No talking behind a teammate's back to anyone inside or outside of the team.
- What happens inside the team stays inside the team. It creates a safety zone that allows players to be vulnerable and to take risks.
- Never take advantage of a teammate and never let a teammate take advantage of you.
- No inside jokes, talking under your breath, whispering, and the like when the team is together. If it cannot be said aloud for all to hear, then do not say it.
- Expect teammates to solve their own problems.

Behavior at Meetings

I also knew that if we were going to use the team-meeting format to examine our behavior, it would be a good idea to ask the team to use these same procedures to create a list of behaviors for conducting team meetings. After all, these meetings were the only time that we were all together in one room to discuss our most sensitive issues as a team. The following is an example of how one team at Minnesota rolled out their expectations for conducting team meetings:

- Be prepared to take notes.
- Be honest when speaking, and your teammates will believe you.
- Maintain eye contact.
- Use a calm but demanding tone.
- In order to be good listeners, we should have positive and open body language.
- When in a group setting, do not become a distraction.
- Don't be overly concerned with the manner in which you are being criticized.
- Always be respectful.
- Eliminate behaviors that discourage interaction.
- Quiet people can't let boisterous people interrupt and speak right over them.
- Don't respond to criticism with bad body language and selfish pouting.
- Do not disrespect the speaker; this is distracting to everyone.

Role-Playing Exercises

Another means for rehearsing the trust principle were the role-playing exercises that I would spring, unannounced, on the team. These usually occurred in the team meeting room, but they could have been enacted anywhere. Of all the mechanisms for learning trusting behaviors, this was one of the most effective. I would start by choosing anywhere from one to four players, depending on what the script called for. The players were asked to act out the scene and supply their own dialogue. The goal was to use trust behaviors to resolve the issue. Here is an example of a role-playing assignment I used recently.

It's Saturday night after a big win over your rival school. You and your teammates are out celebrating at a bar. Some of your teammates begin drinking beer, but a team policy prohibits players from using alcohol, even for players who are 21 or over. You suddenly feel conflicted. Do you show up at practice on Monday and rat out your teammates? Do you confront them right there at the bar? Or do you let it go and do nothing? What should you do?

I set up a table to be used as a bar, and then I assigned the three or four acting parts to random players. Sometimes I felt that a particular player needed to work through how she would handle her role in this particular episode and would assign her to the cast. The rest of us would watch and listen. Each skit would be followed by a brief discussion of how successfully they conveyed their point of view to us. These exercises often created energetic debates over how the situation should be handled. There was rarely a right answer. But the process of working their way through these difficult issues provided significant experience for each player. We believed that by acting out these exercises the team was never allowed to stray very far from facing the challenges of how to build an atmosphere of trust.

Movie Clips and Readings

We also made use of movie clips. I rarely asked the team to watch an entire movie. There simply wasn't enough time. But it was not difficult to find time to view selected clips of varying length, usually 15 to 30 minutes. The clips were very powerful expressions of some of the concepts I was trying hard to convey. They provided reference points that were shared by all. I wouldn't have to provide elaborate explanations if I could simply refer to a scene from a movie. This was faster and allowed all of us to carry with us a video reminder of the message I was trying to illustrate.

For example, let's say that I wanted to discuss my long-standing preference to empower my players to become critical thinkers instead of forcing them to memorize what someone else believes. In other words, I've always wanted my teams to think, and not just memorize their way through their athletic experience. So I would show selected scenes from the movie, *Dead Poets Society*. These clips illustrated precisely what I wanted my team to understand about the pedagogical relationship between coach and player. The clips brought to life the detail, the subtleties, and the body language that can only be conveyed through the medium of motion pictures. You can imagine how much more the players appreciated watching movies rather than listening to me struggle in trying to describe all of this from a standing position at a team meeting.

In addition to the movie clips, I made significant use of printed resources such as books, magazine articles, and blogs. A good example of this option occurred early in my time in Minnesota. I had just finished reading Martin Seligman's outstanding book on positive psychology, *Learned Optimism.* It is one of the best coaching books I have ever read. Seligman enters the discussion where most psychologists leave off. The conventional wisdom of the day (circa 1996) held that athletes could improve their competitive mentality through the use of affirmations and visualizations. An affirmation is the declaration of an intention to accomplish a particular goal. A visualization is the creation in your own mind, through the arrangement of vivid colors and sounds, a visual picture of how the declaration will unfold. By repeating the affirmations and replaying the visualizations, athletes are able to arrange a mind-set that equips them with the determination to succeed. Learned optimism is an outgrowth of this idea of positive thinking: affirmation and visualization.

I selected one of our longer road trips and asked each player to prepare herself for a series of team meetings during which Seligman's concept of learned optimism would be discussed. I had copied each of the book's chapters and assigned them to small groups of two or three to read and report. The meetings were long, but the accomplishments were superb.

We learned about the difference between Seligman's approach and the so-called power of positive thinking. As he put it, positive thinking often involves trying to believe upbeat statements such as "Every day, in every way, I'm getting better and better." If you can actually believe such statements, more power to you. However, Seligman admonishes those who follow this route, arguing that many educated people, trained in skeptical thinking, cannot manage this kind of boosterism. Learned optimism, in contrast, is about accuracy.

Learned Optimism

For those of us who had become skeptical of the power of positive thinking (repeating affirmations and visualizations to oneself) as the road to personal and team success, learned optimism provided a way to take our pursuit to the next level. The following is an outline of some of the fundamental ideas contained in Seligman's book *Learned Optimism*:

> When we fail at something, we all become helpless and depressed *at least momentarily*. We don't initiate voluntary actions as quickly as we would otherwise, or we may not try at all. If we do try, we will not persist. Explanatory style is the great modulator of learned helplessness. Optimists recover from their momentary helplessness immediately. Very soon after failing, they pick themselves up, shrug, and start trying again. For them, defeat is a challenge, a mere setback on their road to inevitable victory. They see defeat as temporary and specific, not pervasive.
>
> Pessimists wallow in defeat, which they see as permanent and pervasive. They become depressed and stay helpless for very long periods. A setback is a defeat. And a defeat in one battle is the loss of the war. They don't begin to try again for weeks or months, and if they try, the slightest new setback throws them back into a helpless state.*

One of the main sources of negative thinking that can lead to poor performance is learned helplessness. This is giving up, the quitting response, the belief there is nothing I can do. Learned helplessness is at the core of failure and defeat.

There are two major risk factors for poor achievement among athletes:

1. *Pessimistic explanatory style*. A person's explanatory style is the manner in which one habitually explains things to oneself. Athletes who see bad events as permanent, pervasive, and personal will, over time, become demoralized and perform poorly.

2. *Bad life events*. Athletes who suffer the most bad events—parents separating, family deaths, family job loss, traumatic athletic injuries, bad experiences with coaches—will do the worst.

---

*Martin E.P. Seligman, *Learned Optimism* (New York: Alfred A. Knopf, 1998), 137.

As coaches we must do our homework. Careful observation of each player will provide the coach with enough information to make the correct evaluation. Learn to recognize the automatic thoughts (phrases, sentences) running through a player's mind when things are going badly. The player may not notice these thoughts. Teach players to dispute these automatic thoughts by thinking of contrary evidence. Players must learn to create different explanations to dispute automatic thoughts, distract themselves from pessimistic thoughts, and recognize and question the pessimistic assumptions governing much of what they do.

There are three basic predictions for sports. First, everything else being equal, the individual with the more optimistic explanatory style will go on to win. She will win because she will try harder, particularly after defeat or under stiff challenge. Second, this prediction holds for teams. If a team can be characterized by its level of optimism, the more optimistic team will win—if talent is equal; this phenomenon will be most apparent under pressure. Third, and most exciting, when athletes' explanatory style is changed from pessimistic to optimistic, they will win more, particularly under pressure.

Key Insights From Practicing Learned Optimism

- Teams, and not just individuals, have a meaningful and measurable explanatory style.
- Explanatory style predicts how teams will do above and beyond how good a team is.
- Success on the playing field is predicted by optimism.
- Failure on the playing field is predicted by pessimism.
- Explanatory style works by means of how a team does under pressure after a loss or late in close games.

Here is what Seligman recommends to coaches (page 166). We must take these findings seriously. They have several immediate, practical implications for us.

- Optimism tells you when to use certain players rather than others. Consider a crucial volleyball match. You have a tall, hard-hitting athlete, but he's a pessimist whose unforced errors in the fifth set were one of the reasons his team lost their last match. Substitute. Use pessimists only after they have done well.

- Optimism tells you who to select and recruit. If two prospects are close in raw talent, recruit the optimist. He'll do better in the long run.
- You can train pessimists to become optimists.

There are several ways for players to overcome the negative spiral caused by pessimism. First, distract yourself when pessimistic thoughts occur. Stop ruminating and shift your attention; this is an important concept. Schedule a later time to review the situation.

You also can dispute the evidence. Ask yourself, "What is the evidence for this belief?" One way to dispute a negative belief is to show that it is factually incorrect.

For example, a player believes "I suck as a passer." What evidence is there for this belief? Imagine she can tell herself: "The truth is I've passed thousands of balls to the target. I just shanked one ball. There is a strong likelihood that my next pass will be closer to the target. I know this because I've proven myself as a passer in the past."

A second way to dispute a pessimistic thought is to scan for alternative causes of the event. Most events have multiple causes. Rarely is anything as simple as "I suck."

For example, a player says "I didn't put a very good move on that last ball. But other factors were at work as well. I was up against the opponent's toughest server. I'm also passing next to a teammate who is very quiet and does not clarify passing responsibilities as she should. This situation may have created momentary tentativeness for me as I attempted to pass that last ball. Not only that, I've been having a tough time passing the deep ball and getting to the net to get a swing at our low outside set. I just hurried that last pass and let it get away. These are all correctable things, and there is no reason to believe I will let them affect my next attempt. I choose to focus on the things I can change in this situation."

A third way to dispute a pessimistic thought is to minimize the severity of the event. Maybe you are not the best passer on the team. Maybe you are prone to making errors. So what? There is no need to conclude that this is a catastrophic event. See it for what it is and move on.

For example, a player may say, "Yeah I blew that one. And the likelihood of getting served again is high. But so far I've only given up this one point. This is not a catastrophe. No need to conclude that I'll shank the next one. Let's bear down here and put a better move on the ball."

A fourth way to dispute a pessimistic thought is to ask if your belief, even if true, is functional for you in the present situation. Instead of disputing your pessimistic thought, ask if your belief is helping you in facing your adversity. This is especially true when, as an athlete, you have to perform now. Distraction (not disputation) might be the tool of choice.

For example, a player may say, "Even the stats show that I am not a good passer. It is not unreasonable to believe that I might shank the next ball as well. But since there is a good chance that I will be served again, I've got to distract myself right now and turn to optimistic thoughts about the next pass. I'll say to myself, 'Stop!' and I'll assign a later time to worry about my passing."

Learning to be an optimist in sports is a difficult assignment. For the pessimist, it might require reversing a lifetime of negative thinking. The more quickly you can rid your players of the pessimism that can engulf a team if left unchecked, the more quickly you can launch your plan to add learned optimism to your list of trust-building skills.

The Triangle of Doom

Like its namesake the Bermuda Triangle, the triangle of doom (figure 8.1) is not a place you want to spend your time. Although I can present no scientific evidence to support this claim, decades of coaching have convinced me that the triangle of doom hovers like the sword of Damocles waiting to drop on unsuspecting athletes. Three distinct behaviors represent the three corners of the triangle. The first is whining and

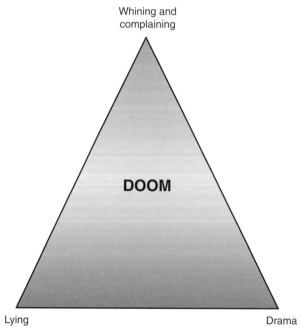

FIGURE 8.1 The triangle of doom.

complaining, followed by the creation of unnecessary drama, concluding with the most widely used of these behaviors—lying.

Whining and Complaining

We don't whine or complain. We want to be individuals who can handle any situation and never complain about anything on or off the court. This particular habit is out of place, annoying, and self-indulgent in today's world of athletics.

Victor Frankl wrote a deeply moving book called *Man's Search for Meaning* (Buccaneer Books 1993). Frankl was a Holocaust survivor and psychiatrist. Clearly, he understood the role of suffering in the human condition. "If there is a meaning in life at all, then there must be a meaning in suffering," he wrote. "Suffering is an ineradicable part of life, even as fate and death. Without suffering and death, human life cannot be complete. The way in which a man accepts his fate and all the suffering it entails, the way in which he takes up his cross, gives him ample opportunity—even under the most difficult circumstances—to add a deeper meaning to his life."

This quote is an indictment of whining and complaining, one of the most destructive aspects of athletics. Frankl writes about the nobility of suffering, and his basic message is that you can't always control the events in your life, but you can control your attitude toward them. Whining not only degrades the person indulging in it, but it also poisons anybody who listens to it and tolerates it. Whiners and complainers don't understand that they are living in a superficial world that prevents them from sacrificing themselves for a greater mission. Athletics doesn't develop whiners and complainers. Instead, it exposes them.

Here is a sample of what I mean. How would you grade yourself according to table 8.1 Teammates Versus Complainers?

Drama

We don't freak out over ridiculous issues or live in fragile states of emotional crisis. We refuse to become overly sensitive, unstable, or volatile over insignificant events. The presence of unnecessary drama within the team can waste enormous amounts of psychological energy, energy that could be invested in other, more productive areas in the team-building process.

I define *unnecessary drama* as any sign of selfishness that distracts the team from its mission. Here are some examples.

A player makes a mistake in practice and rolls her eyes, curses under her breath, and turns away from teammates in a show of self-disgust. This is common among athletes and is one of the most destructively selfish things a player can do during practice and competition. It is a

TABLE 8.1 Teammates Versus Complainers

Teammates	Complainers
Are open to change.	Resist change.
Have "can do" orientation.	See reasons they cannot do things.
Build on successes and strengths.	Focus on finding problems to fix.
Look for the challenge in situations.	Are overwhelmed by problems.
Take responsibility for their actions.	Avoid blame or responsibility.
Think in terms of new possibilities.	Are limited by what worked in the past.
Are good listeners.	Are poor listeners.
Have a continuous supply of energy.	Run out of energy quickly.
Make decisions easily.	Wimp out in the face of tough decisions.
Feel in control of their environment.	Feel victimized by their environment.
Are driven to excel by challenge and risk.	Are afraid to take risks or face challenges.
Work hard all the time.	Work hard only when they feel like it.
Enjoy inner calmness.	Suffer excessive inner stress.
Are present- and future-oriented.	Cannot let go of the past.
Learn and grow from mistakes.	Are devastated by failure.
Have high self-esteem.	Have low self-esteem.
Pursue goals with discipline.	Have trouble managing a commitment to goals.
See past personal differences with teammates and offer support.	Are stuck on petty bickering.

statement of immaturity and a basic lack of awareness of the impact of this behavior on teammates. No one needs or wants to know about the frustrations of others. In addition to the demanding level of energy spent on their own improvement, teammates now have to waste additional energy worrying about where this player's attitude is heading. Players need to get over it and learn how to eliminate these behaviors.

A player walks into practice in a bad mood. She is preoccupied with problems in her life off the court and is letting everyone else know about it. She is emotionally unprepared to practice and starts to withdraw from coaches and teammates during warm-up drills. She chooses to put on a frown and quickly becomes "bitch of the day." Within minutes she has become the center of attention. Teammates are wondering what is wrong. Slowly, as if this player were an emotional magnet, the focus of practice has been sabotaged, and the unfolding drama plays out until every player has become distracted. This player's selfishness has created a very difficult and unnecessary situation for her coaches and teammates to overcome.

A player allows her anxiety level about being told to do sprint work lead to a personal meltdown. She suddenly removes herself from the drill and begins to cry. A few teammates try to console her, but she is committed to the meltdown. This is a result of poor preparation by the player. It is her responsibility as an athlete to learn how to sprint without building up a mountain of anxiety. It is also unfair of her to create a major distraction in front of her teammates, none of whom are interested in her meltdown performance.

You don't have to take the bait when someone is throwing a scene. You can choose to ignore her, and by doing so you will be encouraging her to fix her own behavior. Let's eliminate things like rushing to help a teammate who is breaking down because something has become a significant physical challenge. Let her work it out on her own. Ultimately, this is what we want from each teammate under pressure. Don't reward unnecessary drama by rushing to support it.

Lying

Lying is a behavior that seems to be deeply rooted in the American culture. It may seem harmless to the liar, but it is often one of the reasons teams never reach their potential. More than any other form of behavior, lying creates an atmosphere of distrust.

A lie is a type of deception in the form of an untruthful statement, especially with the intention to deceive others, often with the further intention to maintain a secret or reputation, protect someone's feelings, or to avoid a punishment. *To lie* is to state something that one knows to be false or that one has not reasonably ascertained to be true with the intention that it be accepted as true by oneself or someone else. A liar is a person who is lying, who has previously lied, or who tends by nature to lie repeatedly.

I believe it is important to teach players as much as I can about the lying process. This includes an awareness of the various kinds of lies that make their way into team discussions.

Fabrication A fabrication is a lie told when someone submits a statement as truth, without knowing for certain whether it actually *is* true. Although the statement may be possible or plausible, it is not based on fact. Rather, it is something made up, or it is a misrepresentation of the truth. For instance, a man giving directions to a tourist when he doesn't actually know the directions is lying by fabrication.

Bold-Faced Lie   A bold-faced (also referred to as bare-faced or bald-faced, although all three have slightly different meanings) lie is one that is told when it is obvious to all concerned that it is a lie. For example, a child who has chocolate all around his mouth and denies that he has eaten any chocolate has told a bold-faced lie.

Lying by Omission   One lies by omission by omitting an important fact, deliberately leaving another person with a misconception. Lying by omission includes failures to correct preexisting misconceptions. If a wife asks her husband if he's at a bar, the husband may tell his wife he is shopping, which is true, but lie by omitting the fact that he is shopping at a bar.

White Lie   A white lie would cause only relatively minor discord if it were uncovered, and typically offers some benefit to the hearer. White lies are often used to avoid offense, such as complimenting something one finds unattractive. In this case, the lie is told to avoid the harmful realistic implications of the truth. As a concept, it is largely defined by local custom and cannot be clearly separated from other lies with any authority.

Misleading/Dissembling   A misleading statement is one that contains no outright lie, but still retains the purpose of getting someone to believe in an untruth. Dissembling likewise describes the presentation of facts in a way that is literally true, but intentionally misleading.

Exaggeration   An exaggeration (also called hyperbole) occurs when the most fundamental aspects of a statement are true, but only to a certain degree. It is also seen as stretching the truth or making something appear more powerful, meaningful, or real than it actually is.

Contextual Lies   One can state part of the truth out of context, knowing that without complete information, it gives a false impression. Likewise, one can actually state accurate facts, yet deceive with them. To say, "Yeah, that's right, I slept with your best friend," using a sarcastic, offended tone may cause the listener to assume the speaker did not mean what he said when, in fact, he did.

The impact of lying can be felt throughout the program. Like an army of tiny beetles that kill huge trees by boring, one by one, through to the tree's core, the accumulation of seemingly innocent lies can cause a team to unravel over time.

There is no greater threat to the growth of mutual trust than the ongoing practice of lying. No team can afford to ignore its danger signals. On the other hand, a commitment to truth can create trust and respect. Keep this in mind as you teach your team to navigate their way toward team-wide trust.

Acknowledgment Rule

This rule has been part of my program since the early 1980s. It is one of those simple tools that manages to solve a lot of problems. Without it, or something close to it, the shaping of trusting behaviors would be impossible. Here are the principles of the acknowledgment rule:

- When you are spoken to by a coach or teammate, you must acknowledge to the speaker that you have heard and understood her. Take the emotion out of your response.

- This acknowledgment can be through spoken words or gestures, but it must convey that you have heard what has been said to you.

- Acknowledging that you have been spoken to does not mean that you agree with what has been said.

- Learn to develop an acknowledgment style that invites further communication. Do not leave a coach or teammate thinking that you are unapproachable.

- Respond every time a coach gives you feedback or instruction.

- When a teammate communicates something to you in the heat of battle, and you are momentarily offended, acknowledge in a non-inflammatory manner.

Here is the brief episode from my coaching experience that led to the creation of the acknowledgment rule. I had an athlete who was afflicted with the pessimism disease (see the discussion on learned optimism earlier in the chapter). Virtually every time she made an error in practice she would frown, pout, and grow silent. I would often veer from my intended course and walk toward her, quietly providing some positive reinforcement and instruction as I passed her. Inevitably she would leave me marooned on my coaching island by saying nothing in return, providing no eye contact, and continuing her straight-ahead glare.

For several days it was my perception that she couldn't hear me. After my first attempt to gain her attention failed, I would repeat my comment using a louder voice. Still, no response. Finally, on the third attempt, I would go louder and include a pinch of frustration, which was already building and did not need to be manufactured. "How about creating some balance in your defensive stance?" I would yell. At this point she would spin toward me and respond with the predictable, "I heard you."

Well, how was I supposed to know that she had heard me? Nothing in her body language provided any clues that she had. At that very moment, I decided that this particular form of communication had seen its last day in my gym. All I needed from her was "OK coach, got it," or a slight nod of the head in my direction accompanied by a little eye contact. Of course, a little bit of "Yeah, I'm being pretty selfish here" wouldn't have hurt. She eventually learned to communicate appropriately.

The next day I distributed copies (no laptops yet) of the acknowledgment rule. After all these years, I can see no reason to abandon it.

Embrace Conflict as a Necessary Part of Trust Building

Much of what I have discussed in this chapter involves conflict. It is not easy to be either the enlightener or the enlightenee when confronted with these challenges. Both require the cultivation of a skill base that can handle the constant pressure that accompanies this type of commitment. Once again I turn to Lencioni and *The Five Dysfunctions of a Team* for the definitive explanation of why embracing conflict, not avoiding it, is important in the search for trust:

> All great relationships . . . require productive conflict in order to grow. [Too many teams] spend inordinate amounts of time and energy trying to avoid the kind of passionate debates that are essential to any great team. . . . They emerge [from these debates] with no residual feelings or collateral damage, but with an eagerness and readiness to take on the next important issue. Ironically, teams that avoid . . . conflict often do so in order to avoid hurting team members' feelings, and then end up encouraging dangerous tension. When team members do not openly disagree about important ideas, they often turn to back-channel personal attacks, which are far nastier and more harmful than any heated argument over issues.*

Coaches as Trust Police

Every coach on your staff must learn to teach the mental perspective advocated here. It is understandable that a coach would look me in the eye and say, "You have to be kidding me. I don't have enough time as it is. How am I going to add this to my list of responsibilities?" I am very familiar with the workload facing a full-time coach, but in my view,

---

*Patrick Lencioni, *The Five Dysfunctions of a Team: A Leadership Fable* (San Francisco: Jossey-Bass, 2002), 202-204.

ignoring the monitoring of your players is not an option. Each coach must learn to simultaneously teach the game and also keep an eye focused on the players in order to evaluate their trust-building skills.

Basically, coaches need to watch the interaction patterns among players in every situation. This includes practices, meetings, travel, meals, and any other time that the players interact with one another. A list of items to watch for would include at least the following:

- Acknowledgment rule
- Whining or complaining
- Lying
- Drama
- Feedback patterns
- Dissatisfaction with playing time dissatisfaction
- Gym culture
- Social behavior
- Giver versus taker
- Making others pay to be around you

If a coach catches a player ignoring, violating, or in any way minimizing the importance of these behaviors, the coach should move immediately to adjust the player's conduct. Here are some often-used strategies.

Let's use a commonly occurring example of unacceptable behavior. A player makes a mistake in practice and curses to herself, turns her back on her teammate, and mentally checks out for a few moments. As a member of the trust police, what do you to? Here are some options:

- Initiate dialogue with the player when undermining behavior occurs.
- Ask the player to explain exactly how this unwanted behavior will help to build trust and achieve goals. Use her answers to create a teaching moment.
- Guide the player through the principles of learned optimism, applying them to her behavior.
- Replay the incident and guide her through correct behavior.
- Note the behavior at the moment but postpone the correction until later.

It is important, I believe, to frame each of these moments for the purpose of providing feedback before the event evaporates. These events are just as important as those that are triggered by a volleyball-related mistake. Don't let anything slide. It is fatiguing and frustrating, especially in the beginning before the network of desired behavior gains traction, but it is necessary if the team is going to develop a sense of trust.

Lesson Plan for Trust

Most coaches prepare extensively for volleyball practices every day. Most coaches write out explanations and diagrams of these practices in significant detail. I have never seen a practice plan for managing the teaching of mental skills. About the closest I've witnessed was watching a coach tell her staff to make sure that everyone directs the same type of feedback when addressing one particular player. This was discussed thoroughly at the prepractice staff meeting. But is that enough?

Remember that most of you would agree that a team's mental attitude accounts for at least 50 percent of the probability of a team winning or losing. I think that most of you would extend this logic to agree, therefore, that at least 50 percent of your training time should be devoted to the mental skills we have discussed so far. This would mean that coaches should be writing lesson plans for coaching the mental skills as well, but this is not happening.

I wrote out lesson plans for developing team trust. I scheduled meeting times well in advance. I prepared meeting materials with the same thorough effort that I had devoted to volleyball practices. I had meetings to prepare for meetings. The movie clips, the role-playing exercises, the readings, and the sessions that I used to teach the team about the negative impact of lying, whining, complaining, creating drama, engaging in poor conduct at meetings, and using inadequate communication habits, these were always seen as the fundamentals of creating trusting behavior.

Recognizing Trust-Building Behavior

Through the years I learned to keep an eye trained on the behaviors exhibited by my teams. You never know when you might unintentionally walk in on a trust-building episode being played out. When you do, an unmistakable sense of familiarity will invite your attention. You need to stick around and watch something memorable begin to unfold. These are the moments that are so powerful that they can determine the course of a season.

In 2003 my University of Minnesota team had received a top ten (number 6) preseason ranking. I arranged a tough schedule, thinking that we were going to be a very good team. We opened our season at the Hawaii Tournament, always a tough place to win. We were less than spectacular and winced at our 0-3 record as we boarded the flight to return home. We managed to win a few matches in the following weeks, but a month into our season found us at 7-7, hardly the win–loss record expected of a highly ranked team. That was hard to live with for a team so accustomed to winning. Our last two matches in that streak were conference losses to Big Ten teams Indiana and Purdue. This magnified the emotional impact that the losses were inflicting on all of us. No one had expected such a disappointing early season performance.

Almost everyone had filed out of the Purdue arena, our last stop on the 7-7 tour, except us. Our team was still in the locker room waiting for the coaches to deliver our postmatch comments, but no one had made a move. I don't think they wanted to hear from me, and I don't think the staff wanted to hear from the players. But the postmatch ritual had to unfold, and I was the one who had to make it happen.

I walked into the locker room. I wasn't surprised by what I saw. Every player was staring at the floor in silence. Usually they were in a hurry to pack their bags and get on the bus, but not this time. I saw anger in their faces. I could feel their frustration. I knew that I had to find a way to help them process what had happened, but I just stood there, taking too much time trying to decide what to say.

Then, without warning, our team captain and All-American, Cassie Busse, took the floor. On the rare occasion when she did decide to speak, she chose her words carefully, and she was always brief, very brief. This would be no exception.

"This is my senior year," she said, scanning the room for eye contact. "And this is not how things are going to end." That was it. End of speech. Cassie led the normal postmatch team yell, picked up her bag and walked out. We were all stunned. We followed her to the bus.

At that very moment she had transformed our identity as a team. We finished second in the Big Ten and defeated Pepperdine and Washington in the western regional championship to go to our first Final Four. Cassie's speech seemed to ignite our competitive fuse. It wasn't *what* she said, it was *how* she said it. It was the right thing to say, at the right time, and in the right place. Our senior leader, quiet throughout the frustration of the 7-7 start, chose our most vulnerable moment to stand in front of her team to declare that there was a new sheriff in town.

Conclusion

That's the thing about leaders. They always seem to know what to say and when to say it. In addition to Cassie's leadership declaration, she also engaged her team in a blatant act of trust. Cassie wanted us to know that we could trust her to lead the team on the court and in the locker room. No questions asked. In fact, we could trust her to lead the team in any situation. By accepting the responsibility to lead the team out from the wilderness, she drew a line in the sand. This is as far as it goes, she seemed to be saying. If you can trust in me, I will make sure that we will embrace the challenges that lie ahead.

It was a powerful moment, witnessing the emergence of team trust, touching each of the players one by one. That moment changed all of us. If I ever harbored any doubt regarding the impact that trust can have on a team, those doubts had been permanently deleted.

I wasn't the only one to witness its potential impact. As the U.S. women's Olympic team prepared to compete in the London Games, the coaching staff spent valuable time attempting to practice the fundamentals of positive team chemistry. They had established early in the quadrennial that there would be an increased emphasis on the development of team trust. The team played its way to a number-one world ranking as they prepared for the Games. The staff was quick to cite improved team chemistry as one of the significant factors leading to the team's outstanding performance on the court. Just in case I was tempted to forget about how strongly the U.S. staff felt about their chemistry-building efforts, one of the staff members turned to me following a particularly spirited practice session and offered the following assessment: "For the first time in four years, I feel like we're putting a real team on the floor."

CHAPTER 9

Coaching the Match

The most practical thing I can tell you about coaching the match is that there really shouldn't be that much for you to do. If you have prepared yourself and your team properly, you should be able to sit back and listen to the match as it unfolds, free to respond with an occasional corrective or congratulatory comment when you feel the need. This preparatory work occurs during the weeks and months leading up to competition when coaches put their players through the technical and tactical training regimens with which we are all familiar. This is when coaches devote most of their time to the physical aspects (skills and tactics) of training their teams to compete. If and when there is time left over from this, some of these coaches attempt to squeeze in a few activities designed to cultivate the growth of team trust—trust in themselves and trust in each other—as they prepare for battle.

But a lot of these coaches have it backward. They tend to spend most of their prep time on technical and tactical aspects and, by comparison, little time on the critically important aspects emphasized throughout this book—the development of individual and team trust. Before you start to worry about losing training time in the gym due to increased attention on the mental game, remember that most of the psychological training takes place within the context of a normal practice session. Do you recall back in chapter 8 when you agreed that the pursuit of team-wide trust accounts for at least 50 percent of a winning effort and therefore ought to occupy at least 50 percent of our training time? Well, here is an opportunity to apply that belief. Your next challenge will be to create a training atmosphere that relies on a harmony between the mental (trust) and the physical (skill training, tactical training, and strength training). By opening up your preparation routine to include trust training at the same level (at least) as physical training, you will have resolved your dilemma.

I anchored the sideline as a head coach for 1,345 Division I collegiate matches. Add another 55 U.S. and collegiate international matches, and the total rises to 1,400. Then toss in another 200 or so age-group club matches, and the total levels out at around 1,600. This figure does not include the occasions when I served as a U.S. assistant or bench advisor. This means that I conducted prematch meetings, decided upon and turned in starting lineups, formulated or approved game plans, offered sideline feedback, and held postmatch meetings at nearly every one of those 1,600 matches. I conducted somewhere in the vicinity of 15,000 timeouts. I think I can speak with some degree of experience about how to manage a match.

I have heard many colleagues say that practice was their favorite coaching activity. Not me. The match, the actual moment of competition, was by far the most enjoyable, the most exciting, the most rewarding, and the most compelling of all other coaching duties. For me, practice was interesting because it required so much thought and preparation. But the matches, this is where I found my motivation.

I will admit to carrying around a bit of anxiety with regard to losing. Coaching is a results-oriented job. Winning is good; losing is bad. Often you turn around to find a TV camera and a few print media reporters wanting to know why you lost. Sometimes this seemed more like a statement than a question. There were times when I wanted to return to my days as an assistant professor and high school teacher. I was free to assign a low grade when a student performed poorly in my class. I was never accused of being a bad teacher when this occurred. The blame seemed to rest with the bad student. There were no cameras trying to capture the bad grade moment, no reporters who wanted to interview the student to determine why the bad grade had been assigned. I was never asked, "Was this student the victim of your poorly planned course syllabus?" or "Why aren't your students mentally tougher?" No reporter would ask me, "When do you test your class next?" "Do you plan to change your teaching strategies to avoid low grades in the future?" Or even, "Do you mind if I stop by your study sessions to evaluate progress? I'll send a camera crew over tomorrow."

Coaches grind away under the microscope. They must endure this type of questioning regularly. For many, the competition segments are anxiety producing. The fear of losing can pull the carpet from under even the most confident coach. Listen to how one of the most successful coaches in history put it when asked to describe his game-day outlook. Former Alabama football coaching legend Paul "Bear" Bryant said, "I'm not much of a golfer. I don't have any friends. And, all I like to do the day of a game is go home and be alone and worry about ways not to lose."

This is always an option as we craft our approach to managing competition, but I don't recommend it. Instead, I would urge you to step back, relax, and take a panoramic look at what awaits you as you enter the competition arena. Think about the match as the center of a confluence of several streams of preparation, all aimed at maximizing the team's potential. Replace anxiety with the proactive task of checking on each of these streams, much like a doctor does rounds. It is the coach's responsibility to make sure all streams are flowing freely and are delivering the proper nutrients to the match.

When I was coaching, I always preferred to walk into the match environment completely prepared. I didn't want to arrive at the bench area with important match-related issues still to be resolved. It was important to have time to say hello to the event management personnel that I had come to know in the various arenas across the country and certainly to our own personnel when playing at home. I readied myself for the random appearance of friends, ex-players, fans, and volleyball enthusiasts who often showed up at matches to say hello. These were all wonderful moments that I cherish more now as I look back than I did at the time; they taught me early that it would be a good idea to have completed all of my match preparation *before* walking into the social atmosphere that always preceded matches.

Prematch Meeting

Before the start of any competition, I recommend a final prematch team meeting. The meeting should last no more than 20 minutes and should be held around 90 minutes before match time. Most of the information will have been covered earlier in the week, but it is helpful to conduct a final review. The following is a sample prematch meeting agenda, one that I could easily have written for one of my own meetings:

Meeting Agenda

1. Confirmation of starting line-up, possible match-ups, and substitution patterns
2. Reinforcement of principles of our style of play
3. Brief review of key game plan items (players have this on their computers)

a. Opponent FBA chart and our block and defense chart

b. Opponent block and defense and our FBA chart

4. Motivation

5. Risk management reminder

6. Different life of each match

In the prematch meeting, I would address each item to the team. In the sections that follow, we will cover some of these ideas but in a more shorthand fashion. In addition, I will provide background material to help you understand the items that go into the agenda for the prematch meeting.

Confirm Starting Lineup, Match-Ups, and Substitution Patterns

A coach must follow a few rules when selecting a line-up, choosing match-ups, or using substitutes. The rotation rule stands out as the most significant. It is one of the oldest rules of the game and remains unchanged since its inception in 1912. It is a rule that is unique to our sport and has a profound effect on the way our game is played. Because of it, we have to coach and play our game in six separate chapters, with each chapter representing one of the six rotations. Furthermore, the rule dictates that we play each rotation with different personnel and a different arrangement of players' court positioning.

The rule seems harmless, but it means that each time your team rotates, your offensive and defensive formations undergo a complete overhaul. Every player will be in a different position on the court. Every coach will have to design a set of tactics with different personnel who are subject to different overlap restrictions for each of the six rotations. The rule has also resulted in the tendency for teams to line up according to the concept of symmetry.

Symmetry in a line-up means that, in the traditional 5-1 system for example, OHs are placed opposite each other, as are MBs. The OPP and setter are also lined up opposite each other in the rotation sequence. The goal of symmetry is to make sure each rotation features an OH, a MB, and either the setter or an OPP. Specific physical characteristics are important in building a line-up. OHs should be gifted jumpers who can swing for kills on both the left and right sides, as well as from the back row. They also should demonstrate high-level skills as passers. MBs should be tall, jump well from lateral footwork patterns, and possess lightning quick read-and-react skills. An OPP must be able to attack well from the right side, be an intimidating blocker against the opponent's left side attack, and be an offensive threat from the back row (especially position one). The setter must possess all-around skills, but more than anything else, the setter must be able to run the offense with confidence, skill, and intelligence.

In an earlier book, *Insights and Strategies for Winning Volleyball* (Human Kinetics 1991), I claimed that championship team chemistry started with the piecing together of specific personality types on the court. I described each role and how it contributes to chemistry (pages 138-141). Things haven't changed much since then, although I have added leadership as a fourth role. I feel it is an essential building block for team chemistry. And I have added a recommendation. If you are at all confused by the idea that chemistry attributes can trump athleticism, you should dig out your old video copy of *Miracle,* the story of the 1980 U.S. gold-medal-winning hockey team, arguably the most unexpected, incredible, miraculous upset in the history of team sports. Locate the following scene and watch it again.

At an early team tryout, the head coach (Herb Brooks) made a series of what, to many, were curious selections. In addition to posting the final "you made the team" list on the first day of a seven-day tryout, Brooks' list included players who were questionable from an athletic standpoint and left out others who were popular choices. "Herb," I paraphrase on behalf of the assistant coach, "what are you doing? Some of the best athletes aren't on this list!"

"I'm not looking for the *best* athletes," said Brooks, "I'm looking for the *right* ones."

It is within this spirit that I offer the following. It is my latest attempt to formalize my list of chemistry roles.

- **Stud.** Every great team has at least one player on its roster that everyone considers a stud. This player is so accomplished that everyone in the gym knows that he can take over the match at any time. The mere presence of a stud gives a team a tremendous psychological edge. Studs may be short on other attributes, but they are physically intimidating. Preferably a stud is a left-side hitter, but anyone can ascend to this role. His dramatic performances get your attention. He wants the ball at critical moments. He always shows up and never hides. The stud is usually the reason the team wins a close match. The stud doesn't mind carrying a heavy load. This is a difficult role to accept, requiring that a player possess an enormous level of confidence and competitive drive bordering on cockiness.

- **Winner.** Every great team is blessed with at least one all-out winner. A winner is a player who never, ever, contemplates the possibility of losing. No matter what the circumstances, no matter how far behind, no matter how much bad fortune has come her way, the winner plays every point as if she has a chance to win the match. This player is courageous and takes risks. The commitment to winning is infectious, and the winner often carries the emotional load for her team. She is a rare breed. The winner is preferably a setter, but anyone can play this role. Her key ingredient is an unshakeable belief that her team can win under any circumstances. She will always be able to infect the rest of the team with this belief. She is a great communicator and is not afraid to express her feelings in front of teammates. She makes everyone around her feel good about herself. She presents a positive, enthusiastic version of herself at all times. She must have enough game to be credible. Her most important skill is her belief and her ability to make everyone else believe.

• **Stabilizer.** Most athletes are not sufficiently skilled to be studs or psychologically equipped to be winners. Championship teams are heavily populated with players who fit neither of these roles. Instead, many of them play a stabilizing role. The stabilizer is usually a low-error player who is seldom the primary reason the team wins but never the reason it loses. Often he is referred to by coaches and sports commentators as a role player. He sets the stage so the headliners—the studs and the winners—can function. The stabilizer is motivated to be a role player; he is not disappointed in realizing that he is not a headliner. He makes very few errors and focuses entirely on what he is asked to do within the system. He gets along with everyone. He keeps everyone else on an even keel and is quick to sniff out brush fires. He is a great teammate who is consistent and reliable. He assists team leaders in keeping teammates accountable to team guidelines. He is a good influence in the locker room with a mature perspective on life.

• **Leader.** A championship team must have a leader, someone who always does the right thing. The leader uses the right voice inflection, picks the right time to address a situation, knows how to approach each teammate, knows how to energize the team when it starts to sag, and is in command of her emotions at all times. The leader always knows what button to push when the team needs to be rescued from going down the wrong path. Quite simply, this player accepts the role of holding her team together and yells "Attack" when everyone seems to be in full retreat. This player must command the respect of her teammates. She has the courage to stand alone. She is fearless in confronting team-mates and situations that need attention. The leader is a skilled liaison between players and coaches and knows when to involve coaches. She is respected by all and is willing to live a life that models championship

behaviors. This is a people-skill role not necessarily tied to playing ability. The leader initiates comebacks during competition. She is fearless
and charismatic. The leader has to earn the right to lead since the first
person you have to lead is yourself. Teammates won't listen if the leader
doesn't walk the walk. Some people respond to the leader, but others
will be a pain in the butt. Some people will fight the leader every step
of the way. A leader knows she has to take them with her anyway. A
great leader never gives up on anyone. A great leader is not judgmental;
she shows an equal loyalty to everyone on the team. She will have to
make uncomfortable decisions that will cause people to dislike her. The
leader's job is not to be everyone's friend. Her job is to lead!

The point to be taken from this discussion is that line-up selection,
match-ups, and substitution patterns involve the combining of two lines
of thought that ultimately must converge into one. First are the tactical
and positional considerations that determine where in the rotational
order each athlete would best function within the system of play. And
second, which collection of players would best express the combination
of chemistry roles? The coach should review line-up decisions with the
team before every match. Players deserve to know how line-up selections are being made.

One of your chief responsibilities is to make sure that your team projects the style of play that you have created for them. Here is an example
of how a coach can identify the various elements that make up a system
of play. The system of play I describe here is based on the 2004 University
of Minnesota team that reached the finals of the NCAA Championship.

My first decision was to play a genuine 6-2 offense. By *genuine* I mean
that our two setters would play in all six rotations. They would not be
replaced when they rotated to the front row. Our two setters would
stay in the front row and would be counted on to hit, block, and pass.

This was a huge risk that very few coaches would consider taking.
Neither of our setters had ever played in a 6-2. One of them, Lindsey
Taatjes, had never before played as a hitter. Could she learn to hit at a
high enough level to warrant our playing this system? Neither Lindsey
nor Kelly Bowman, the other setter, had ever been a primary passer.
At 5 feet 10 they were a serious downgrade in the size of our right-side
block. These facts alone were enough to give us cold feet as we pieced
together our system of play.

But we didn't stop there. We decided to use our libero to sub in for our
outside hitters and not use the customary system of subbing the libero
for the middle blockers. This may not sound like much, but opponents
were clearly distracted by our unique style of play.

Kelly Bowman (preparing to spike) and Lindsey Taatjes (covering for Bowman as she swings) were the two setters in Minnesota's 6-2 system in 2004 when we played in the NCAA Women's Volleyball tournament championship match.
Darryl Dennis/Icon SMI

There were some advantages to the system we chose to play. Our two setters were also two of our best defenders. Keeping them both on the floor full time meant that we could not only use our best defender (libero) in every rotation, but we could also sub in our excellent defensive specialists for our outside hitters. This meant that our best defenders would be on the floor for every rotation.

An additional wrinkle was now possible. Our two setters could conceal their respective rotational position and run fake patterns at the blockers as they converged together at the setter's contact. It took a lot of reading ability for a team to know which one was front row and which one was back row. As a result we were able to achieve maximum use of the specialization options made available under the liberal collegiate rules.

We were also able to dial down the degree of difficulty in our serving game and make fewer errors because our blocking and defense were excellent. There was no point in risking serving or hitting errors. It would have been foolish to take our defense and counterattack game out of the equation by giving away free points. Finally, we were able to give our outstanding libero Paula Gentil the green light, allowing her to go anywhere at any time to play the ball.

This was the culmination of three years of grooming my team to play great defense. Our emphasis on low errors, creative substitution patterns, and a deceptive 6-2 offense became our signature style of play.

I always felt that it was important to review the ingredients of the team's style of play, punctuating those areas that might need special attention in the upcoming match.

Scouting and Game Planning

I first became excited about scouting and game planning in the late 1970s and early 1980s, well before the appearance of personal computers. Pencils and legal pads preceded keyboards and hard drives. I remember vividly how proud I felt when I realized that our sport could be statistically quantified and broken down in a fashion similar to baseball, football, and basketball. The first popular statistic was hitting efficiency (kills – errors / total attempts), otherwise known as kill efficiency (KEff). This became the gold standard for measuring a player's offensive abilities. The groundbreaking work of Dr. Jim Coleman inspired coaches, researchers, and other analysts in the volleyball community to develop statistics for measuring passing, blocking, and serving efficiency as well. These numbers allowed us to assess the overall strengths of a player or a team.

Next came a series of formulas that allowed us to evaluate the match by rotation. Volleyball coaches were suddenly debating the merit of things like the net points won or lost in, say, rotation 4. As a result we could easily identify weak rotations and, with some investigative work, trace our way through a statistical report of a match to determine if the problem in rotation 4 was a serving, passing, hitting, blocking, or attacking issue. This type of statistical analysis revolutionized the approach to volleyball coaching throughout the world.

The stat sheet is a statistical report of what happened in a particular match or practice drill. Its value lies in the information it generates about that match. It has no predictive powers, except to those who believe that recorded tendencies shape future performance. During this period, the proliferation of computers and the development of volleyball software accelerated the gathering of statistics, and an army of statistical recorders began to spread across the national volleyball landscape; I was among them!

I was one of those coaches who could be seen pouring over stat sheets after every match. I couldn't get enough. I kept up with and knew the performance numbers for my players, for our opponents, even for selected international teams and players. I recall how impatient I would become if I had to wait too long after a match for my copy of the stat sheet. I must have been an effective ambassador for stat sheets. The players began reading them. To my regret, so did some of the parents. At its peak, the postmatch meal resembled a prayer service with everyone's gaze trained on the stat sheet in an atmosphere of reverent silence.

It was right around that period—I'm going to say early to mid 1980s— that I started to question the value of recording and distributing stats. The excitement I had felt earlier was beginning to wear off. One look at the team benches in any volleyball arena, and I'd see at least one person recording statistics, usually with a computer. I cannot remember attending any match at any level (well, maybe a match in the 12-year-old age group several years ago) where this has not been the case. I began to ask myself why I was devoting so much staff and personal time collecting and embracing all of these numbers. After all, statistics really only tell you what happened in the past. Yes, I know that many coaches keep real-time statistics, presumably to stay informed during a match to get a quick read on who is performing well and who isn't. Does this obsession with statistics warrant the amount of time we devote to it? It seems to me that this information should be quite obvious to anyone who is not encumbered with having to switch his attention away from the match to either write on a clipboard or strike a keyboard. Personally, I would choose to train my focus on other, more relevant tasks. The statistics will be there if and when I need them.

Think about it. There are only a limited number of reasons for recording these stats. First, they are the only means available to the press to use for journalistic analysis (you can assign a promotions person to generate these stats). Second, all award-giving agencies (institutional, conference, regional, and national) rely on these statistics to evaluate candidates for their awards (these stats can also be retrieved from the promotions person). Third, they provide ironclad information, according to some parents, to justify why their child should be a starter (you're on your own to regulate who does and does not receive a copy). If any of these are important for your program, then knock yourself out, but unless someone can demonstrate a causal relationship between stats and future performance, I am comfortable with de-emphasizing and cutting back on the current levels of gathering statistics. My personal postmatch desire to read through the stat sheet, nurtured originally by the early days of the growth of volleyball statistics, does not justify the time and effort being currently expended.

Fortunately, and simultaneously with the growth of the stats movement, a parallel practice was beginning to emerge. We call it game planning (I'm not sure why we don't call it match planning). Whereas I have difficulty answering the question "Why do we take stats?" I find it much easier answering the question "What do I need to know about our opponent to enhance our chances of winning the match?" Instead of recording our findings as numbers in rows and columns, we prefer to *chart* the information.

I am fully aware that charting a team's movement patterns also relies on past information, the very thing I use to criticize statistical information gathering. But charting a match and keeping statistics are two different things. Statistics do not reveal anything about team movement, substitution patterns, defensive vulnerabilities, and the like. While both approaches rely on data from the past, charts yield a much wider array of information than stats. Stats do not provide anything beyond that which charting can provide. Charting involves the use of geometric shapes and a series of arrows to replicate, for example, the opponent's serve-receive patterns, their FBA and CA tendencies, and their blocking and defensive alignments. Charting becomes a pictorial presentation of the opponent's system of play. I believe this is a more valuable resource than a stat sheet when preparing for a match.

Missing from this equation is the opportunity for programs to either limit or revise their approach to collecting stats. Those who have purchased the computer hardware and software to collect and process stats—and this includes just about everyone—may find it difficult to break ranks and step outside the mainstream. It can seem that once you own the equipment, you lose the freedom to decide if taking stats is a good idea or not. Am I against using statistics of any kind? No. Do I recommend that coaches think through their approach to statistics and *not* simply follow the herd? Yes. What can be concluded from this information other than what each player and team accomplished in a previous match? Yet this is the most commonly produced report by all of the volleyball tech cadres at work around the world. Marginally useful? Yes. Essential to winning the next match? Unlikely.

Remember the stat sheet supplies only limited information. It is an arithmetic summary of specific actions by a player or team and yields nothing in the way of team alignment patterns, systems of play, serving tendencies, and the like. On the other hand, charting a match provides all this and more. These charts can be the coach's ticket to the creative world of game planning. This is where I would recommend that you spend your time. Examine the FBA chart. The coach can use this to develop blocking schemes and decide on which areas to serve in each rotation. Where stat sheets leave the coach almost empty-handed, the charts equip the game planner with vital information about probable opponent systems and tactics.

But neither of these approaches captures all that you need to know about your opponent. If you have been following one of the primary themes of this book, you can probably anticipate what comes next. The stat sheets and the charts provide only cold, inanimate glimpses into the inner workings of a team. If you wish to know your opponent, if you wish to understand their psychological makeup, then you must search to discover what makes their hearts beat as one. Only then can you know what has to be done in order to establish a chance to win the match. The charts add significantly to the formation of the game plan, but in my opinion, it is the psychological element that gives the game plan its finality. It provides the mortar that holds the team together.

The trouble is there is no stat, no chart available for recording a team's psychology. Instead, coaches must rely on their own skills of observation resulting from the experience gained by years of watching players play the game. Good coaches can watch a team play and connect the psychological dots that serve as a basis for understanding a team's style. Unlike the clear-cut arithmetic and geometric responses that are derived from stat taking and charting, these game-plan items stem from confident and creative artistry by the head coach. Here is a brief sample of what I am talking about. This was taken from an actual game plan I prepared for a collegiate match late in the 2010 season.

Our upcoming opponent likes to play fast. We have to stay ahead of, or at least keep up with their pace. For example, they clear a dead ball from the court quickly. Their server is already at the baseline ready to serve on the referee's whistle. They leave very little time for their opponent to share information or to prepare for the next FBA sequence. We have to become comfortable with this style immediately. It cannot distract us.

We normally stay with our standard package defense throughout the match. But for this match we are going with it up to 20 points in each set. But from 20 on, we will switch into our double-team mode against their two top hitters. We will not let those two hitters beat us. We are quite comfortable in allowing their second-line hitters to take their best shot late in each set (after 20).

Motivation

I firmly believe that athletes should be self-motivated. But sometimes a team will come out flat and not ready to play. When this happens, when the team fails to self-motivate, the coach should have a plan B ready. This happened to me at a home match during my last season as head coach at Minnesota. I had seen it coming all week in practice, and I came to the match prepared.

What you are about to read occurred on a day when I was already pretty jacked up. My team had needlessly handed over a victory to our opponent the night before. While "celebrating" this unexpected outcome, I received a phone call from our top recruit announcing that she would be signing with one of our archrivals. Then, to keep the string alive, I stopped at an arena concession stand to dine on one of their delicately prepared hot dogs. I looked at the ketchup label and could have sworn later that it read, "Best if used before December 1936."

Traditional motivation strategies seemed inappropriate, given the way the weekend was unfolding. I decided, therefore, not to use my favorite and most inspirational speech, which went something like this: "Go, win!" No. Tonight I would reach deep into the backpack and create something that might be a little more reflective of my mood at the time. I needed to get my team going by doing something out of the ordinary. I walked solo into the team meeting room and, treating the moment as if I were reading a press release, unfolded what would become later known as the manifesto (see "Volleyball Team Announces Decision to Become a Team").

I really think I nailed it that night. My team had become complacent and in need of an attitude intervention. Sometimes you just have to go with your gut feeling. This time things worked out for me. The manifesto contained just enough sarcasm and truth to get my team's attention. I wouldn't go to this type of motivation strategy every night, but I trusted my instincts, we came back to win the match, and the manifesto stayed with us as a season-long reminder that a plan B must be within reach when things go flat.

Volleyball Team Announces Decision to Become a Team

In a prepared statement, the volleyball team declared that, on the eve of the NCAA Tournament, they were finally ready to put aside the disruptive behaviors that had kept them from reaching their potential. The team met together after Tuesday's practice to address the issues.

"We have struggled all season with our team chemistry," said coach Mike Hebert. "It has been a roller coaster. We have experienced moments of greatness and moments of sheer frustration. I am thrilled that the team has decided to take control of its own destiny."

A copy of the team's formal statement follows.

We, the members of the volleyball team, unanimously agree to the following principles and actions:

- No whining or complaining. We agreed to this in August, but we still whined and complained on a regular basis. The constant carping and picking during practice, in hotel rooms, on the bus, during matches—this is now over.

- We will eliminate unnecessary drama.

- We will put a stop to all selfish behavior. Some of our teammates are self-absorbed and think only of themselves. They give very little to team chemistry. These players will start thinking of others immediately.

- We are tired of watching teammates play with fear. The players who have this problem will have to get over it and be ready to play this weekend as if they are actually college level athletes, motivated by the desire to compete.

- We are equally aggravated by teammates whose performance level is wildly inconsistent. They seem to decide when and where they are willing to give their best. These people represent the height of selfishness, and they have to figure out a way to be at their best at all times.

- Pouting, sulking, and looks of frustration during competition are hereby forbidden.

- The use of foul language during competition is hereby forbidden.

- The tone used between and among players during competition will be positive and encouraging in nature. We are tired of players giving each other dirty looks, rolling their eyes, displaying irritation with one another, and so on. We agree to grow up and manage these potential distractions more successfully.

We realize that not much time is left in the season, and that we will have to be very specific in certain cases where change needs to occur. For example:

- Our setter will have to realize the impact her presentation of self has on the team and how we play. Drawing inward and becoming silent, distant, and uninvolved has become old and suffocates our team. She will have to figure out how to live up to her responsibilities as a player and co-captain.

- Maria will have to stop keeping teammates and coaches in suspense from match to match by performing so inconsistently. She has to stop blaming others and start controlling her game. She needs to get rid of her wimpy side and play like a competitor.

- Nao needs to shut up and play. She is a leader when she plays at her best, but she is a complete distraction when she starts yapping and frowning. This is her final chance to fix this.

- Anne has to stop being afraid to compete. People are tired of waiting.

- LaShawn needs to hit the ball in the court. The occasional in-bounds nuclear blast cannot overcome the high number of hitting errors she commits.

- Sharon needs to stop being knocked off balance by things people say, things people do, things that bother her. She needs to become more resilient.

- Kathleen needs to demonstrate more patience with others and not be so defensive after mistakes.

Risk Management Reminder

Risk management is about choosing the shot or serve that maximizes the degree of difficulty for the opponent and at the same time minimizes the chance of failure (giving up an easy point) by your team. Each opportunity to spike or serve, for example, presents a choice to be made. You have to ask, "What level of risk (making a mistake that leads to a point for the opponent) needs to be factored into the equation as I choose a particular shot?"

When hitting, a player must ask herself, "Am I in good position to execute my shot? How about my timing? Am I early or late? Can I contact the ball with maximum reach, or am I confined to hitting the ball low to the tape? Can I see the block well? What shots has the block taken away or made available?" The player needs to be able to put all of these variables into an equation and, without hesitation, select the proper shot dictated by the situations.

When serving, consider the score of the set and the level of risk that is acceptable in each situation. This calculation will be different for each server, depending on the skill level of the server and the passing abilities of the opponents. Generally speaking, it does not make sense to make an error on a high-risk serve and thereby give up an opportunity for our block, defense, and counterattack to go to work. This is especially true if the opponent is within only a few points of winning the set. We have to make them earn their points. We won't hand over a point because of a bad decision to go with a high-risk serve.

Risk management is worked on every day in practice. It is such an important concept that I include it in every prematch meeting. I present it as a review session. I do not want confusion over risk management decisions to be the reason we lose.

Control your game.

Every Match Has a Different Life

The phrase "Every match has its own life" was passed along to me by an excellent volleyball coach when we worked together in 1986. His name is Wuqiang Pang, and he taught me a lot about the sport from the Chinese perspective. One day he and I were talking about how unpredictable a volleyball match could be. I was claiming that there must be a way to pick a winner with more confidence than I was able to muster. He looked at me with a commanding facial expression designed to close the conversation. "No guessing," he said sternly. "Every match has its own life." As usual he was right. This nugget of knowledge is what enabled me to insist to my players that, in preparing for a match, no team can ever be taken lightly. You must respect your opponent at all times because they could rise up and play—within the context of this particular match's life—like the greatest team on the planet.

I believe there are only three ways that a match can develop. First, both teams can play well and there is no need for either coach to become desperate in his managing of the match. The match will be close, and the team making the most good plays at crunch time will probably win. Second, one team plays well, and the other does not. This match normally goes to the former. The winning coach need only apply continued maintenance to the team, while the losing coach must function in emergency mode throughout. A third option is that both teams play poorly. This is also likely to be a close match. Both coaches are in for a long night and must pay close attention to every rally. These matches are usually won by the team making the fewest errors. In my experience, the psychological outlook for both player and coach can be affected significantly by which of these three paths the match takes. How will you respond once you determine which of the three competition options this match will embrace?

Tonight's match presents one clearly visible feature. Our opponent comes in very hungry. They need at least two more wins to qualify for postseason play, but they lost their top hitter to an injury last week. Their

Brazil sends a hard spike over the net at the 2008 Olympics in Beijing. Play on a volleyball court is fluid, and every match has its own life, whatever the level of play.
Millereau/DPPI-SIPA/Icon SMI

team leaders, however, will still be in the line-up. It is unlikely that our opponent's level of play will decline. In fact, it is more likely that they will put forth an inspired performance. It will be essential that *our* team leaders guard against any sort of injury-related letdown. This match will probably "live" a life that no one could expect.

Additional Preparation to Coach the Match

OK. The prematch meeting is over. The players scatter to the training room for last minute repairs. I change clothes to continue my visits with friends, premium seat holders, and booster club members.

It's about 45 minutes before match time now, and the players reappear on the floor for their warm-up. This is also the time for me to return to the bench area to review my match notes one more time. I hand my line-up sheet to the referee and begin to wonder who will sing our national anthem tonight. I am certain that no one else in the arena is concerned about this, but that moment, the one snugged between the line-up being turned in and the first note of the national anthem, is one of the most genuine I will encounter all night. It captures the brief but meaningful realization that we (staff and players) are gathering in the bench area to prepare for battle once again. It may be signaled by only a small glance or a low hand slap, but it is a magnificent moment that is shared only among and by combatants. It is very special.

Line-ups are announced, and the teams are ready for the prematch handshake. This seems like a good time to march backward in time to paint a more detailed picture of what is involved in the phrase *coaching the match*.

By now it should be clear that the title of this chapter should be Preparing to Coach the Match instead of Coaching the Match. Think of the match as an event requiring a series of decisions. You have been privy to some already, but there are several more that a coach is likely to encounter. Using the following examples, I will illustrate some of the possible answers regarding a wide range of issues.

Playing Time

To earn playing time, each player must learn to play one of these championship roles: stud, winner, stabilizer, or leader. She must practice the skills of optimism, be an energetic communicator on the court, embrace conflict, and learn to trust and be trusted. She must display mental toughness and resiliency and play with commitment and passion. She must never be a distraction. Each player must believe in herself and her team. She has to play a low-error game and display a competitive attitude during practice and competition.

Players also will be evaluated according to several intangibles, such as their ability to inspire others and their ability to play well during critical moments in a match. A player who is not on the court during a match might assume that she knows my reasons for not playing her, but her assumption could be wrong. There are many factors that may be operating, such as limited substitution availability during that set, preferred match-ups, or quality of practice performance leading up to the match. If a player wishes clarification regarding playing time status, she should select a time apart from practice or competition to talk to me about my decisions.

I will, whenever possible, attempt to provide playing time for every athlete on the roster, but these opportunities cannot be guaranteed. My perception of when or if an athlete plays may not coincide with the player's perception. Players must understand that above all, playing time decisions are motivated by my obligation to produce a team that will defeat our opponent. I will always put the players on the floor that I think have the best chance to win. It is likely that at some point a player will disagree with my decisions. This is to be expected at this level of competition. The player's job is to control her emotions and contribute to team chemistry at all times. When a player doesn't play as much as she would like, she should be noble and supportive of the team and its mission. This remarkably noble, self-sacrificing, generous human being *always* places the team before herself.

Understanding Competition

Players need to understand what it means to be competitive. Be your best at the end of sets. Find a way to make a big play to win the set. Think throughout the match. Never find yourself uttering mindless chatter. Everything you say must have a purpose. Every thought you have must be about trying to win the match. Where did they serve me last time in this rotation? Who on my team needs to be pumped up after a mistake? Who and where should I be serving in this rotation? This hitter keeps hitting to my left, I will adjust! This quick hitter gets on the ball fast, I have to keep my hands high!

Look your opponent in the eye and declare to yourself that you will beat her. Use body language that sends this message every second of every match.

Feel free to show more than happiness over a good play. Learn to display a deep down competitiveness that goes beyond just sharing your joy with teammates over a successful moment. Learn to let yourself go and express your competitive side. Remember, you are trying to beat your opponent. There is no disgrace or lack of class involved in making this clear. This is what competitive athletics is all about. Let it come out. I'm not asking you to be unethical and trash talk. I'm talking about going beyond happy. I'm talking about letting your fierce desire to win take over your personality during competition. All great competitors do this, and they ride a fine line. The more you do it, the better you'll get at it, and the more you will enjoy playing the game.

Never take time off from being a competitor. No hiding or zoning out for periods of time during a match, no matter how brief.

Tell yourself you've got to stretch yourself out of your comfort zone on defense. You have to play at another level to be competitive. You've got to leave the slow, undisciplined mental habits of high school and club ball behind as you try to play defense at a high level.

Perfect free ball passing. If you put a ball on the 5-to-8 foot line, you take away our offensive advantage, and everyone must adjust to what should have been a strong offensive opportunity. Remember, if we get a free ball, the opponent must pay!

Always be ready away from the ball. Never be caught by surprise.

Pump up your teammates when they need it. Make sure that players understand that holding each other accountable does not always mean trying to correct a teammate's mistakes. This can lead to insanity for everyone. No one responds well after a mistake with five other people telling her what she did wrong.

For my final take on competitiveness, I turn to the master, Coach John Wooden, who wrote in *Wooden on Leadership,* coauthored with Steve Jamison, these words:

> Competitive greatness is a real love for a hard battle, knowing it offers the opportunity to be at your best when your best is required. Only in this supreme effort is there an opportunity to summon your best, a personal greatness that cannot be diminished, dismissed, or derided because of a final score or bottom line. Competitive greatness is not defined by victory nor denied by defeat. It exists in the effort that precedes those two 'imposters,' two measurements of success that you should reject.
>
> Focus on the process instead of the prize. Never fixate on winning. Don't even mention it. Rather, do everything you can to make sure you give everything you have, both in practice and in matches. The score will take care of itself when you take care of the effort that precedes the score. Do not judge success based on the number of championships you win. Instead, judge it based on how close you come to realizing your potential.*

Unusual Circumstances

Always check to see if there are any unusual circumstances that may affect the match. Here are some examples:

- My team played in a 2.5-hour match the night before, and we didn't leave the gym until 11:00 pm. I will have to use substitutes carefully to keep key players fresh.

- The first referee is notorious for whistling violations on setters. I want my setter to avoid high-risk attempts that could result in a whistle and to remain focused if she *is* called for a violation.

- The referee stand is positioned very close to the sideline. When we run slides to that side, I want our hitters to use a shorter approach to avoid possible injuries.

---

*John Wooden and Steve Jamison, *Wooden on Leadership* (New York: McGraw-Hill, 2005), 52-53.

Division of Labor on the Bench

How do you want to establish your division of labor on the bench? Once the match begins, I will monitor the psychology of the match. In addition I will call timeouts, make substitutions, and oversee the application of the game plan. Monitoring the psychology of the match includes observing trust behavior, rescuing a player or the team, checking to make sure each player fulfills her chemistry role, ensuring that players are earning their playing time, and verifying that leaders are leading the team. Other staff will be assigned to carry out tasks as assigned.

Team Timeouts

What protocol will govern team timeouts? Team timeouts can be called only by the head coach. There will be a brief staff meeting separate from the players for topic clarification before talking with the team. In a noisy arena, the coach will make sure to speak loudly enough to convey the message. The coach will provide the team with specific instructions regarding what to do next and ask for player feedback. He will ask the court players: How does it feel out there? Any suggestions? He will ask noncourt players: What do you see out there? Any suggestions? Timeouts are for player and team adjustments, not venting by the coach.

Managing Injuries

How will I manage possible injury situations? Go through your roster to examine all possible options for replacing an injured player. Do not allow an injury to become a distraction. Make sure that you have a plan in place to shield the injured player from the rest of the team. If you have access to medical personnel, ask them to manage the situation.

Managing Success

How will you manage the two inevitable by-products of success—complacency and selfishness? Team leadership must cultivate an atmosphere of trust in order to stifle these two maladies. Maintain a vivid awareness that some team is on your heels planning to overtake you at the earliest opportunity. Success often leads to a feeling of selfish entitlement, followed by questionable effort. Fight against this probability.

Preparing for a Fifth Set

What are your lineup options for a possible fifth set? Will you go for a blocking matchup, strong serving order, a hot hitter in position four, or use the same lineup used in the other sets? As I look back at my time on the bench for all of those 1,600 matches, I think I can say that I was fascinated by how the matches ran their course and by how quickly a coach had to operate in order to keep up with all that was unfolding. Each second brought a new opportunity to impact the match with a decision. One moment I found myself looking at the referee to see if he was upset with my player who had just given her a dirty look. A second later I was watching our opponent go into a bunch read blocking base they hadn't used before in the match. I then leaned toward my assistant to ask about the opponent's next FBA formation and who was likely to be set. Next I stole a glance at the opponent's timeout to see how the coach was handling his team's run of errors. Then I turned my head to watch our setter's footwork to the next pass. (She had been injured, and I wanted to make sure she was moving with confidence.) Then I glanced at the scoreboard to determine if there were enough rotations left in the set to sub for my outside hitter. That ate up about 30 seconds. Love it!

Watching the Opponent

Watching your opponent with a trained eye will teach you more about the game than any stat sheet can. Watch how the team plays away from the ball rather than how hard they hit the ball on an open net. Can they create order out of chaos? Do they commit careless errors? Do they communicate intelligently on the court?

Game Plan

What is the purpose of your game plan? Identify how the opponent scores points. Take away what they like to do and make them feel uncomfortable in the match. Plan for specific blocking matchups. Create a specific serving strategy.

Communication

How will you deliver scouting information to your team? Provide an informal summary on court just before the match begins. Watch a 30- to 45-minute video and review a written summary any time before the match. Distribute this material to each player via computer access. Or use a combination of these elements.

Handling an Underperformance

Ask yourself how you will manage an underperforming starter. You could take her out of the match early and allow her time to regroup. You could sit her down for the rest of the match because her attitude is poor and heading south. Or you could leave her alone and trust that she will recover on her own.

Listen to the Match

Most coaches I know personally or from watching them coach are guilty of the crime of overindulgence. What they have in common is that they are not listening to the match. Instead they are fascinated with their ability to attract attention to their respective coaching styles. Some are "pissed-off pacers" (POPs). You can spot them as they march up and down the sideline glaring at players, referees, and anyone else who can be suspected of contaminating the coach's night. Others are among a group of coaches who go by the sit-down-and-stare (SDS) moniker. Their vital signs should be monitored throughout the match to make sure they remain medically responsive. Then there are the "hateful hothead" (HHH) coaches who excel as loud and obnoxious irritants and who seem to be downright unhappy. And of course there are the "you're killing me" (YKM) coaches with their pathetic, sorrowful palms-up appeals for referees to stop ruining their lives.

These coaches are consumed with their own self-anointed routines. The match provides a stage for them to indulge their alleged fan base. Although these coaches seem content to stay within their scripted behavioral paradigms, they would be far more effective if they would arrive at the bench with a commitment to listen to the match. The match has a lot to say if only we would turn up the volume and listen.

Here is an example. Down two sets to none in a recent match, my players were leaving the court to attend the traditional midmatch meeting, which is allowed under U.S. women's collegiate rules. We needed to find a way to climb back into contention in the match. As my staff paused in the outer hall before going inside, they were steaming with anger. They wanted me to come down hard on the team for playing so poorly, but I asked them to hold off. I had been watching our players enter the meeting. There were no slumping shoulders, no staring at shoe tops. They had played with great effort over the last 20 minutes of the match, but they just could not score points with any regularity. I saw no quit in their eyes as they filed into the meeting room. Everyone seemed to be on task.

So I chose to create a calm, business-like approach for the meeting. I treated the situation as if it were an explanation of a practice drill. My message was calm and brief. There would be no wholesale tactical changes, no personnel changes. In fact, I told them that I was proud of the way they had held their mental ground in the match. I told them that the necessary ingredients to launch a comeback were within reach. I told them to be patient and to play with an inner calmness that had been missing up to that point.

I spoke for approximately one minute and withdrew to the bench area with my staff in tow. I felt a strong sense of confidence in how I handled the midmatch meeting. I had coached in almost 2,000 matches up to that point. I had learned how to listen to matches. I was hearing, loud and clear, that my team still had plenty of fuel in the tank.

Almost two hours later, the match—complete with live TV and a sell-out crowd of nearly 6,000 people—was over. Our players melted into a victory pile in the middle of the court. I had read the match correctly, choosing to trust them instead of pounding on them to give more.

This is a decision you will have to make. As you observe the match from your position in the bench area, you should decide whether you are going to hone your listening skills or your venting skills. By listening carefully, you can discover everything you need to know unless, of course, you let your old coaching habits get in the way. If you decide you wish to refine your listening skills, here are some of the things you might consider:

- Particularly watch your setter's body language and presentation of self toward teammates. This is often the litmus test for how your team is adjusting to the match.

- Scan the body language of each player immediately following an error. This will tell you who is fully engaged or not. This is often viewed as the time for venting. Don't do it yourself, and don't let any players do it.

- Listen, literally, to your team while they are playing. Who is doing most of the talking? I sometimes close my eyes momentarily and listen. I want to know who is engaged in the match and who is dishing out mindless chatter.

- Observe how the opposition coach behaves when his team has made uncharacteristic mistakes. Has player trust in their coach broken down?

- Notice how your team greets substitutes as they enter the court. This can signal a reflection of the team's level of confidence in this player.

There is no limit to what can be discovered when one zooms in to hear what the match is saying. What you decide to do about what you discover is another matter requiring another set of decisions, but your starting point has to be developing an awareness that the match has a lot to say. Everything you hear has a bearing on the match. Either it produces a confirmation of what you had already observed, or it provides an opportunity or a decision. It is this constant tracking of the emotional ebb and flow of your team that will occupy most of your time.

I have heard from many observers who ask why I appear to be so detached from the action while I sit on the bench. I'm not detached. It just looks that way. I am actually very busy. I am listening to the match.

Postmatch

Win or lose, the postmatch environment should project a similarity of purpose that will keep everyone on same page as the team winds down. First the staff and players should all know what is expected of them after the match is over. Exactly when and where do you want your athletes to report? This is the last time you will have access to your team before the next practice, match, or other team activity. You will want their attention. But you will also want them to have a few minutes to greet the parents, friends, and relatives who have shown up to see the team play. One of the many solutions to this issue is to ask your team to note the time as soon as the final whistle has been blown. Everyone must be in the meeting room at exactly 3 minutes (or whatever time you prefer) after the match has ended.

This meeting is *not* the time for the coaches' critical review of the match. It is a time for the staff and team leaders to make sure that, when the meeting is over, everyone feels good about the team and leaves the room feeling excited about the next team gathering! Be a role model for your players. Make sure that you act like someone who wants to share in the future of the team, not someone who looks as though he wants to escape after a tough loss.

As for the actual items to be covered in the meeting, this can vary according to circumstances. Was it a program-affirming win or a devastating loss? Are we under pressure to board a waiting bus or airplane, or do we have plenty of time for a longer meeting? Did we sustain any serious injuries, or did we avoid them? Were there any chemistry breakdowns during the match, or did we earn high marks? Select the top three or four items and briefly discuss them at this meeting. An alternative is to select three or four players and ask them to respond to these same issues.

If you can, find a way to applaud the role of B-side players during last week's practices and how they figured prominently in each win. (Thank you to my good friend Shelton Collier, currently the head coach at Wingate College in North Carolina, for planting that idea with me many years ago.)

Make sure that you ask the team captain if she wishes to speak. The head coach should always be the final speaker and should deliver the wrap-up. End as soon as you can and start thinking about your next practice.

Conclusion

The longer I coached, the more I realized that every opponent has an Achilles heel, a vulnerability that could be identified and exposed if I looked closely enough. Once identified, the opponent's ability to maintain its composure and confidence would be in jeopardy. It is different from team to team. But there is always something about the opponent that could be targeted for disruption. And that would be enough to give us a chance to win.

It is in this arena that I spent most of my game-planning time and energy. The rest of the staff created the charts and rotational information. But I watched and studied each opposing team to discover what their vulnerability might be. Once identified, I would create a strategy for attacking this particular vulnerability and present it to my team as part of the game plan. I secretly called this "Mike's message." It was my unique way of always trying to derail the opponent's plan to beat us. I wanted to find a way to make our opponent feel distracted, uncomfortable in the match.

The first of these "messages" fell into my lap. Illinois was preparing to play highly-ranked Western Michigan in a first round NCAA playoff match on *their* home court. The Broncos were heavy favorites to win and to advance to the regionals at Nebraska.

During the week leading up to the match I had been noticing that Sandy Scholtens, one of our freshman outside hitters, was tearing it up in practice. She had established a history of not liking Western Michigan that dated back to the early attempts by the WMU staff to recruit her. It seemed that all we needed to do was say "Western Michigan," and Sandy would turn into a fierce giant-killer.

The first 45 to 60 minutes of the match were highly competitive. But as the match wore on, we started to pull away. Sandy began to play with a special fire that gave us inspiration but was beginning to distract the WMU team. She was passing, digging, serving, and hitting off the block for key points. At 5'7" she was the glue holding us together. And she was the reason Western Michigan began to unravel. Illinois won the match, outscoring the Broncos 15-2 in the final set.

Illinois went on to face Western Michigan several more times over the next few seasons and Scholtens—not normally a starter—started every one of those matches. It was one of those quirky things that happens in sports. In this case, Sandy's mere appearance on the court seemed to serve as kryptonite to Western Michigan's superwomen. In each of the remaining matches between the two teams, Illinois prevailed. Sandy led the way in each victory. Clearly, the Broncos were either annoyed or unnerved with Sandy on the court against them. All I had to do was insert her into the starting lineup, and the Western Michigan players—taller and more athletic than Illinois—would become slightly distracted.

On another occasion against a different opponent I created a message that called for our block to double-team the opponent's star hitter, leaving the lesser hitters in one-on-one situations. Since they were going against only one blocker, I figured that these hitters would start getting more sets as long as our block did a good job of taking away their big gun. This meant that as the teams battled each other into a fifth set, for example, our opponent would have to rely on hitters other than their traditional terminator(s) to win the match. But I reasoned that these second-line hitters rarely played the closer role. And if the match came down to our top hitters vs. their second-line hitters, we would be the favorite to win the match. Teams simply don't function as well when they have to rely on nonkey personnel at crunch time.

Here are some of the questions I would routinely asked about our opponent as I created Mike's messages:

- What is their signature style, and how can we force them into a different style of play?
- Who are the players they rely on the most at crunch time, and what can we do to prevent those players from winning the key points?
- What is my "take" on how the match will unfold and what we need to do in order to prevent things from evolving according to their expectations?
- How well do they play in spontaneous situations? What can we do to disrupt their ability to create order out of chaos?
- What is their offensive style when they are out of system?

My final recommendations can be reduced to these two. First, be sure to develop a coach's eye. Don't settle for watching the match as a spectator, riding an emotional roller coaster with each point won and lost. Watch players as they react to situations that develop away from the ball. How are they reading each play? Are they making good decisions?

Second, remember that people management skills are more important than anything else when directing your team in a match. You are the maestro conducting an orchestra. You are the Commissioner of the

Trust Police. You are the air traffic controller, evaluating and directing court movement patterns. And you are the CEO of the entire operation. If you can marshal all of your forces to produce an environment that allows athletes to compete at a high level and to simultaneously enjoy what they are doing, you will have placed yourself and your team in a position to win.

CHAPTER 10

Thinking Outside the Box

I am staring at a manuscript page on my computer that has only one phrase neatly centered on its screen. "Thinking Outside the Box" is what it says. It is the title of this chapter, the one that anchors this book, but the more I read the phrase, the more uncertain I become as to its meaning. I know that it appeared not too long ago in our linguistic history. Its intention, I believe, is to identify an occasion when someone is speaking from an unusual or unorthodox point of view. We say that one is speaking outside the box.

But now I start to wonder. If someone is outside the box, who is *in* the box? How does one qualify for being outside or inside? When this location is identified, does the person face lifetime membership in one or the other? Are you permitted to roam back and forth between in and out, framing your opinions as you go? These are the kinds of dilemmas I grind on every day.

It is important to me that I get this right. I am about to discuss the impact of outside the box thinking as it applies to volleyball. I don't want to misrepresent anyone's opinion. So here goes my working definition of outside the box.

What we're talking about here are points of view. I'm going to start by characterizing the posture of those people who are already inside the box. This is the orthodox, conventional wing of the volleyball nation. They gain admission to the box either by believing the conservative message or by not caring about the outcome of any volleyball-related issues. Doesn't matter.

One leaves the box either by request or as a result of banishment by the insiders. These people are known as the troublemakers, weirdos, rule changers, and disruptive activists who lurk in the hallways of the volleyball universe. They often carry the reputation of being agents of change. They can live with risk, whereas the insiders cannot. For example, outsiders may be able to live with the threat of their blocking scheme leaving a hitter wide open, whereas this kind of risky tactic would keep an insider awake at night.

For me there are different classes of folk escaping to the outside. Some simply have to make tough but necessary decisions that cast them overboard. Others have threatened to modify long-standing customs with regard to skills and tactics. Still others threaten to be tossed from the box because they stumble upon an idea that could disrupt the volleyball world as we know it.

Were you around when the FIVB announced that the first touch by the block would not be considered an official contact? When Bill Neville and Doug Beal masterminded the two-passer, swing-hitter system? Or when Brazil began jump serving as a basic staple of their attack? All of these people would have been considered as operating from outside the box. This is where most of our exciting ideas come from. I want people to ask questions and not immediately embrace the prevailing orthodoxy when it comes to anything related to volleyball. Ask questions, investigate, do research, use trial and error, and steal good ideas if you have to.

You never know when something is going to threaten to derail your program. In fact, I learned over the years to keep my guard up constantly to prevent being blindsided by unpredictable events. While this tactic may help in preventing *some* of the turmoil headed your way, something always slips through your guard and smacks you while you're looking in the other direction. These are the times when it is beneficial to think outside the box and to be prepared to make some tough decisions.

Stocking the Toolkit

If you are going to coach volleyball today, you better be properly equipped. The era of a clipboard and whistle sufficing has long past. The current coaching toolbox should consist of the following.

Cell Phone

A cell phone is mandatory; otherwise you will not be able to contact your players. You will recognize the cell phone. It will be the wafer thin electronic device that is never more than one meter from its owner. With this cell phone, your players will be able to send and receive text messages. If you refuse to participate in this mode of communication, you will become isolated from everyone with whom you need to stay connected. The telephone feature of this device appears to work, but for reasons known only to the current youth generation, the telephone function is rarely used.

Laptop

You must also have a portable computer, whether a laptop, tablet, or the next generation device. These devices are similar to the cell phone because they are used as a back-up communication system. The laptop is an ancient, bulky storage device that can be used to take stats, learn game plans, and send emails. However, its primary function today is to watch movies and short videos on a strangely irreverent site called YouTube. One can also locate and watch volleyball matches from around the world on the laptop.

Sociology Text

You will also need a modern sociology textbook. This is because you will not be able to understand what motivates today's youth, and they will not be able to understand what you are saying, ever. They have grown up in a world with which you are not now and never will be familiar. You will need help. Your only shot at being able to communicate with your players is to start reading that book as soon as you can!

These are not the only tools you will need, but they will get you started. Be sure to check out the Mindset List, published annually by Beloit College (www.beloit.edu/mindset). It describes the culture—material, social, attitudinal—of the incoming freshman class. It will serve as a wonderful supplement to your coaching manual as well as provide a dictionary of words and events to give you valuable insights into each new class of recruits.

Bridging the Generation Gap

In case you hadn't noticed, coaches of all sports seem to be pushed to the absolute end of their stress ranges by the conduct of many of today's athletes. Athletes are viewed as selfish and entitled. They seem to see little need to give back to their sport, they don't appear to mind watching their parents fight their battles for them, and they have little or no appreciation for the history of their sport or for the people who

Each new class of players brings something different to the game. Katherine Harms at the 2011 NCAA Tournament spiking against North Dakota State.
Zuma Press/Icon SMI

have laid the foundation that enables them to participate. I don't think it would be much of a stretch for me if I said that communication between coaches and each new generation of players has broken down. And this is a problem.

While we seek to improve our communication with each other on and off the court, let's add another layer of concern that has recently materialized in the world of sport. Let's take a closer look at the generational differences that seem to be a severely troubling aspect of our present sport environment.

A few years ago, my team suffered a particularly humiliating loss at home. It wasn't the loss that sent me reeling, it was *how* we lost. We were sloppy in our execution. Poor communication. Sketchy effort. The usual list of culprits. My sense of frustration had been building through-out the match. I walked briskly to the locker room when the match was over. I wanted to be the first one there so that each player would have to suffer my glare as she filed into the room. If you coach long enough, you will inevitably encounter one of these moments.

The postmatch wrap-up meeting following a bad loss is not a good time to rip into a team for performing poorly. Emotions run high. Players and coaches are likely to say things they might later regret. This discussion can take place any time before the next practice. But on this particular evening, I was not going to conceal my emotions behind the "Let's use this loss to get better" speech. Instead of saying a few words and dis-missing the team, which is what I would normally do, I found myself poised to launch into an unprecedented (for me) locker room tirade. I wanted them to feel my disappointment and pain. I wasn't going to be the only person in the room who was going to suffer.

But as I opened my mouth to speak, and without any warning, I decided to skip past the part where I was supposed to hammer the team for their poor execution and lack of effort. Instead, I gave what I consider was one of the most poignant, inspiring, and spontaneous speeches I have ever delivered. For me, the loss was a reflection of where we were as a program. Our team had allowed itself to play at an unacceptably poor level in front of more than 5,000 fans. I began by tracing the growth of collegiate women's volleyball from the early 1970s to the present. I praised the contributions of the pioneers who had worked hard to build the sport. I invoked the names of the great players and coaches who were part of the generation that incrementally pushed volleyball further down the path toward respectability as a sport during a time when it was not popular to do so.

I wanted every member of that team to understand the debt she owed to her predecessors, to the players who had done so much to bring the sport to its current level. I wanted them to realize that they had an obligation to perform at a higher level and to display a keen sense of respect for all who had gone on before them. When I finally started to wind down, I had been talking for almost 30 minutes. I had a good feeling about the power of my appeal to the history of the sport and the obligations that accompany an understanding of this history. I felt that I had connected with my team in a way that I never had before. I really thought that I had scored a major breakthrough.

After pausing for dramatic effect, I scanned the room to get eye con-tact with everyone. This would be the moment of truth. I would call on selected players to voice their deep appreciation of the history of the game that we all had come to love. I was looking forward to the mystical experience that all of us would share. This would be the moment when I would emotionally lock arms with my players and march together toward the newly discovered historical imperative that we never, ever would allow ourselves to play as poorly as we had played earlier that evening.

I waited with great anticipation, but not a peep. There were lots of eyes staring at shoe tops. Not one player spoke up. Could it be that I had struck such a sensitive nerve with the team that they were overwhelmed with the magnitude of my message? Still no one raised a hand. The uncomfortable silence continued. Finally, one of the players, slowly and with great trepidation, raised her eyes to meet mine. "I have a question," she stammered. Good. Finally someone is willing to punctuate the serious nature of my appeal by asking a question that would lead us all to a higher level of discourse regarding our future obligations. But that's not what happened. Instead, the moment unfolded in this fashion.

"Who," she asked with a quivering voice, "is Flo Hyman?"

What? Flo Hyman, an African-American volleyball player in the 1980s, was possibly the most iconic female volleyball player of all time before she died unexpectedly of complications from Marfan's syndrome while competing for her professional team in Japan. For me, Flo embodied the significant cultural trends of the 1960s and '70s. She was a product of much of what we had all worked for during that era—civil rights, women's rights, and Title IX. How could my players not know about Flo Hyman?

This question, and my lukewarm reaction to it, brought the meeting to a skidding halt. It seemed that nothing I said had achieved any traction. There I stood, having just been struck by the reality club. In an instant I realized the importance of keeping up with the generational changes in outlook that occur every 5 to 10 years among our respective athlete populations.

Being Aware of Age-Time Differences

I came of age in the 1960s and '70s. Social justice and the struggle for human rights dominated the cultural landscape. It would have been well within my comfort zone to present this same speech to my earliest teams in the 1970s and maybe early 1980s. This was the language to which they were accustomed; they felt comfortable within its confines. It was also the language that I brought with me to the coaching profession.

But by the mid-1980s the rebel hippie generation that had shaped so much of how I thought about social issues had given way to the yuppie generation. People of this era were the recipients of the social gains made in the previous era. They no longer felt the need to go to war on the domestic social front. They were sometimes referred to as the "me" generation because they began to pursue a more selfish agenda.

I can remember when this generational overhaul occurred. I noticed that players were much less likely to initiate change on their own. They were the first in a line of generations to feel that everything was owed them. The sense of appreciation displayed by the earlier freedom fighters gave way to the self-empowering expectations of the yuppies. The yuppies were followed by Generation X. They managed to out-duel the yuppies when it came to expecting the world to provide them with services and easy solutions. Now we have the millennials. I'll say more about them in a moment.

Why is this analysis important? For me the answer was embedded in a conversation I had in the mid-1980s with Lou Henson, the highly respected basketball coach at the University of Illinois. His teams were extremely selfless and disciplined, and they managed to achieve those two qualities consistently every year I watched them play. "How do you do it?" I asked him.

"You have to listen very carefully to what matters to the players," he told me. "You can't let them sneak past you because you aren't listening." He continued, "You can't scold them for being who they are. When they change, you change. If you can't keep up with what they think is important, you'll lose them."

Lou knew what he was talking about. I wish I had solicited his advice earlier. But after hearing the question "Who is Flo Hyman?" I knew that I had some work to do. At that locker room meeting, I was venting from the point of view of social justice. I simply could not allow my players to ignore their responsibility to uphold the ongoing fight to solidify a place for women's volleyball.

But I was talking to a room full of players who were influenced by the "who cares" posture of their generation. They were locked into looking out for themselves. Flo Hyman was a name they didn't know; players winced at the thought of having to find out who she was. It felt too much like a homework assignment. They would have responded more favorably to me had I stayed with the usual next practice announcement. This would have been something their generation could embrace. They would have been content to sidestep the discussion of Flo's historical significance in favor of receiving routine information that could be copied into their plan book.

Designing and teaching a system of communication is one of the responsibilities of the coach. An important element of the system is adjusting annually to the communication styles of each new generation of athletes. This is something that doesn't appear in coaching manuals, but it should. As the coach grows one year older each season, the new roster players remain young, and the distance between their ages can lead to severe mistakes unless the coach manages to keep up with the evolving generational culture.

Coaching Millennials

Today's generation is referred to by many as the millennials. They are unlike any previous generation. They are motivated by a sense of justice but are also very comfortable as pursuers of their own selfish needs. Here is a portrait of today's millennial generation. For more information, see Susan M. Heathfield's article "11 Tips for Managing Millennials" at http://humanresources.about.com/od/managementtips/a/millenials.htm.

Millennials often are protected by helicopter parents. They identify with their parents' values and schedules. Often they have conventional values and appreciate family and friends. Religion is popular. They seek leadership but with no history of self-direction. They tend to be confident, but often this is false due to parental hyperbole. They have not faced much adversity. They are great multitaskers. Many come from homes in which both parents work, so they are latchkey kids. A great diversity of activities is available to them. They are motivated to become involved. They can feel pressured by the demanding time schedule imposed by their many opportunities and activities. Their cell phones are always nearby, keeping them connected via texts, email, and social media. They are fascinated by new technology and have little sympathy or patience for those who are not connected. They want and give frequent feedback and appreciate diversity. They are team oriented and competitive due to an early exposure to sports. They are needy because they have not had to fend for themselves as much as earlier generations.

When coaching millennials, fix generational misunderstandings if they exist and improve relationships with players through consideration of their generational personalities. Get to know them as people first and players second. Millennials want to be led, so establish clear expectations and standards for behavior. They are driven to achieve, but they need a clear plan to follow. Provide organizational clarity through the use of calendars, email, and other means. Their multitasking creates tight schedules, so try to avoid last second changes in schedules.

Millennials are used to belonging to a family unit. Make sure everyone on the team perceives that she has a role. Have a plan for the parents; they are an undeniable part of the process.

Find ways to enhance training. Make practices challenging, upbeat, innovative, and technologically current. It is important for coaches to be perceived as making the experience comprehensive, moving beyond volleyball.

Give players opportunities to connect with each other when stretching, during the warm-up, on the bus, and other appropriate situations. This is an expectation of millennial athletes.

Millennials will fight for what they believe in. They are constantly in touch with each other and with athletes from other teams. You need to assist dissatisfied players because their problem-solving strategies are insufficient.

Coaches must improve their listening skills. Don't just speak. Listen and then speak. Each coach should connect with an athlete daily in addition to weekly meetings. Leave the past and stay in the present. It is very important to conduct informal and frequent meetings, especially individual meetings. The day of publicly calling out a player is over.

Keep team issues in-house, although this is very tough to do in a world of technological connectedness. Seek feedback from players. They are driven. Millennials are open to being led but are skeptical. Overcome their skepticism through genuine appreciation of them as people.

Millennials keep their options open. They can bail out sooner than we are used to seeing.

Millennials have to be forced to acquire self-discipline. They have high expectations but are not used to paying dues. They are not automatically aware of things such as the rookie duties of shagging balls, cleaning the locker room, and so on.

Do not fall into the trap of assuming that your players will simply work things out on their own. A team's communication protocol functions at the same level of importance as a team's system of play. Without proper attention to meaningful rehearsal, the communication system will unravel.

I carefully rehearsed the on-court communication patterns with my players. I sent some of the quiet players to the speech therapist so they could learn how to project their voices. I held meetings with staff and players to discuss solutions to the generational issues. Speech therapy and cross-generational communication—both were definitely outside the box decisions. But by now none of this came as a surprise to anyone. I had long before declared my allegiance to coaches who had labored to push volleyball toward respectability as a sport. I felt that I was acting in step with these colleagues.

By calling attention to the millennial generation's agenda as something we needed to learn about, I had again planted both feet outside that box. I realize now, as I look back on my career, that this is where I had spent most of my time—outside the box. It was where I felt comfortable, where I felt free to think independently about coaching volleyball.

I remained passionate about these things and kept driving home the point that no team ever has the right to disgrace the game as we had just done that night. It was an affront to all of the people who had done so much to make that evening even possible. The volleyball-specific uniforms (not the basketball hand-me-downs), the volleyball-specific court (without the confusing multiple set of lines used by the dozen other sports using the facility), the season ticket plans and over 5,000 butts in seats (not the double-digit parent-driven crowds and the roll of tear-off raffle tickets of the 1970s), the 40-member strong pep band (not the portable tape player)—all of these and more were improvements in our sport that had been earned, one item at a time, through hand-to-hand administrative combat.

The DS and the All-American

I relay this story to you not because I want to ridicule anyone, but because I want to celebrate the remarkable rise to prominence of a most unlikely player, in a most unlikely situation.

We were playing on the road against a formidable conference opponent. In the days leading up to the match, I had noticed a change in attitude by our All-American outside hitter. She seemed to be less responsive to coaching. She had allowed her locker room behavior to deteriorate to the point where teammates were expressing frustration to the coaching staff. She became very judgmental. Teammates were walking on eggshells around her. The environment had become toxic, and this player was right in the middle of it.

I asked the player if we could meet after our pregame meal before the match. "What's the topic?" was her terse response. Not accustomed to being spoken to in that tone, I answered her directly. "Your playing time and your attitude," I said, "and your performance on the court. You are not playing well."

An already sour conversation turned more sour and ended with my telling her to warm up before the match to determine whether or not she would be even able to play that night since she had developed a sore back. After being told by our athletic trainer that she was healthy enough to play, I watched her warm up at the arena. Apart from displaying the same poor body language that had accompanied her throughout the previous week, she seemed to be ready to play. So I gave her the benefit of a doubt and started her in the match.

I made a bad decision. She played well below her ability and displayed a sense of irritability toward teammates and coaches. She needed to be taken out of the match, and that is what I did. We were short on outside hitters that year, and she was replaced by a defensive specialist (DS) who had not played the position since her high school and club days. We lost the match, but not because of the defensive specialist. She had played brilliantly. After a brief postmatch meeting, we dressed quickly and left the arena in a state of disarray. This was turning into a major drama episode, and it needed to be dealt with immediately.

We had to play another match the following night. I scrambled to set up another meeting with the offending player. I told her that she had lost her starting position to the defensive specialist. She did not receive the news well. When it was time for our on-court warm-up before the match, she showed up with head phones, chewing gum, and no ankle braces, all of which were violations of team rules. Her answer to my questioning was, "Why should I warm up like everyone else if I am not going to play?" All I had said up to that point was that she had lost her *starting* position. There was never any talk of her not being allowed to play should I need her. By now she had dug a very deep hole for herself. To make matters worse, she sat (players usually stand) at the end of the bench and sulked throughout the match, a match we ended up winning with our DS hitting outside!

Later that night we returned to campus. As soon as we entered the building, I asked the player, our captain, and our coaching staff to meet me in our office. There was no time to waste. I sat her down and launched into my perception of where things stood. "Let's not draw this out," I told her. "Either you are in or you are out. Which will it be?"

After a few seconds of quiet deliberation, she turned to me and announced, "I guess I'm out." And with that she got up and left. She had quit the team.

I was not surprised by her departure. She had told me two years earlier that she was having a hard time liking volleyball. She had lost her passion for the game and was anxious to move on in life. In that brief moment, she took her first step in that direction.

We still had almost a half of the season left to play, and we had to play it without our All-American outside hitter. There was some serious hand wringing going on. Who was going to be the permanent solution on the outside? Were we going to win another match? Why did this player walk out on her team?

We decided to ask the DS to become our starting outside hitter. At 5'9" she would never be as dominant a hitter as her now departed teammate, but she had a nice repertoire of shots and could serve, pass, and defend at a high level. She started, and she excelled. When given the opportunity, she grabbed it and ran. Simultaneously, the team felt that a burden had been lifted from them when their teammate decided to quit. The daily drama was gone. Players were free to assert themselves without being pinned to the wall for feeling the wrong way about something. The removal of this

> continued

> continued

one player loosened the ropes that had been holding the team hostage. We suddenly became a team.

In fact, we became a very, very good team. We won our NCAA Regional Championship and qualified for yet another Final Four. We did this despite the mid-season drama surrounding one player.

This is less a story about a player who walked away from her teammates and more a story about an undersized DS who became a starting outside hitter on a Final Four team and was named to the All-Tournament team at that year's Final Four. How was it that this team could lose such a tremendous All-American athlete and feel as though more could be accomplished *without* her than *with* her? To follow through on the threat to remove the player from the roster and to follow that decision with moving a DS to a starting outside hitter position? And then to watch the team come within one match of playing for a national championship? It was a remarkable series of events. This is legendary stuff. And it all happened because of the willingness of the coaches to make some tough decisions outside the box.

Using Statistics

Jump with me into the time machine and dial up a volleyball tournament from the early days of our sport. In fact, let's go back to the last year before official stats were taken, whenever that was. Let's assume, for argument's sake, that 1950 is the year in question. We get out of our machine, and we take a look around. The uniforms and shoes look odd. No antennae fixed to each end of the net. No protective padding on the net posts or on the referee stand. The ball is not completely round, and it is made of hard leather. As we keep looking, we stop to watch a little of the tournament's final match. We notice that there are no computers. In fact, we notice that there are no stats being taken, not even by hand.

It appears that in 1950 stats were not all that important. There is simply no evidence that volleyball folks, all except the scorer, felt that they should be recording numbers during the match. But most people today would argue that the steady deluge of statistics threatening to drown our sport has become a necessary staple on the volleyball benches and in the video machines across the land. Many are proud to say that volleyball has become a leader in statistical evaluation of sport performance.

This may be true, but I would still like to hang around that 1950s gym and talk to some of the local keepers of the volleyball tradition. I would like to ask them if they had ever considered using statistics to evaluate their matches and, if so, what they would like to know as a result.

Then I would like to return to the present to ask my contemporaries to take their own look back and tell me, after all these years, how the game has changed—if it all—as a result of using statistics. How different would that final match in the 1950 tournament finals have looked had it been played in the stat-saturated atmosphere of the present? Would they have discovered something new about the game? Or are stats merely a bunch of answers in search of questions?

The problems with statistics have been well-documented. They measure only the physical. They tell us nothing about the mental strengths of a player, nor can they measure aggressiveness and tentativeness. Stats often ignore the timing of an action. When were those errors committed? In the early stages of a match or late in the fifth set? And what about those annoying per set statistics? This is a topic I covered in a blog I wrote for the January 2012 edition of the AVCA's Coaching Volleyball 2.0. (See the sidebar titled Per Set Statistics.)

Per Set Statistics

Why do volleyball people attribute meaning to *per set statistics*? I have read discussions on volleyball chat rooms where contributors argue that team A is a better blocking team than team B because they average more blocks per set. Even worse, per set statistics are used to evaluate All-Region and All-American candidates!

Here is the problem. The top team in a conference (team A) can play against the last place team (team B) and win in a 3-0 blowout. As a result, both teams participate in a relatively low number of total rotations, thereby limiting the total number of blocking opportunities available to each team. Both teams' blocks per set will be low when compared to the totals accumulated in a match between two evenly matched teams where the score can be 3-2, and the total number of blocking opportunities much higher than the earlier example.

Consider that the first place team will likely play in a higher number of 3-0, low rotation matches and might average, say, 1.7 blocks per set. Another team, which competes in more 3-2 and 3-1, high rotation matches can average, say, 2.2 blocks per set. This is not because they are a better blocking team, but because they play longer matches that provide significantly more opportunities to post a blocking stat.

All per set statistics suffer from the same flaw. Only per *attempt* statistics have value. And the only per attempt statistic available to us is kill efficiency. Our sport needs to overhaul its approach to statistical evaluation to rid itself of per-set stats. How many times do I have to listen to someone tell me that blocker B is better than blocker A because she has a higher blocks-per-set average. Blocker A plays on a powerhouse team

> continued

> continued

that wins most of its matches 3-0. Blocker B, on the other hand, plays on an average team that battles its way to 4 or 5 sets virtually every time they play. It is conceivable that blocker B can post a higher blocks-per-set average merely because she plays on a team that provides her with more opportunities to block.

Further complicating this issue are the following:

a. Some teams prefer to use their block to channel the ball to their diggers. They are likely to block fewer balls simply because of their system.

b. Others want to block every ball they can with less concern for channeling to diggers. They are likely to have higher blocks-per-set numbers; again, because of their system.

c. Some teams emphasize control blocking, making it possible to pass the ball accurately to their setter for a counterattack opportunity. This can be a very effective system choice, but there is no stat recorded for a control block.

d. Some teams are very physical and can put up an intimidating block, forcing the opponent's attacker into a tip or roll shot that is easily scooped up by the blocking team. But again, no blocking stat is posted.

All of the above have a significant impact on the accumulation of blocks per set. But they lead to a wide variance in team blocking totals. They are an unreliable indicator of which teams are the better blocking teams. There is no scientific correlation between the *blocks-per-set statistic* and the *actual blocking ability* of a team.

Mike Hebert, January 2012, *AVCA Coaching Volleyball 2.0*. Used with permission from American Volleyball Coaches Association.

Long ago, when I was an upstart, younger coach, I preached the value of recording statistics as loudly as anyone. As time and interest waned, I began to question their worth. I asked myself what they could provide that is of use to coaches during matches. I never had the chance to listen to the answer that the 1950s players would have given me, so all we can do is imagine a time when there were no stats. What would we want to know that only stats could provide?

I am not calling for volleyball coaches to abandon statistics. I can often see the value in keeping them. But I do wish to encourage people to go back to the starting line, take a good look at what lies ahead, step out of the box, and begin shaping your own plan for using statistics.

For me the most important statistics-related question has become: Do the data generated by our stats program justify the amount of staff energy and time we devote to it? I would guess that there would be a variety of answers to this question. Whatever your decision, this is a topic that will be on the drawing board for a long time.

Covering

I explain coverage to players like this. A cover is the first contact resulting from a teammate's attack being blocked. Covering the hitter is one of those lost arts talked about by volleyball's old timers. It is a phase of the game that we will remain committed to as a team. Always remember: a cover is not a cover if we can't set the next contact.

Team coverage resembles fast-break basketball. It also adds a significant layer of hard work. It is fatiguing to execute the constant movement required of the coverage game. Most coverage situations are unique. Players have to know where their teammates are and move to fill an open spot on the floor. Covering is not a regimented activity. Instead, players are asked to be creative and follow their instincts when looking for the right place to align for the cover attempt.

The old guys claim, with some hyperbole, to have actually seen blocked balls kept off the floor and converted for kills. Like the softball players at the bar after a game or the basketball warriors gathering in the park, these old guys spin tales of embellishment to anyone who will listen. Sometimes the topic of hitter coverage finds its way into the discussion, but it remains one of the least developed phases of the game.

My observation has been that when teams play good hitter coverage, it is almost always the result of one of two things. First, some players absolutely love to cover blocked balls, and they fly around the court looking for action. They give the impression that the entire team has taken on hitter coverage as a strong priority, but in reality it is the work of one or two players.

The other possibility is that the team *has* been trained in specific and detailed movement patterns designed to have every player stationed in a preassigned coverage location, determined by which hitter receives the set. This system relies upon how well each coverage player can memorize the correct location responsibilities and remain prepared to cover the ball.

I'm not a fan of either solution. In the first instance, there are too few players committed to covering the entire court. In the second example, there are enough players, but they are locked into a tightly mapped grid that restricts the freedom to go after any ball.

Borrowing from my basketball playing days, I taught a coverage system that relied more on vision and instinct than on memorizing where one was supposed to stand at the moment the hitter contacts the ball. Instead, each player looks for an open area and moves to fill it. I called this the fast-break system of covering. To cover the hitter successfully, a player must calculate the location of each teammate, read the attack angle of the hitter and the platform angle of the blocker, and then take up a position near and under the blocker's attempt to block your teammate. Where each player goes to form the coverage pattern may be different every time.

Many have tried to discourage me from using this system. They worry that players will be unable to make the correct read when deciding where to go for the cover. But I point to the fact that in tens of thousands of gyms across the country, there are basketball players of all ages doing exactly that. They easily calculate where they are supposed to be as the rebound and fast-break sequence develops. If the basketball players can do it, why not volleyball players?

I couldn't be any further out of the box on this one.

Serving

My sole purpose in discussing serving is to call attention to a particular serving philosophy that is common among men's teams and becoming more popular with women's teams. I am referring to the decision to let your server pound away on his toughest serve even when an error would result in losing a point and the set in a critical part of the match.

I have watched match after match follow the same script. The serving team has made a comeback and is serving at 23-24. Let's say that this server's jump-serve has, according to team statistics, a 30 percent chance of scoring either a direct or indirect point, but it also carries with it (according to their stats) a 35 percent chance of being an error. The serving team is on fire and within one point of surging into a 24-24 tie in the set if they only can win one more rally! Then their jump server knocks the serve 25 feet out of bounds. It doesn't sit right with me. It seems to violate the purpose of knowing the statistical facts of the match. You know going in that the match would be close. Is there no plan B for such a situation? It all seems pointless (no pun intended) to me. If someone were going to give you a 5 percent situational advantage, would you take it as your first option? I would.

I find myself wondering why a coach would accept that 5-percentage point disadvantage in such a critical situation late in a set. I would rather serve with a greater chance of the ball being in and take my chances with my block-defend-counterattack game to stay in the set. My chance of this strategy working is 5 percent greater than telling my server to go for the big bomber.

Making Position Changes

If a player ever confronts a coach who is threatening to change her roster position, tell the player the odds are high that the change is in her favor; the player almost always blossoms under the circumstances of the new position. I can't count the number of times I have seen this situation work out better for the player, but every time I propose a position change to a player there is initial resistance.

While coaching at Minnesota in 2004, I had a setter named Lindsey Taatjes. Her nickname Hobbs (borrowed from the movie *The Natural*) was given to her early in her career by Aame Amundson. Hobbs was a very good high school and club setter, but she had never once played as a hitter on any team. She didn't know how to hit.

I wanted to play a genuine 6-2 system that season, and everything was in place to do it. Kelly Bowman, an All-American setter and opposite, was back for her final year, and the only questionable element was Hobbs' lack of experience as a hitter. So I told her she had about four months to pull some kind of hitting game together so she could play opposite Bowman in our newly hatched 6-2.

Hobbs put in some serious work time on her own to develop an armswing. By the beginning of the 2004 season, she had become functional as an attacker. She kept improving. By NCAA Tournament time she was in full bloom. In fact, she put up such great numbers at the Regional Championships, she was voted the tournament's Most Valuable Player. We advanced to the Final Four where we defeated USC and lost to Stanford in the championship match.

None of this could have happened if it were not for the bold decision to teach Hobbs how to hit and ask her to do it at a championship level.

Creating Team Moments

This one is going to be a stretch for most of you. Frankly, it was for me too. I was coaching at the University of Illinois at the time, and we were competing at Providence College in a tournament. We had some down time, so I loaded up the van with the players, and we drove to Newport,

Rhode Island, to see the local scene. As I was making my way through town, one of the players sitting in the back seat let out a blood-curdling scream, the kind of scream one might hear as you fall from the top of a skyscraper. I jammed on the brakes and threaded through traffic until I could find a place to pull up to the curb safely. I jumped from my seat to see what had happened. This is how it was explained to me.

As we had turned the corner into the intersection in which we were now illegally parked, one of the players had suddenly glanced out her window and let out the horrible scream described. "What's wrong?" I asked, fearing the worst.

"Oh, it's OK, coach," they told me. One of our players had spotted a Gap store. "With six floors!" she said. "I've never seen one that big!"

The next weekend we played against Texas A & M in the finals of a tournament in Chicago. It was a long and well-played match by both teams. Down 12-9 in the fifth set, I called my last timeout. I reviewed our next rotation with the team and settled on the offensive play we were going to run. We had been in this situation before, and I trusted the team to push back in the match. There were only 15 to 20 seconds left in the timeout.

Then the unexplainable occurred. I suddenly remembered the Gap event from the weekend before. Sitting next to me on a chair was a roll of athletic tape. I tore off a small piece, wrote the initials "Gap" on it, and stuck it on the back of my tie where the manufacturer's label usually goes. At the very instant the team was ready to break their timeout huddle, I spun around and twisted my tie so they could see the hastily drawn manufacturer label on the back. The players went berserk, yelling "Gap, Gap, Gap!" Then they took the court and made quick work of the Aggies. They displayed a level of enthusiasm and joy that I hadn't seen before. "What the hell?" I asked myself. "What just happened?"

Well, I'm not sure what happened, but I knew enough to let it go. We had experienced a moment as a group. There were similar moments throughout my career that I could describe. There were times when I tried to artificially induce a moment of this type, but they never materialized, and I ended up looking goofy.

Just so you don't dismiss this incident as completely crazy, the Gap made a curtain call later that season. We were scheduled to play both Penn State (ranked number 10) and Ohio State (ranked number 6) on the road, by far the most difficult road trip in the Big Ten Conference. We celebrated Thanksgiving dinner on Thursday night before taking on Penn State on Friday. Meanwhile, my wife, Sherry, had purchased for me a genuine Gap tie and presented it to me at the dinner. "This tie has

Destinee Hooker of the United States spikes hard against a shaky block at the London Olympics in 2012. Destinee was a standout All-American at Texas who has continued to showcase her skills on the international stage.

OC Register/Zuma Press/Icon SMI

special powers," she told the players in a tongue-in-cheek style. "Don't worry, everything will be OK."

I know many coaching friends who would have shut down the whole Gap thing the minute it happened. "There is no place for this kind of nonsense in volleyball!" would have been their assessment. But something happens during these moments that create a genuine impact on the mood and outlook of the team. If you stay in the box, you will feel pressure from the volleyball regulars to keep things moving along on a conservative track, but if you are operating from outside the box, you might want to stand back, evaluate, and choose how you want to manage these kinds of moments.

Oh we beat Penn State 3-2 and Ohio State 3-1 for the rare sweep. Can you convince me that the Gap tie had nothing to do with these results?

Staying Fresh

There are many coaches who subscribe to the conventional wisdom that in the sport of volleyball, practices must be at least three hours long. I believe this derives from the highly publicized Japanese coaching styles of the 1960s and 1970s. They were characterized by long hours in the gym and brutal training regimens. American volleyball was looking for role model programs during those years, and there were none more well-known and bragged about than the Japanese, so we tried to become as Japanese as we could.

Whenever there would be a question regarding how long to practice, the answer would always be, "We need the reps, so let's go for four hours." It was as if the Japanese were secretly listening to our staff meetings, and we were not going to allow anyone, especially the Japanese, to label us as soft. We were marching to a different drumbeat. Despite the fact that all the other sports were limiting practice sessions to 1.5 or 2.0 hours, volleyball coaches evaluated progress in their sport by how many units of time they demanded from their athletes.

I decided to step out of this box early in my career. During long training periods, I elected to train on a three-days-on, one-day-off cycle even though everyone else was practicing Monday to Friday with weekends off. Why did I make this choice? The 3-1 system provided a better spacing for stress and recovery. Athletes remained fresh, and there was no weekend overcrowding in the training room.

As seasons wore down, I started tapering practice length in an attempt to keep players fresh for the late season playoff run. While early season practices may have lasted for 2.5 to 3 hours, the final practices at the end of a season were sometimes only an hour, maybe less. And I sometimes cancelled practice when I could see that too many players were exhausted or injured. Tapering isn't only for swimmers.

Taking Notes

Don't be afraid of being labeled a volleyball geek just because you carry with you some means of taking notes as you wander in and out of gyms during your career. I will tell you first hand that you can sometimes learn more by taking random notes than by attending formal clinics. I have a hefty supply of volleyball insights in cardboard boxes stored in my garage. Here is an example of one of my lists.

10 Prototypes of Problem Players

1. The Pavlovian server. This server hears the referee's whistle to beckon the serve and turns instantly into one of Ivan Pavlov's classically conditioned dogs. Just as the dogs respond immediately and in the same way to salivary stimuli, most servers respond to the whistle by hitting the one and only serve they know. There is no room for variety, such as changing the speed, location, timing, or type of serve.

2. The nervous defender. This defender gives up a balanced, ready defensive posture at the moment of contact by the attacker. She is often airborne as the ball is attacked.

3. The clueless ball watcher. Usually this is a blocker whose eyes are fixed on the set ball at the very instant the eyes should be fixed on the opponent's setter and hitters.

4. The bodyline hitter. This hitter sends every shot straight ahead within the bodyline established by the hips and shoulders. Easy to block, easy to dig.

5. The window washer. This blocker extends the arms and hands straight up from the shoulders and risks having the ball rearrange his face.

6. The leaning tower of Pisa. This is the digger who refuses to execute a jab step to close on the ball and instead topples to the floor like a fallen tree.

7. The loan shark. This player is unable to calculate the odds of a ball landing anywhere in the opponent's court in situations calling for the player to simply get the ball over the net.

8. Tiger Woods. This name is given to hitters who put a max swing on every ball but only a handful find the court.

9. Late for your date. This is the quick hitter who is always late getting up to hit a one set.

10. Shank-o-potamus. This is a primary passer who struggles to get the ball to the target.

Getting Evaluated

By now you should have a reasonable feel for how I would set up and run a program. I want to leave you with a snapshot of some of the basic principles that provided content as I pieced together my style, but I'm going to provide that snapshot from someone else's camera.

Several years ago I invited Chuck Rey to join my staff at Minnesota as a volunteer assistant. He agreed, and he did a wonderful job. Chuck is resourceful, loyal, and creative, and he carries around a 16 handicap. He was always smart enough to let me win, although he could have won whenever he wanted. I also appreciated his effort to learn how to say "Great shot, Mike!" with his best Morgan Freeman voice.

Chuck was attentive at every staff meeting and took great quantities of notes. I learned later these jottings were the seedlings of what would eventually grow into a thoughtful evaluation of my program and me.

It is a rare occasion when one coach is invited to experience the internal operation of another coach's program since all of us are protective of everything we say or do. Our program philosophy is our version of intellectual property. Naturally we are going to be sensitive toward anything critical that might be said about it. Nevertheless, I asked Chuck if he would mind sharing some parting thoughts with me before he left our program. Chuck is now the lead assistant at Miami University in Ohio. He did, indeed, turn in his homework assignment on the way out of town. Here is an excerpt from that document.

My Time at Minnesota by Chuck Rey

In coming to the University of Minnesota, I was under the impression that great coaches were rigid and strict and created an environment that disciplined players are to follow "the way." Although at Minnesota there is an underlying coach-created paradigm, it is not noticeably evident. Instead, the coaching staff is calm and poised and empowers players to allow their individualism to shine within the underlying limitations of the team concept. It is their individualism that enables players to grow into great players, thus building a unique chemistry of greatness throughout the team.

My philosophy and belief in striving for perfection of fundamentals focused on physical skills (passing, setting, serving, hitting, blocking, defense). What I learned from Mike is that the real fundamentals of communication and reading the game supersede these physical building blocks of individual players. These are true root and core that enable a team of six players to work in harmony in a confining 30-x-30-foot space. My philosophy on fundamentals has expanded from the individual to the team.

Mike was calm and poised during matches. He did not get overcome emotionally by the atmosphere or the situation, which enabled him to focus throughout the entire match and provide direction to the players. I found I would get caught up in the emotion of the match and became a cheerleader instead of a coach. I am learning.

Conclusion

Living outside the box means questioning just about everything that comes your way. Asking questions makes you more curious, and finding answers to these questions builds confidence. As I look back from the vantage point of retirement, I can find more clarity in decisions made late in my career. I even started to believe that I knew why my teams won a lot of volleyball matches.

I was never supposed to be a coach. I earned a PhD in philosophy of education at Indiana University and was on target to become an assistant professor. But the magnetic tug of volleyball pulled me into the coaching profession before my academic career ever took off. Ironically, the resulting lack of formal training in coaching might have been one of the reasons for my success. I was free to learn on my own. I was a blank screen waiting to be filled with relevant information. And I was the decider with regard to what was and was not relevant. I was able to reject without penalty those things that I judged to be less than useful to my coaching career.

I succeeded as a volleyball coach because I was able to wrap my head around the mental side of the job. I knew enough about the game of volleyball to put a competitive team on the floor, but coaching taught me more than this. I learned how to treat people the right way. I know that some would disagree with that last claim, but I am certain that what separated me from the rest of the coaching population was my ability to engage people without making them feel inferior or disrespected. I have always believed that people will provide higher quality work for you if they can feel accepted, rather than not rejected.

I took this outlook to the gym as well. I felt that if I could build a program on positive ground, I would always have a chance to win. I rejected the harsh, belittling style of coaching that so many of my colleagues chose. There were times when I attempted to convert to this other side, but it wasn't me. I was the nice guy, and I did the best I could with it. I know that it was used against me in recruiting, but I couldn't help that. We all know the saying about coaching. I have to know who I am and become the best "me" that I can be.

I was committed to building a different kind of success that would be measured by the ability to set and pursue goals. I wanted players to become critical thinkers and not just physical performers. I wanted them to share the challenge of attempting to win volleyball matches, not wait for me to beat it out of them. I wanted to empower them to become champions as a result of the choices they made on a daily basis. I wanted *them* to make the decision to want to excel.

Luckily, many of my players understood what I was after. We won our share of matches and celebrated some wonderful accomplishments.

With this as a backdrop I think it would be fair to say that my entire career was spent outside the box. By not accepting the harsh style of interacting with my players, I set myself apart from many of my colleagues. Others wondered why I devoted so much time to becoming a program developer and not a clipboard coach.

Regardless of where you stand in evaluating my career path, my final message to you is this. Find out all you can about the game of volleyball. There are plenty of opportunities for decision-making. Design practices so that your players are put in situations they will likely face in matches. Create drills that will challenge them to become decision-makers. Choose a situation and be creative, but remember that decisions are a process. Don't be afraid to step outside the box and go to work. Finally, activate the Trust Police to ensure that your team embraces the goal of cultivating an environment that nurtures team trust.

This is what thinking volleyball coaches do.

INDEX

Note: Page references followed by an italicized *f* or *t* indicate information contained in figures and tables, respectively.

ABOUT THE AUTHOR

Mike Hebert began coaching in 1976. During his career, he coached the University of Pittsburgh men's and women's teams, the University of New Mexico women's team, the University of Illinois women's team, and the University of Minnesota women's team. In 35 years of coaching, Mike earned a career record of 952-392 and led teams to the Division I Final Four on five occasions. He reached the semifinals of the EAIAW Championships all four of his years at Pittsburgh, winning two regional championships. He was named the American Volleyball Coaches Association (AVCA) National Coach of the Year in 1985  and served as the president of the AVCA from 1987 to 1990. Hebert was a part-time member of USA Volleyball's coaching staff for over 30 years and was honored with their All-Time Great Volleyball Coaches Award.

Now retired from coaching, Mike continues to work with USA volleyball and is a member of both the University of Minnesota and AVCA halls of fame.